A Path Twice Traveled

FAIRBANK CENTER FOR CHINESE STUDIES AT HARVARD UNIVERSITY

A Path Twice Traveled

My Journey as a Historian of China

Paul A. Cohen

Published by the Fairbank Center for
Chinese Studies at Harvard University
Distributed by Harvard University Press
Cambridge (Massachusetts) and London 2019

Founded in 1955 by Professor John King Fairbank, the Fairbank Center advances scholarship in all fields of Chinese studies at Harvard. The Center sponsors seminars and conferences, supports faculty and student research, maintains Harvard's research library on contemporary China, hosts postdoctoral fellows, visiting scholars, and associates in research, and publishes new research.

Library of Congress Cataloging-in-Publication Data

Names: Cohen, Paul A., author.
Title: A path twice traveled : my journey as a historian of China / Paul A. Cohen.
Description: Cambridge, Massachusetts : The Fairbank Center for Chinese Studies at
    Harvard University, 2019. | Includes bibliographical references and index.
Identifiers: LCCN 2018034046 | ISBN 9780674237292 (pbk. : alk. paper)
Subjects: LCSH: Cohen, Paul A. | Historians—United States—Biography. |
    China—Historiography.
Classification: LCC DS734.7 .C68 2019 | DDC 951.0072/02 [B]—dc23 LC record available
    at https://lccn.loc.gov/2018034046

Index by Anne Holmes of EdIndex

♾ Printed on acid-free paper

Last figure below indicates year of this printing
28 27 26 25 24 23 22 21 20 19

For Elizabeth

Contents

Figures

Acknowledgments

This memoir, a genre completely new to me, has benefited immensely from the advice and encouragement of friends and colleagues. I was persuaded to write it in the first instance by my longtime partner, Elizabeth Sinn, to whom the memoir is dedicated. The first person to read it after Elizabeth was Alan Lebowitz, who brought to the reading two special qualities: first, his field of professional interest, American and English literature, could not be further from mine, and second, he and I have been good friends for more than sixty-five years. Alan's insightful comments on the first draft—and later on a revised draft—were extremely helpful. Others who agreed to read it and give me their thoughts, all either China or Japan specialists, were John Israel, Jeff Wasserstrom, Irv Scheiner, Ross Terrill, Tom Havens, Chris Munn, and Michael Szonyi. I am indebted to them all for their suggestions for improvement.

Since Harvard's Fairbank Center for Chinese Studies does not regularly publish books, a committee was formed to work out publication arrangements. Aside from me, the committee consisted of Michael Szonyi (director of the Fairbank Center), Daniel Murphy (executive director of the Center), and Bob Graham (director of the Harvard University Asia Center's Publications Program). At all stages of preparation of the work, I received much sound advice from Bob, who also lined up professional talent to assist in the book's production. Thanks go also to Lisa Cohen, who prepared the illustrations for publication, Justin Wong for making available photographic material in the possession of the Fairbank Center, and Holly Fairbank for advice on procuring photographs of her father. The copyediting of the manuscript was expertly done by Laura Poole. Also, Jeff Cosloy exercised patience and imagination in the design of the book cover.

Finally, I thank the Fairbank Center for Chinese Studies, which has been an intellectual home to me for over half a century, and the Centre of Asian Studies and Hong Kong Institute for the Humanities and Social Sciences at the University of Hong Kong, which during my frequent visits to Hong Kong over the past two decades have generously provided me with office space, administrative support, and a congenial and stimulating intellectual environment.

INTRODUCTION

I certainly was not born to history. In fact, how I came to be a historian is a fairly involved story. Born in 1934, I grew up in the town of Great Neck, on the north shore of Long Island. My best subject in high school was math, and the vocational aptitude tests I took suggested that I was probably headed for engineering or something of that sort. My father, Wilfred, who along with his brothers and my grandfather (Joseph) was in the business of manufacturing men's clothing, thought I might be interested in the production end of their operation. So one day, when I was around sixteen, my dad and I flew in a propeller-driven plane from La Guardia Airport to Philadelphia, where the company factory was located (the business and sales offices were in New York City). We spent the day inspecting the machinery that was used to make men's suits, sport coats, and trousers and talking to the people who worked at and ran the plant. Then we went back to the airport, hopped on a plane, and were home in time for dinner. From an early age, I had developed a negative attitude toward business in general, which seemed to be all about making money and not much else. (As my dad wrote me in early 1954, "You spent the first seventeen years of your life devaluating the dollar, and putting money on a very low basis. It was a crime to have money.") I don't think my parents, who had long known of my feelings, were surprised when I told them some time later that the clothing business was not for me.

In the late 1940s and early 1950s, when I was in high school, some women held jobs outside the home, and it was not unheard of for them to have full-fledged careers. But it was a very different world from today, when, for example, enrollments in law school and medical school in the United States are fairly evenly divided between men and women. Although one of my aunts taught Spanish in the New York City school system and another was a celebrated dancer and choreographer, my mom, Rose, like many women of her generation, had no career of her own. Aside from engaging in volunteer work, she was basically a homemaker for most of her married life. For her only son, on the other hand, a career of some sort was assumed, and the important thing in my case was that once I elected not to become a maker of men's clothing, what I would be in the future was entirely my choice (Fig I.1).

It took me many years to fully realize how lucky I was to have the freedom to choose what I would do with my life and not be pressured into something. My dad, although a little disappointed that I would not be going into the family business, made it clear that I should do what I wanted and he would support my decision and even help me out financially, if necessary. He was more than happy to give me opportunities he had been denied in his youth. In the spring term of my second year in college he wrote me: "Be sure you make a point of doing what *you* want to do. So few people ever accomplish this. . . . Nothing would please me more [than] if you became interested in something and went off on a mission for a year, just satisfying some impulses and desires you had, because you will feel awfully good when you do what you want to do, not what a lot of other people think would be the right thing for you to do." In another letter, my father told me about his own experience when he was my age. When he finished high school, my grandfather didn't take kindly to my dad's desire to attend City College of New York (CCNY). My grandfather had "the old-fashioned idea that boys should work as soon as they were through with high school." He went on, "So, believe me, that one year I spent going to CCNY during the day was a luxury for me. Every night at dinner, I couldn't mention any college stuff at all because I had to keep it quiet—so much so that after that first year I decided I had better start work. I went to college for three years at night and worked every day for $8 a week—and hard, too."

My dad recalled that when he got out of the navy at the end of World War I, within forty-eight hours of being discharged from service, still wearing his uniform, he visited my grandfather in his New York City

INTRO.1. The author, still a boy here, not yet thinking about the future, but perhaps displaying early interest in a wider world.

office. He was sitting in the showroom, having come down just for a visit, and his father, who was hard-pressed at the time and working long hours, passed a crack to someone, "Look, he sits there like a king," and told my father that he should report for work Monday morning. As my dad often told me, his dream when he got out of the navy had been to go to medical school and become a surgeon, but he said he had no regrets over having gone into the clothing business, which he and his brother Isidore in particular eventually built into a leading manufacturer of men's clothing. As he also reminded me from time to time, "I did not have the opportunity of making my own choice."

My father was a resourceful man and compensated for the disappointments of his youth in many ways. He was a founder, trustee, and past president of the North Shore University Hospital (Manhasset, New York), a founder and trustee of the Long Island Jewish Hospital (New Hyde Park, New York), and a founder and board member of the Hospital of the Albert Einstein College of Medicine (the Bronx, New York City). Although he never said as much to me, I'm sure that his involvement in the operations of three major medical institutions was a vicarious way of satisfying his frustrated ambition to become a doctor. He also served as president of Temple Beth-El, Great Neck's main Reform Jewish synagogue, and contributed to a range of Jewish philanthropies. On top of his other involvements, he became an accomplished amateur painter, with several one-man exhibitions to his credit. With the proceeds from the sales of his paintings, he established the Wilfred P. Cohen Foundation, which made grants to young artists and art students.

Few things were more gratifying to my father than being able to give me the freedom to shape my life that he had been denied in his youth. This applied to his daughters as well. My youngest sister, Alice, owned and operated an antiques shop, first in Manhasset, and then in Greenport, New York. Barbara, my oldest sister, after earning her master's degree at the Columbia University School of Social Work, had a private practice as a psychiatric social worker in the New York area and was a certified family therapist at a school in New Rochelle, New York. When my dad died in 1992, I was in my late fifties and several decades into my career as a historian of China. In eulogizing him, I made it a special point to acknowledge his generosity. At this point in my life, having learned of the experiences other people in my generation had

had with their fathers, I realized more clearly than ever that this quality was rare.

I began my university career in the fall of 1952 as an engineering student at Cornell University. Once in college, however, my mind was quickly opened to other subjects; by the end of my first semester, I had transferred out of engineering into arts and sciences. My last two years of college were spent at the University of Chicago, where, under the influence of the innovative curriculum introduced some years earlier by Robert M. Hutchins, I was exposed to a wide range of courses in the humanities, social sciences, and natural sciences, along with several courses of an integrative nature—but no field of concentration, no major. As my undergraduate education neared its close, the lack of a major presented a problem. In the mid-1950s it was generally expected that all healthy men would spend two years in the military, something I did not look forward to. My first year at the University of Chicago (1953–1954) was immensely important for me. I loved the intellectual environment Chicago offered, and for the first time in my life I became an avid reader. Although I still didn't have a specific sense of what I wanted to do in the future, I knew with great clarity that it was going to have to be something that engaged me intellectually. This meant continuing my education at the graduate level, which at the time was also the simplest way to obtain a deferment from the draft. There was only one problem: without an undergraduate major, the number of graduate programs prepared to accept someone like me was limited.

I worried a lot about this, and during my final year at Chicago I explored a range of different career possibilities, each of which involved additional schooling. I was interested in art and, with my talent for mathematics, thought that maybe architecture might work for me. But after arranging to have lunch with a young architect in the Chicago area and being told that beginning architects often ended up spending the first ten years designing staircases, architecture was dropped from my list. I was also attracted to psychology and flirted with the idea of becoming a psychiatrist, but the prospect of spending many years in medical school soured me on that possibility as well. As I became increasingly discouraged over my unsuccessful efforts to find a suitable career path, I thought that maybe I should just throw in the towel and go into the military for a couple of years after my graduation. I wrote Alan Lebowitz and Daniel

Stern, two close friends who were juniors at Harvard at the time, sharing my frustration with them. They immediately got back to me with a telegram, the gist of which was "Don't go into the Army. Come to Harvard over spring break."

And that was what I did. At the time Danny was taking an introductory course in East Asian civilization. He was very upbeat about the class, especially the new intellectual doors it opened, and after looking over the syllabus I was hooked. On a lark, I tracked down Japan historian Edwin O. Reischauer, one of the two main instructors of the course. I explained my situation to him and asked him, since Harvard's M.A. program in East Asian Studies was interdisciplinary (i.e., no specific major requirement), whether there was any chance of someone with my background being accepted into it. He told me to apply. Although still without my undergraduate degree from Chicago (I had one more course requirement to fulfill over the summer), I was admitted "on trial" and began at Harvard in fall 1955.

What captivated me at this point, interestingly, was not history, which I still knew precious little about, but Asia, particularly China. Ever since spending a few months in Europe in summer 1954 (my first foray outside North America), I had become intrigued by the differences among cultures, and this discovery was the major factor pulling me in the direction of a country and culture concerning which I was almost totally ignorant (my only exposure to China having been Pearl Buck's novel *The Good Earth*). We usually think of cultural difference in spatial terms. Thus, Benedict Anderson commented in his autobiography on the specialness of fieldwork: "The experience of strangeness makes all your senses much more sensitive than normal, and your attachment to comparison grows deeper."[1] Although I didn't realize it at the time, cultural difference can also be expressed in temporal terms, linking it inextricably to history, which is what British historian David Lowenthal (drawing on the first line of L. P. Hartley's novel *The Go-Between*) had in mind when he referred in one of his books to the past as a "foreign country."[2] Not long after my arrival at Harvard, I came under the spell of renowned China historian John King Fairbank, who cotaught "Rice Paddies"—the nickname students gave to the introductory course in East Asian civilization—with Reischauer. This, I learned very quickly, meant that at Harvard the focus of my study would be not just China but Chinese *history*, which was what Fairbank did.

That all happened well over a half century ago. I didn't fall in love instantly with history, but increasingly, as I realized how different understandings of the subject (including mine from Fairbank's) could be, history as an exciting and intellectually challenging field of learning grew on me. Initially, this meant Chinese history, and in 1984 I published a book titled *Discovering History in China: American Historical Writing on the Recent Chinese Past* (Columbia University Press), in which I adopted a critical stance toward the Western-centric biases of the leading U.S. approaches to recent Chinese history and argued strongly in favor of a more China-centered understanding. Thinking through the issues raised in the book, I became more fascinated with what history, broadly speaking, was all about. So much so that in my next book, *History in Three Keys: The Boxers as Event, Experience, and Myth* (Columbia University Press, 1997), I made it clear at the outset that although the specific example I focused on was the Boxer movement and uprising at the turn of the twentieth century in China, what I hoped to explore extended well beyond China and the Boxers.

In October 2015, I was introduced to Dr. Rao Shurong, editor of the influential Chinese literary monthly *Dushu* (Reading). She invited me to submit something for publication in her journal. I wrote Rao in January 2016 with a possible idea for an article. In the course of a sixty-year career as a historian of China, my thinking about Chinese history—and about history in general—had undergone a number of shifts and turns, and since I was well known among Chinese historians (both of the above-mentioned books having been published in multiple Chinese editions), I thought it might be of some interest to describe for *Dushu* readers the evolution of one non-Chinese scholar's thinking about Chinese history. Rao liked my suggestion and agreed to it. Alas, once I began to work on the piece, it became clear that it was a much larger undertaking than I had anticipated and I would not be able to come even close to the length limit suggested by *Dushu*. My thinking now was that rather than a short journal article, what I really needed to write was something a good deal more substantial, probably resulting in a small book.

As this change in plans was taking place, I received much encouragement from my partner, Elizabeth Sinn, who suggested that with the expanded project, I would be able to delve into some of the more hidden aspects of my career—the backstories, for example, pertaining to the sometimes thorny process of getting a work published or to decisions I have made as a writer but haven't felt impelled to share with my readers. I've followed her suggestion (see in particular chapters 4 and 7) and found that by doing so, the processes of writing and publishing have been illuminated in ways that otherwise would not have been possible. Aside from enriching my story, the material on my encounters with presses over the years may be of help to younger scholars, who are just beginning to publish and often have little sense of what the process entails. This is a fragile time in a scholar's career, and one thing he or she needs to know is that publishing houses are run by human beings, and just as human beings sometimes err in their judgments, presses don't always make good decisions.

Conveying such information, however, is hardly the principal aim of this memoir. My main point is to share with readers the sense of exhilaration and deep satisfaction I have enjoyed from the process of coming to grips with history as a discipline and, more specifically, the history of a country that, although very different from my own, has turned out to be not quite as different as I once thought as my understanding of history in general has deepened.

A memoir, of course, is itself a form of history. Which means that for a historian, writing a memoir on his or her career is very different from building that career in the first place. Two distinct forms of consciousness are involved. This is what my chosen title—*A Path Twice Traveled*—alludes to. It gets at the crucially important disparity between the past as originally experienced and the past as later reconstructed historically. Experience is outcome-blind—we don't know how things are going to turn out or what will come next, whereas in historical reconstruction the outcome is known in advance and the historian's effort is directed toward understanding and explaining how it came to pass. I have more to say on this in the final chapter.

Let me also say a bit here about the sources for this memoir and its intended readership. The two main sources are my own writings and talks (published and unpublished) and the voluminous correspondence and notes in my files. After completing a first draft of the memoir, it occurred to me that it might also be of value to read some of the memoirs written by other historians, for which purpose I found Jeremy D. Popkin's *History,*

Historians, and Autobiography (University of Chicago Press, 2005) to be a marvelous guide.

Although in places I have touched on aspects of my personal life that clearly bore on my professional career, this is not in any sense an account of my private life. It is, first and foremost, the largely public story of my intellectual evolution as a historian of China. Because a number of my books have exerted considerable influence on the field of Chinese history in the Euro-American world and in East Asia, the memoir should be of interest to China historians and to people with a special interest in Chinese history. I hope parts of the memoir will also be of interest to historians in general. I have in mind particularly those sections that deal with *Discovering History in China* (1984), *History in Three Keys* (1997), *Speaking to History: The Story of King Goujian in Twentieth-Century China* (2009), and my most recent publication, *History and Popular Memory: The Power of Story in Moments of Crisis* (Columbia University Press, 2014).

Finally, on showing an early draft of this book to several friends, each pointed out the failure to contextualize my account in terms of what was going on in the world or my personal life at the time of writing. As one of them put it, "It reads as if you were sitting on a cloud somewhere, flipping from one book to the next, but there was no sense of who Paul Cohen was or where he was or what else was going on in his life and the world." I got the message and made a serious effort in subsequent drafts to address the issue of context. The memoir is still more a public account than a private one, but now with a greater recognition of the key role that my private life and happenings around the world played at various junctures. Hopefully this will make it of greater interest to people who are not China historians—or, for that matter, historians of anything else.

CHAPTER I

Beginnings

It seems to me, given the Chinese view of the importance of sixty-year cycles and the fact that it is now just over sixty years since I began my study of Chinese history, that this is probably a good time to take stock of the path I have followed: where I started, how and why my views changed at certain points, and where I find myself now. Although most of my scholarly work has focused on the nineteenth and twentieth centuries and has therefore almost inevitably dealt in some way with the interactions between China and the West (or a Western-influenced Japan), an abiding concern through much of my career has been my determination to get inside China, to reconstruct Chinese history as much as possible as the Chinese themselves experienced it, rather than in terms of what people in the West thought was important, natural, or normal. In short, I wanted to move beyond approaches to the Chinese past that bore a heavy burden of Eurocentric or Western-centric preconceptions. An early example of this was my first book, *China and Christianity* (1963), in which I explicitly distanced myself from the older approach to China missions, with its focus "on missions history, not on Chinese history." With the coming of age of Chinese studies in the postwar era, "the inadequacies of this old Western-centered approach" had become apparent, and a new approach had been suggested—the pioneer here was one of my teachers at Harvard, John King Fairbank—that was "more concerned with understanding and evaluating the role played by Christian missions in Chinese history."[1] I adopted this approach in the book.

To put it in a slightly different way, what I attempted to do in *China and Christianity*—and I crib here from Ryan Dunch in his illuminating comment—was "not to write on China missions as an aspect of American experience, but to examine the missionary engagement with China from a Chinese perspective." "So," Dunch continues,

> he travelled, to Paris, to London, and, vitally, to Taipei, where he was the first American scholar to make extensive use of the Zongli Yamen archives there. From these disparate sources he wove an intricate and multi-dimensional argument pivoting around four main sets of actors, the Chinese local elite, Chinese officials, Western consuls and governments, and missionaries. In doing so he opened up questions not envisaged in the work of his peers about how to embed the missionaries and their effects into Chinese history. He was already "discovering history in China" where his contemporaries saw Westerners as acting *upon* China.[2]

Career Preparation: The Guidance of John King Fairbank

I'm getting ahead of myself. A lot happened in the way of preparation before I got to that first book. My two main teachers in graduate school were John Fairbank and Benjamin Schwartz. They were very different. Fairbank (fig. 1.1) was deeply preoccupied with China. You had the sense at times that that was all he wanted to talk about. He did things in addition to teaching that made us graduate students feel like we were a special group. Every Thursday afternoon, he and his wife, Wilma, had tea at their home in Cambridge, and anybody who happened to be in town—scholars, mostly China scholars, from France, Japan, and elsewhere—were invited, and you got to meet them and talk with them. Another thing Fairbank did was organize informal Friday night get-togethers with people with significant China experience. He had a wide range of nonacademic friends, such as Edgar Snow, Owen Lattimore, and John Carter Vincent, people who had been in the diplomatic corps (Vincent) or were scholars (Lattimore) or journalists (Snow). He would schedule an evening with them at somebody's home, often Vincent's home since

1.1. Fairbank in front of his longtime home in Cambridge. *Source:* cover of Paul A. Cohen and Merle Goldman, comps., *Fairbank Remembered* (Cambridge, MA: John K. Fairbank Center for East Asian Research, Harvard University, 1992).

he lived in Cambridge. So we graduate students got a chance to spend a few hours talking with these people and discussing their China experiences. I began to feel as though, "Hey, this is, this is real. This is real stuff."[3]

At that point (the latter half of the 1950s), the China field in the United States was still very underdeveloped. Book publication was minimal. You could easily read just about every book in every discipline relating to China and Japan. Mainstream journals like the *American Historical Review* weren't open to articles on East Asian history. There were very few English-language journals that dealt specifically with Asian subject matter, the best known being the *Far Eastern Quarterly*, which in September 1956 was renamed the *Journal of Asian Studies*, and the *Harvard Journal of Asiatic Studies*. One of the things Fairbank decided to do was to fill this gap a bit by publishing, once a year, an informal graduate student journal called *Papers on China*. The top five or six seminar papers produced annually by Harvard graduate students working on China were selected for the journal, which was distributed to libraries all over the world. If one of your seminar papers was included, it made you feel like a professional, a real scholar.

Schwartz (fig. 1.2) was very different from Fairbank. He would come to lunch all the time. There was a table where many of the China and Japan scholars ate lunch. Ed Reischauer would frequently come there and Fairbank occasionally. Schwartz was a regular participant in these lunches. Unlike Fairbank, he liked to talk about everything—anything that was interesting to him, not just China. Both men were vitally important influences on me but in different ways. There were a number of things about Fairbank that were special. For example, after I started teaching, any time I published an article and sent it to him, within a week he would write back with comments and encouragement. But if I sent it to Schwartz, it could take six months to hear a reply. If one went to see Schwartz in his office, on the other hand, one could sit down and talk with him for an hour. But there would be a line outside Fairbank's door, and everyone was allotted five minutes of his time. So you had to get to the point. I don't think Fairbank had more students than Schwartz, but he took on many more administrative responsibilities. Schwartz was the anti-administrator; although he served a year as acting director of the East

1.2. Benjamin Schwartz. Photograph by Jane Reed.

Asian Research Center, Fairbank was the regular director until his retirement in 1973.

Although intellectually Schwartz was very important in terms of how I thought about history and how I formulated problems, Fairbank was clearly the greater influence during the early years of my career as a China historian. The two seminars I took as a graduate student were both with Fairbank. In the first of these, which was in the spring of 1957, my Chinese (a demanding language I had only begun to study at Harvard in the fall of 1955 at age twenty-one) was not good enough to use for research purposes, so I chose a paper topic that relied entirely on English-language materials. It was a comparison of the approaches used by two of the most important Protestant missionaries of the late nineteenth century in China: Timothy Richard and Hudson Taylor. I had never taken a graduate seminar before, and when it was my turn to give an oral report on my progress to the rest of the class, things did not go well. With little sense of the time allotted me, I went on and on, until finally Fairbank got up and noisily raised and lowered the window shades in the classroom. It was his way of signaling that my time was up and I should bring my report to a quick close. His behavior on that occasion was so lacking in grace that one of the other students in the class phoned me at home that evening to apologize and commiserate. After that rocky start, things could only get better. Later in 1957 my seminar paper was selected to be published in *Papers on China*.[4] With the passage of time, my relationship with Fairbank steadily improved.

The second seminar I took with Fairbank was on Qing documents. In addition to getting an introduction to documentary Chinese—the special language used in the edicts and memorials that formed the lion's share of communication between the throne and the provinces during the Qing dynasty—each student in the seminar was responsible for writing a paper making use of sources in the Qing documentary style. Mine focused on a number of antimissionary incidents—they were called *jiao'an* or "church cases" in Chinese—that took place in the provinces of Hunan and Jiangxi in 1862. When I began to do the research, it took me ages to read just one page of text, but the more I read, the faster my speed became. Fairbank, who had himself recently published a pathbreaking article on *jiao'an*,[5] liked what I had done and encouraged me. I also benefited from the generous help of Kwang-Ching Liu, a former Fairbank student who was at Harvard that year and sat in on the Qing documents course (fig. 1.3). K.C. (as he was generally known) spent three hours with me after one seminar meeting helping me decipher a particularly difficult essay that was germane to my topic. Again, my seminar paper was chosen for publication in *Papers on China*.[6] Its key themes figured prominently in part of my doctoral dissertation and in one chapter of the book that eventually resulted from the dissertation.[7]

Although I continued to take courses, much of my time during the next few years was spent researching and writing my dissertation. At the outset I had hoped to work with both Fairbank and Schwartz, but in the end my involvement was much closer with Fairbank, partly because of his strong interest in the missionary topic that was the focus of my dissertation (Schwartz's interests lay elsewhere) and partly because, as director of the East Asian Research Center, he was the person I had to consult with periodically about administrative matters relating to my course work and future plans. As my dissertation work was nearing an end, I applied for and received a fellowship in a Ford Foundation–funded,

1.3. Fairbank teaching in his Widener Library study.

Cornell-administered program for further training in the Chinese language in Taipei. (For political reasons, it was then impossible for Americans to go to the People's Republic of China. U.S. recognition of the Nationalist government in Taipei as the sole legitimate government of China did not begin to change until the secret contacts between President Richard Nixon and Chairman Mao Zedong that began in 1969–70.) The main emphasis of the Cornell program was on improving spoken Chinese capability. But as valuable as that was, it paled before the opportunity the program afforded to live in a Chinese cultural and physical environment for nearly a year and a half.

Living in Taipei

After spending the summer of 1960 at Yale taking intensive Chinese language courses,[8] I arrived in Taipei in September with my wife Andrea and our young daughter, Joanna (who had been born in May 1959 when Andrea and I were still living in Cambridge), and began the Cornell program in early October. Andrea had been a year behind me in high school, but we did not know each other very well until, by chance, we both signed up for a course in French language to be given in Paris in the summer of 1954. We became close during that summer, and two years later we married.

Readers in the twenty-first century may, at the abrupt introduction of my wife, wonder what her career interests were and how it was decided that she would go to Taipei with me. Times were very different then. During my early years in graduate school, Andrea, who had been born in Berlin and was fluent in German, was just winding up her undergraduate career at Barnard College with an honors thesis on the political situation in the Weimar period. After joining me at Harvard, she did some editorial work for the Harvard Business School and began to study Chinese in preparation for our eventual travel to Taiwan. As I look back on my fellow male graduate students in Chinese studies at the time, not one (unless my memory fails me) had a wife with a career of her own, and this continued to be the case more or less after our arrival in Taipei, when we became friends with American China scholars from places other than

Harvard. Wives generally did some tutorial work in spoken Chinese. Although they often had interests of their own—Andrea did editorial work for the prominent Taiwanese psychologist Lin Tsung-yi, preparing his English-language writings for publication—whatever career aspirations they may have had were put on hold as they followed their husbands into the field.[9]

This asymmetrical pattern with respect to men's and women's career aspirations began to change dramatically in the course of the 1960s and after, largely a reflection of the civil rights movement. But in the early 1960s, it was accepted as the norm that my wife would follow me not only to Taipei but also, as my teaching career began, to a succession of teaching posts in different parts of the United States. Andrea was not alone in this regard. Natalie Zemon Davis, who later served as president of the American Historical Association, became passionately interested in history while an undergraduate at Smith College, but her professors there assumed a married woman couldn't have a professional career and, although her husband was supportive and believed in "equality of careers," the two of them took it for granted that she would go where his jobs were.[10] This asymmetry was by no means confined to the academic world. Jane Kramer, in a recent review of Paul Freedman's *Ten Restaurants That Changed America*, had to remind herself that in the Eisenhower 1950s, "women were not seated in most New York restaurants without a man to order, and pay, for them."[11] There were dozens of other respects in which the situations of men and women in U.S. society were far from equal. As Massachusetts Senator Elizabeth Warren put it, women had, for decades, been "shut out of lots of things."[12]

When I think back on the time I spent in Taipei, now more than a half-century ago, what sticks in my mind is less the mechanics of studying Chinese language than the experience of inhabiting an authentic Chinese milieu. Like many other foreigners (and some Chinese), we lived in a Japanese-style home, a vestige of the decades of Japanese colonial rule over Taiwan (which lasted from 1895 until 1945). Occasionally, responding to a bout of homesickness, we prevailed on our cook to make *Faguo kaomianbao* (French toast) for breakfast instead of serving up something more typically Chinese, like *shaobing jia youtiao* (a deep-fried twisted dough stick sandwiched between the halves of a sesame seed bun), which could be purchased for very little money at a streetside stand not far from our house. But like our Chinese neighbors, we lived in a basically Chinese fashion. Our home, like many of theirs, was surrounded by a high wall with broken glass on top, the major purpose of which (we were told) was to keep people engaged in the illegal dog meat trade from climbing the wall and making off with the family hound. Generally speaking, most of our meals consisted of food excellently prepared by our Sichuanese cook, Hsieh (Xie) Sufang, which was how we wanted it. How well I remember the first meal Sufang made after coming to work for us. The main dish consisted of scrambled eggs and shrimp with no sauce and was extremely bland. I knew this was not a typical example of Sichuanese cuisine and so I asked her about it. Her response: "Ai, Chuancai tai la—Meiguoren pa chi" (Oh, Sichuan cooking is too spicy—Americans wouldn't like it). We asked her where she got the idea of making us scrambled eggs and shrimp. She said she had once seen people eating this dish in an American movie. We made it clear that we actually liked spicy food and wanted her to make only authentic Chinese dishes for us. For the most part, she ate what we ate, so she was only too happy to go along with that plan.

The black market was rife in Taipei when I lived there. Most everyone was involved in it. Indeed, one of the first things I did after my arrival was bike to the commercial sector of the city with John Israel (fig. 1.4), a friend from graduate school who had gotten to Taipei before me, so he could introduce me to his "banker." The quotation marks are absolutely essential in this instance as the "banker" was a guy who sat at a desk in the back of a jewelry shop. It seemed pretty shady at first. But John, who had already dealt with this man, introduced me; we shook hands, and it was made clear that henceforth whenever I was running short of local money, all I had to do was write a check on my home bank in Massachusetts, indicating in U.S. dollars the amount I needed. The "banker" would give me the equivalent sum in Taiwanese money based on that day's black market rate. This system worked for the entirety of my stay in Taiwan. Whenever I needed money, I would bike into town and see my "banker." He always remembered who I was, took my check, and gave me the correct equivalent in Taiwanese money without asking to see my passport or any other form of identification. If there was any single event that convinced me I was no longer in America, this was it. All it took was an introduction and a handshake—very Chinese.

1.4. John Israel (left) and Lloyd Eastman, two fellow graduate students at Harvard, enjoying themselves in a Taiwan restaurant, 1961. Photograph by author.

Another characteristically Chinese aspect of the environment in which we lived in Taipei consisted in the sounds coming from the streets. In those days Taipei had a large population of peddlers, who sold services (such as knife sharpening or massages) or things (fresh eggs, baby rabbits, steamed bread, sugarcane, and many other items too numerous to name). The peddlers didn't ring your front doorbell. That wasn't necessary, as most had a special tune they would intone or instrument they would play, which identified what they were selling for the people living behind the high walls. Unfortunately, foreign children sometimes got things a little mixed up. There was the time, for example, when we bought several small rabbits as pets for our daughter. One morning, not long after,

Joanna decided that they might appreciate a bit of the *mantou* she was having for breakfast. It didn't take long for all the bunnies, unaccustomed to a diet of steamed bread, to die. Other street sounds commonly heard were the tinkling of bells of pedicabs and bicycles passing by, the barking of a neighbor's dog, and the voices of people chatting or greeting one another or shouting to make way for a moving vehicle that was fast approaching along the crowded street.

One thing that quickly became apparent after a while was that the city was in many ways a third-world place, unlike the Taipei of today. Children squatted over open sewers in the roads to pee. Trucks, referred to humorously as "honey wagons," circulated through the city periodically collecting night soil (human excrement) from homes and buildings, which was then used by farmers to fertilize their fields. Many shopkeepers lived behind their shops in structures so ramshackle that in the event of destruction by a typhoon, they were often rebuilt in a matter of days as if nothing had happened. For poor Chinese, the health situation was also fairly primitive: children at play in the streets often displayed serious-looking skin diseases, while their parents not infrequently suffered from trachoma, which put them in grave danger of going blind if it was untreated. Chinese girls, no more than six or seven years old themselves, helped care for their younger siblings, keeping them out of trouble by carrying them about on their backs. A lot of activities we generally think of as taking place indoors—cooking meals, mending clothes, doing the laundry, the sale of fresh vegetables and fruit, haggling over prices (generally expected as part of the process of selling and buying)—were performed outside for all to see, hear, and (in the case of food preparation) smell.

For a visitor from the United States, just walking or biking through the streets of Taipei often proved a fascinating experience. It was common to encounter an elaborate funeral procession, which typically included many women clad entirely in white wailing mournfully for the dead as they marched. These women were often not relatives or even friends of the deceased, and after their part in the drama was over, they would abruptly cease their wailing, take off their white hoods, turn around, and, chattering animatedly with each other, walk away. When a religious festival (commonly referred to locally as a *baibai*) was to take place, you might see a truck pass, loaded with freshly slaughtered pigs to

be used for sacrificial purposes. One of the most unusual sights for someone like myself was the snake meat shop just a few blocks from where we
lived. Walking or biking past the shop, you were as likely as not to see a
snake or several snakes nailed (just under the head) to a post or wall, enabling the proprietor to make an incision around the neck of the snake,
strip off the skin, and carefully separate the snake's flesh (to be eaten) from
its entrails (to be discarded).

Of course, our primary entrée into Chinese life—and from a
language-learning standpoint the most important—came from speaking
and hearing Chinese all day long. In the early 1960s, Taipei was not a
place where everyone had at least a modest familiarity with spoken
English. Some people did, most did not. When you wanted to give instructions to the cook or have your bicycle tuned or a roll of film developed, or you needed to cash a check or negotiate the cost of a ride with a
pedicab driver (fig. 1.5) or communicate with the person in charge of
your child's nursery school, you needed to be able to make yourself understood in Chinese and, equally important, understand what the other
person said to you.

Another aspect of my months of living in Taipei that was a new experience for me was the political environment. When I first arrived in
Taiwan in fall 1960, it was only eleven years since the communist victory
in the civil war (1945–49). Some two million of Taiwan's residents were
refugees from the Chinese mainland who had fled to the island during
the civil war years. Chiang Kai-shek's government, which in late 1949 and
early 1950 had been readying itself for an amphibious communist inva-
sion that appeared imminent, was given a new lease on life by the outbreak of the Korean War in June 1950. Communist forces assembling in
southeastern China for the final act of the civil war were redeployed to
the north, and the United States, determining that Taiwan was now an
important part of its defense perimeter in East Asia, moved units of the
Seventh Fleet into the Taiwan Strait.

Magically provided with the breathing space it had previously been
denied, the Chiang government during the 1950s moved in a number of
broad directions that distinguished the Taiwan scene for the next three
decades. The Guomindang (Nationalists) reorganized and rebuilt their
armed forces, by the end of the 1950s creating a military that was 600,000
strong and bore little resemblance to the disorganized, demoralized units

1.5. My daughter Joanna in a pedicab, which took her to and from nursery school (Taipei, 1961). Photograph by author.

that had fled the mainland in 1949. For the civilian population, education became nearly universal in these years, with over 90 percent of children of primary school age enrolled in school as of the late 1950s. A much-praised land reform program was initiated in 1949, which greatly reduced the power of the landlord class in the countryside and transformed Taiwan's agriculture into an owner-cultivator system. The infrastructure the Japanese had created during the colonial era, substantial U.S. economic aid from 1950 on, and the actions of an impressive group of Western-educated Chinese technocrats who had migrated to Taiwan were additional factors favoring the island's economic growth in the 1950s and after.

The foundational policy that drove these developments and that, for several decades after 1950, was enunciated incessantly was the goal of retaking the Chinese mainland. The manifestations of this goal, succinctly embodied in such slogans as *fangong fuguo* (launch a counterattack and recover the nation) and *fangong dalu* (launch a counterattack against the mainland), were encountered everywhere: on billboards in public venues, in magazines and books, in school primers, in political speeches, on radio and television, and in the press. The ideological handmaiden to the core political objective of retaking the mainland was a spirited emphasis, in the school system and elsewhere, on the inculcation of Confucian values. This was partly for the purpose of refurbishing the Republic of China's credentials as the repository of the authentic traditions of Chinese culture at a time when, from the Nationalist perspective, these traditions were being foreignized, falsified, and destroyed under the communists. It was certainly also aimed at the Taiwanese majority on the island who had recently spent a half-century living under Japanese colonial rule. Many mainland Chinese viewed the Taiwanese as wartime collaborators in dire need of being reintroduced to such time-honored Confucian precepts as loyalty and integrity.

The emergency decree of martial law enacted by the Nationalists in 1949 was not lifted until 1987, not long before the death of Chiang Kai-shek's son and successor, Chiang Ching-kuo. Living under a single-party authoritarian political system in a police state environment was a new experience for American students of Chinese. How did it impinge on our lives? In most cases, it didn't really affect us in a serious way (fig. 1.6). But it was eminently noticeable and something we bumped into all the

1.6. With friend singing in a Taiwan restaurant, 1961.

time. I have already alluded to the pervasive presence of written Nationalist propaganda to which we were exposed. U.S. students were told—whether true or not I cannot say—that our cooks and amahs made weekly reports to the authorities about our activities. Students of twentieth-century Chinese literature may have encountered difficulty getting the reading materials needed for their studies. The writings of many of the top literary figures of twentieth-century China (Lu Xun, for example) were not available in the bookstores and could be accessed, if at all, only if you had privileged entrée to a special library collection (e.g., at Academia Sinica). This restriction was mainly directed not at American graduate students but at the local Taiwan population—people like the young Taiwanese soldier I became friendly with who complained to me incessantly about the lack of access to much of twentieth-century China's best writing.

Revising My Dissertation and Looking for a Teaching Job

I had been in constant touch with Fairbank by mail during spring 1960, when he was away touring China centers around the world. Despite being abroad, he dutifully read the chapters of my dissertation and sent me comments. He passed on to me the names of people in Japan and elsewhere who were working on Christian missions in China and with whom I might eventually want to get in touch. Once I was settled in Taipei, I had to decide whether I should aim for quick publication of the revised dissertation or wait until I had done further research in the archives of Tokyo, London, and Paris, after my sojourn in Taiwan was over. During my stay in New Haven over the summer, I had asked Professor Mary Wright at Yale to have a look at the dissertation and give me her opinion. She strongly suggested I revise it for publication immediately and not put it off until after I had done the additional research.

In mid-November I received a long letter from Fairbank giving detailed comments on the dissertation. He felt that it was "an excellent beginning toward a book but [would] require considerable editorial revision in order to get by the Harvard Press, which we would like it to do as soon as possible." The basic problem with the manuscript in his view was that by structuring it in a very analytical way, I had neglected to give the reader a sense of the build-up of tension in the course of the 1860s culminating in "that excellent and horrifying Tientsin Massacre which wraps up all the angles of analysis in one crescendo. If you can pull this off as an editorial *tour de force*, you will have almost a best-seller because the story is one that builds to a remarkable climax."[13]

No one was better than Fairbank at combining praise with pressure. In February 1961 my article "The Anti-Christian Tradition in China" was published in the *Journal of Asian Studies*, and I sent him an offprint. His response: "I think the article is really very impressive and gives you the pioneer position in opening up an entire field. I think you should follow up with a revision of your manuscript as soon as possible. Can you tell me what your timetable is for its development? Do you gain anything by the passage of time? Can we expect the manuscript in September?"[14] That was vintage Fairbank.

Since I wanted to get started with my teaching career after my stay in Asia, another topic of endless back-and-forth correspondence with Fairbank related to the job market in the United States. The China field in the early 1960s, although on the cusp of a major expansion later in the decade, was still very small, and from his Harvard office Fairbank operated a one-man employment service for his former students, informing them of new openings, giving them advice, writing letters commending this or that person's special strengths and skills, and so on. There were a number of complicating factors in my case. The main one was my presence in Asia, which made it impossible or at least prohibitively expensive to interview at institutions I was interested in or that had shown interest in me. Another consideration was that I was done as a student and anxious to move on to the next phase of my career and start teaching. In the end, what I decided to do was take a one-year appointment replacing economic historian Albert Feuerwerker at the University of Michigan during a sabbatical. This had the disadvantage of being a position with no possibility of permanence. But it was a great university with an already established program of Chinese studies in various fields and, because it was only a one-year job and Feuerwerker and I knew each other, there was no pressing need for me to travel to Ann Arbor for an interview.

Before receiving an offer from Michigan, matters became more complicated as other options opened and then closed. Northwestern University was looking for an East Asian specialist to replace Roger Hackett, who had recently accepted a Japanese history position at Michigan. Fairbank was pushing Northwestern for me because it was a real job that could lead to something. I saw his point, although I was not persuaded. In mid-December I heard from Feuerwerker outlining the courses I would likely be asked to teach if I went to Michigan. He said that although he could not commit the History Department definitely, he was personally convinced that the position was mine if I wanted it.[15] Earlier I had received two rather urgent-sounding letters from Northwestern asking me to let them know immediately if I was interested in being considered for the job. I wrote back that I would like a little more time to go over my options. Not long after this, I heard from Northwestern that they had hired someone else for the opening, and shortly thereafter I received a formal offer from Michigan.

On January 11, 1962, I got a cable from Fairbank: "Unknowing preferable alternative recommend accepting Michigan." After waiting a few days, I sent Michigan my acceptance. But then, on January 15, while eating breakfast, I received another cable from Fairbank stating that a University of Chicago offer was now a possibility and recommending that I delay accepting Michigan. I rushed down to the post office and asked whether there was any possibility of my taking back the letter to Michigan. The post office people told me that there was no plane leaving for the United States that day and that it was indeed possible to retrieve my letter if it could be found. After going through stack after stack of mail I finally found my letter and was thus able to intercept it. On January 22 I received a letter from Fairbank, the substance of which was that he had just heard that the Chicago appointment had to go through both the History Department and the East Asian Studies Committee—a double hurdle that would take a considerable period of time. He had recently stopped at the University of Michigan to inaugurate its new Center for Chinese Studies and was much impressed with the youthful enthusiasm and general morale of the community. He recommended that I accept Feuerwerker's offer without further ado, which I did. I also wrote to the University of Chicago, explaining my decision and asking to be considered as a candidate the following year if they were still looking for someone.

During my time in Taipei, Fairbank and I corresponded about multiple other topics besides jobs and the reworking of my dissertation into a book. In the fall of 1960, when the presidential election campaign was in progress in the United States, I regularly sent him clippings from the Guomindang newspaper *Zhongyang ribao* (*Central Daily News*), which was strongly pro-Nixon and attacked Fairbank as a running dog of the American left (John F. Kennedy). Fairbank had been attacked before in the Chinese communist press and, possessed of a wry sense of humor, he was somewhat amused to learn now that he had enemies on both sides of the Taiwan Strait. After discovering on a visit to the Institute of Modern History of Academia Sinica that they had an original copy of the scabrous anti-Christian pamphlet *Pi-hsieh shih-lu* (*Bixie shilu*), which had been translated and published by missionaries under the title *Death Blow to Corrupt Doctrines*, I had a microfilm copy made and sent it to Fairbank at his request.[16] I also kept him informed about reprinted works, such as H. B. Morse's three-volume *The International Relations of the Chinese Empire*, originally published in 1910–1918 and long unavailable. He bought three copies for his personal use and wrote that "the [Harvard] Coop has bought some fifty copies . . . , which we will try to get all graduate students to buy in the coming year." He asked me to suggest English-language books "that might be sent to deserving [Asian] research scholars in Taipei to help them in their work."[17] An inveterate networker, Fairbank wrote me in June that he had asked Fox Butterfield (later a prominent journalist with the *New York Times*), who had just graduated from Harvard summa cum laude in history, to look me up when he got to Taiwan at the end of the summer for language work. "Your advice and example can, I know, be very instructive to him in one way or another, and I hope you will see something of each other."[18]

In August I wrote Fairbank the following:

> The Cornell program is over and it was a great success this year. To symbolize the progress that most of the fellows made in the spoken language, we put on a one-act Chinese play early in July in the United States Information Service (USIS) auditorium. We rehearsed it for six weeks, had a professional Chinese director to guide us, got decked out in traditional Chinese costume, make-up, beards, wigs, scenery—in a word, the works [fig. 1.7]. It was a sell-out, generously praised in all the local papers, and probably the best thing that ever happened to the USIS in Taipei, which it fully realized, as evidenced by the fact that it tried to persuade us to take the play on tour to Taichung and Tainan. Very unpatriotically, we decided that a one-night stand was enough.[19]

Although the Cornell program ended in the early summer of 1961, I remained in Taiwan until January 1962. During my final six months on the island, my time was taken up with a number of activities. I made frequent day trips to Nankang (Nangang), where the Institute of Modern History, Academia Sinica, was located, to do archival research relating to my book. Among the archives housed at the institute were those of the Zongli Yamen (a prototype foreign office that the Qing had created in March 1861), which included a great deal of material on church cases (*jiao'an*). Because these archives were being prepared for publication at the time, when I encountered difficult passages in Chinese, I benefited

1.7. With Jonathan Mirsky (right) performing in Chinese play, Taipei, 1961.

greatly from consultation with Wang Ermin and Lü Shiqiang, the two main resident scholars in charge of the work. I also continued with one-on-one tutorials I had begun while the Cornell program was still in operation. One of these, taught by Ma Jingheng, involved reading and discussing two famous Chinese novels, *Rulin waishi* (*The scholars*) and *Hong lou meng* (*Dream of the red chamber*). In the other tutorial, in which my teacher was Liang Pao-shuo (Baoshuo), we read through in their entirety both the Confucian *Analects* (*Lunyu*) and the *Book of Mencius* (*Mengzi*), my job being to translate passages from the classical language into modern Chinese and then discuss their meaning with Liang. Both courses did a great deal to strengthen my spoken Chinese skills and, like taking part in the Chinese play, represented a fitting conclusion to a marvelous all-around language learning experience.

The Start of My Academic Career

The end of our stay in Taiwan was anything but smooth and trouble-free. Right around the time the problems relating to my job hunt were becoming resolved (mid-January 1962), Joanna came down with chickenpox and a nasty staph infection, only days before Andrea and the two children (our son, Nathaniel, had been added to the family in August) were scheduled to fly to London to stay with my wife's sister while I paid a short visit to Tokyo. The plan was for me to join the family in London after a month in Tokyo, and London would serve as our base for the next few months while I did archival research there and in Paris. Then, as if Joanna's ill health wasn't trouble enough, five-month-old Nathaniel contracted amebic dysentery, could not hold anything down, and had to be hospitalized for a few days and fed intravenously. Andrea's original flight plans were changed. The children improved significantly, and they and she left on January 22. I flew to Tokyo the following day. (I had once thought it might be a good idea to spend a much longer period in Japan, mainly to work on my Japanese, but partly for family reasons and partly because I really wanted to start teaching, this idea had been scrapped months earlier.)

One of the benefits of writing a memoir is that you get to recall earlier moments in your life from the (hopefully wiser) perspective of a much later point in time. After the passage of more than fifty years, I look back on the experience I've just recounted with more than a small measure of guilt. Earlier I wrote about the gender imbalance that still existed at the start of the 1960s. My job at the time was to look after my career, while my wife's primary responsibility was to take care of our children. One of the inescapable consequences of this arrangement was that the man had an exaggerated sense of entitlement. He did what was necessary for the furthering of his career, and the rest of the family adapted. It didn't matter that taking a long plane trip with two small children, both of whom had recently been ill, was bound to be stressful for Andrea. It simply never occurred to me that I might go with them to London, make sure that they were well settled there, and *then* fly to Tokyo. My thinking at the time was different from what it is now.

In Tokyo I met with Japanese scholars whose interests were related to mine. I also began what was to become a lifelong friendship with Irwin Scheiner, who, like me, was a student of Christianity's involvement in East Asia, although his focus was Meiji Japan.[20] In late February I flew to London to join my family. For the balance of February and the whole month of March, I conducted research at the Public Record Office in London and the French Foreign Ministry archives at the Quai d'Orsay in Paris. In early April we returned to the United States, where we stayed with my parents on Long Island for several months before going to Ann Arbor, where we had arranged with the Feuerwerkers to live in their home for the year they were abroad.

The next few years were important and exciting ones in my professional life. Not long after I began to teach at Michigan, I wrote Fairbank (now addressed more familiarly as John) about how much I really enjoyed the process. This didn't come as a huge surprise by any means, but since teaching was what I planned to be doing for the remaining decades of my working life, it was a welcome discovery nevertheless.[21] Aside from the teaching, during my year in Ann Arbor I became good friends with Alexander Eckstein, a China economist who had previously spent time at Harvard. The University of Michigan was moving rapidly to strengthen its position in Chinese studies generally, and during Feuerwerker's absence, Alex played a very active role in this process. Since I had just spent sixteen months in Taiwan and had gotten to know some of the top people who were, like me, entering the job market but, unlike me, didn't have a John Fairbank for guidance, I was well positioned to be of assistance to Alex.[22] Michigan needed good Chinese language teaching and I knew just the person—my teacher and close friend Ma Jingheng. Alex touched base with the language people at the university, and they were interested. This led to a lengthy and involved correspondence with Jingheng dealing with family dependents, visas, and so forth. Everything got worked out in the end, and she and her family moved to Ann Arbor in the summer of 1963; she began to teach Chinese at Michigan in the fall (by which time I had moved on to Amherst College). Another good friend I had gotten to know in Taipei was Donald J. Munro, a China philosopher, who just happened to be living temporarily in the Detroit area while I was in Ann Arbor. Don was finishing up his doctoral work at Columbia University and wasn't ready to start teaching right away. But I knew he was looking for a job in fall 1964, and because there weren't a lot of universities in the country interested in hiring in the area of Chinese philosophy, I mentioned Don to Alex and suggested that Alex speak to the people in the Michigan Philosophy Department. They interviewed Don and offered him a position as assistant professor beginning in the fall of 1964. Don remained at Michigan for more than three decades, enjoying a distinguished teaching and writing career in the areas of Chinese philosophy and thought, retiring in 1996.

It didn't escape my notice, as I became engaged in these job placement activities, that this was something else I had learned how to do from Fairbank, although my contributions in this vein were minuscule in comparison. I can't resist also pointing out that my extensive correspondence with John and many others in the early 1960s took place prior to the advent of email. The days of instantaneous response hadn't yet dawned. We were still in the "Age of the Tortoise," and what a difference that made, especially when a quick decision needed to be made.

One Book Is Accepted for Publication and Another Commenced

Another important development took place during my year in Ann Arbor. I got the news in June 1962 that Harvard had accepted my book manuscript,[23] which meant that during much of the next year the process of book production, which was new to me, was going to consume a good bit of my energy. But I still had time to sink my teeth into something new. Some scholars, as they finish up with one book, know exactly what they want to do next. It has never been that way with me. I had a lot of time to think about this during the summer of 1962, before getting to Michigan, and once I got to Ann Arbor, which had a good Chinese collection, I began to collect materials on a fascinating late Qing intellectual named Wang Tao (1828–97).[24] There were a number of reasons I was attracted to Wang, some of them intellectual, others practical. First, unlike other Chinese in the latter half of the nineteenth century who had extensive contact with Westerners and had traveled or lived abroad, Wang was a prolific and accomplished writer, so the sources on his life and career were abundant. I encountered him initially in Ssu-yü Teng and John Fairbank's classic work *China's Response to the West* (1954), which I had read as a graduate student. This is an example of a common phenomenon in the scholarly world: the influence that prior scholarship—and the choices made in it—exerts on the choices made by later scholars. If Teng and Fairbank hadn't decided to include Wang in their work, chances are it would have been a long time before I had even heard of him, and it is doubtful I would have elected to spend ten years of my life reading his work and writing a book about him. (Something not dissimilar to this happened in the case of *China and Christianity*. In 1941, two Chinese scholars, Chen Zenghui and Wu Shengde, had compiled a comprehensive bibliography of Chinese source materials dealing with incidents involving Christian missions. When I first corresponded with Chen in 1985, I told him that their bibliography had saved me months of time when I was doing the research for my dissertation in the late 1950s. "In fact," I wrote him, "given the state of my Chinese language ability at that time, I seriously doubt whether I would have done my dissertation on that topic at all if it hadn't been for your bibliography."[25])

Practical considerations also take an important part in shaping academic careers, as a past president of the American Historical Association observed in the February 2007 issue of *Perspectives*, and this points to an additional reason for my being attracted to Wang Tao. When I taught at Amherst College, the nearest first-rate Chinese library (Harvard's) was two hours away by car. So it was helpful to have a book project focused on a single person, who also happened to be a high-volume writer, much of whose work had been collected in a few key books that I could have copies made of or borrow from the Harvard-Yenching Library on long-term loan. I remained at Amherst for two years, after which I accepted a position at Wellesley College, a half-hour drive from Cambridge.

There were several reasons for Wellesley's appeal in comparison to Amherst. One of these was the chance it offered to become affiliated with Harvard's East Asian Research Center, where I was given an office and had frequent contact with other China scholars.[26] As I wrote my older sister, Barbara, in March 1965, telling her of the new appointment, "I will no longer be isolated, as I am here [at Amherst]. Here, nobody reads the same books I read, and for intellectual stimulation I must talk to the wall." Another was Wellesley's openness to introducing Chinese language instruction at the college, whereas at the time Amherst seemed indifferent to making East Asian studies a more significant part of the curriculum. Another factor, of course, was the proximity of the Harvard-Yenching Library, the strongest Chinese collection in the country after the Library of Congress. During the earlier phase of my research on Wang Tao, I could get by as long as I had a few key works by Wang. But as I got deeper into the research, the need for more extensive access to a good Chinese collection became pressing.

Another appeal of Wellesley related more broadly to my role as a teacher. From the very start of my career at the college, which lasted some thirty-five years, it was clear that at Wellesley China was viewed as an important part of the world. As I wrote in a short piece in the *Wellesley Alumnae Magazine* in November 1966, there were "few undergraduate institutions in the country . . . able to match Wellesley's commitment to Chinese studies." During my first year at the college (1965–66), I taught a new extradepartmental course on Chinese civilization, which was taken by 242 students. The following year, Chinese language was offered for the first time under the expert guidance of Helen Lin, who had previously taught Chinese at the Foreign Service Language Institute in Taichung, Taiwan, and at Yale's Far Eastern Language Institute. Even before this, enthusiastic students had formed a Chinese lunch table that met weekly, along with interested faculty (like myself), to converse in Chinese (Mandarin). At the end of nine years of Chinese language instruction, as I wrote in a report in September 1974, Wellesley could compare favorably with any undergraduate Chinese program in the country. By that time, in a typical year, we had fifty to sixty students taking Chinese at all levels. Some had used Chinese for research purposes in their senior honors theses, and a growing number went on to more advanced work in the best graduate programs.

In 1966–67, China was the focal point of a number of major extra-curricular events at the college sponsored by the Barnette Miller Foundation and the Mayling Soong Foundation, included among which was an exhibition of traditional Chinese art forms organized by Max Loehr of Harvard. Of course, for the student who became seriously involved in China, there were substantial advantages to be derived from Wellesley's proximity to Harvard.

A fair number of my Wellesley students over the years went on to do graduate work in Chinese studies and from there to careers teaching some aspect of China in colleges and universities across the United States and abroad. At the same time, my close involvement with the East Asian Research Center (later renamed the Fairbank Center for Chinese Studies) at Harvard gave me access to a kind of teaching experience that Wellesley did not offer: the opportunity to enjoy close contact with graduate students, those either studying at Harvard or visiting from elsewhere. I took an active part in the life of the center, launching the New England China Seminar in the 1970s, at the request of then-director Ezra Vogel. This seminar series met monthly, the format consisting of a late afternoon talk by an invited scholar (generally, though not invariably, from the New England area), followed by dinner for the speaker and registered guests, and then an after-dinner talk by a second invited scholar. In 1980 I was asked to serve on the center's executive committee, which at that point met frequently and took an important part in decisions pertaining to running the center. The invitation came from Philip Kuhn, a fellow graduate student from the late 1950s, who was director of the center at the time. Merle Goldman and I were among the first non-Harvard faculty to serve on the executive committee, and I have served on it continuously from 1980 to the present.

Over the years I was at Wellesley I managed, even during the teaching season, to spend two or three days a week at Harvard, where aside from going to (and at times giving) talks at the East Asian Research Center, I was often asked to read and critique graduate student dissertations and the writings of colleagues. As I published more and became better known in the China field generally, my reading of the work in progress of scholars (and occasionally graduate students) at other institutions around the country became a feature of my academic life that I took (and continue to take) with utmost seriousness. All of these factors together convince me that the move I made to Wellesley College and the greater Boston area in fall 1965 was a stroke of good fortune. It presented a unique combination of opportunities that embraced teaching at one of the top undergraduate institutions in the United States while becoming an integral part of one of the country's leading centers for research on Chinese history. In the ensuing chapters of this memoir, I try to convey to the reader how I put the second of these opportunities to use.

CHAPTER 2

Wang Tao

The Problem of Change in the Late Qing

One of the core issues that the career of Wang Tao challenged—a prime reason for my intellectual attraction to him—was the Western impact–Chinese response approach, which had been dominant in U.S. scholarship during the 1950s and 1960s. This approach, as we shall see in the next chapter, was intimately linked to the broader European and American assumption, with deep roots in nineteenth-century Western thought, that meaningful endogenous change was nearly impossible in China, that the only real change that could be expected to happen there was change resulting from the Western impact and patterned after the Western example. Although it was not until the latter half of the 1970s that I undertook to examine this mode of thinking in a comprehensive way, it is clear in retrospect that I had already become deeply uncomfortable with it a decade earlier in the course of my intellectual probing into Wang Tao's life and work.[1]

Wang Tao's Life (1828–97) in Brief

Wang Tao (fig. 2.1) spent his early life in the Suzhou area. After failing to qualify for the Chinese civil service examination for the second degree in 1846, he worked as an editor at the London Missionary Society Press in Shanghai, where he contributed to a new Chinese translation of

2.1. Wang Tao. *Source: Shanghai yanjiu ziliao* (Shanghai: Zhonghua Shuju, 1936).

the Bible. Although baptized in 1854, Wang's leisure-time activities in Shanghai were not exactly an advertisement for Christian rectitude. He and a few close friends regularly went drinking and visited the courtesans, whose world and rituals he recorded in loving detail in his writings. In 1862, the Qing authorities in Shanghai charged Wang with engaging in traitorous communication with the Taiping rebels then threatening the city (see chapter 3). With British help, he fled Shanghai and went to Hong Kong, where arrangements had been made for him to take employment assisting James Legge in the latter's monumental translation of the Chinese Classics. Legge placed such a high value on Wang's help that in 1867 he invited Wang to join him in Scotland to continue with the translation work.

After more than two years abroad, which included visits to continental Europe, Wang returned to Hong Kong in 1870 and began writing about the West. The most influential of his works in this vein was an account of the Franco-Prussian War (published in 1873). This book, the first in Chinese to scrutinize a major episode in recent European history, brought Wang instant fame as an expert on foreign matters. Around this time, Wang embarked on a career in journalism and in 1874 was named editor of the newly launched Chinese daily *Xunhuan ribao* (Universal circulating herald), the first newspaper to be wholly capitalized and operated by Chinese. Although the commercial nature of *Xunhuan ribao* was unmistakable, it was seriously committed to providing information on the outside world and offering advice on current affairs. Wang's essays were regularly published in the paper. Free to express himself at will in British Hong Kong, his use of the press to advocate reform was part of a pioneering trend that was further developed at the turn of the twentieth century by such renowned publicists as Wang Kangnian and Liang Qichao, with far-reaching consequences for modern China.

Wang witnessed in Hong Kong a commercial society in action and associated himself, socially and economically, with a highly successful breed of Chinese merchants. He joined them in their periodic delegations to the governor of Hong Kong and even developed a friendly relationship with Governor John Pope Hennessy. Through his newspaper, Wang urged Chinese officials to strengthen their support of commerce and raise the status of merchants in the Chinese social order.

In 1879, Wang Tao visited Japan for four months and was warmly welcomed by Japanese intellectuals as a celebrated Chinese man of letters and scholar of Western learning.

After two productive decades in Hong Kong, in 1884 Wang Tao returned to Shanghai, where he continued to publicize his reformist ideas. In 1894, he helped Sun Yat-sen draft a reform petition to Li Hongzhang, the leading Qing official of the day. Li was, however, preoccupied with more pressing matters (war with Japan was in the offing), the effort to communicate with him was aborted, and Sun henceforth turned his attention to revolution. Wang Tao, a different kind of revolutionary, died in May 1897, just shy of his seventieth birthday, on the eve of changes that he, as much as any Chinese of his generation, anticipated.[2]

Since Wang Tao spent his entire adult life grappling with complicated questions relating to change, in the course of trying to make sense of his thinking I had to confront these questions myself. In the prologues to the four parts of my book on Wang, I touched on a number of broad change-related issues as they pertained to him: the relationship between incremental change and revolution, the differences between generational and historical change, the virtue of measuring societal change by internal points of reference, the complex relationship between "tradition" and "modernity," differences between the actual historical past of China and "Chinese tradition," technological change versus value change, the geo-cultural sources of change in nineteenth- and twentieth-century China, and so on. In much of my discussion of these issues, as the account of Wang Tao's thinking in the following section suggests, there was still a residual tendency—even as I was beginning to raise questions concerning it—to overstate the relative importance of Western influence as the key measure of change in late Qing China.[3]

Wang Tao's Prescriptions for a New China

"In our new land," John Fairbank wrote, "we helped invent the modern world; the Chinese had it thrust upon them and rammed down their throats."[4] As the West closed in on China in the nineteenth century, it caught the Chinese off-balance—so off-balance that it took decades before they began to comprehend, even dimly, the nature and depth of the challenge facing them. In these circumstances, it was far from self-evident how the challenge was to be met, and it was not uncommon to encounter approaches such as the following:

According to Daoism, softness can overcome hardness and the way to advance is by retreating. Therefore, if one uses one's weakness with skill, it can be turned to strength. When something becomes too hard it must snap; when one advances too hastily one must stumble. Therefore, if one uses one's strength imprudently it will invariably turn to weakness. A glance at history shows that no dynasty ruled longer than the Zhou, despite the fact that after the shift [of its capital] eastward under King Ping [r. 770–719 BCE], the [Zhou] was weakened to the point of being virtually powerless. . . . [Similarly], the Song was the feeblest of houses, yet it was able to contend successively with the Liao, Jin, and Yuan, and to prolong its rule for over three hundred years. Through weakness, it was able to survive.[5]

This passage appeared in a Hong Kong newspaper article in the late 1860s. The intent was to show that Chinese were fooling themselves if they believed that the way to meet the Western challenge was to exchange the time-honored usages of China for those of the West. China's best defense consisted not in training armies, manufacturing weapons, and constructing fortifications, but in exercising Daoist passivity and such hallowed Confucian virtues as righteousness, loyalty, and trust.

The editor of the newspaper sent the article to Wang Tao in Scotland (where he was staying with Legge), and Wang wrote a lengthy rebuttal, spelling out his position on the need for change and articulating an intellectual framework for coping with the Western menace.[6]

He began by boldly proclaiming that the world was undergoing changes of such magnitude that the customs and institutions that had been preserved by Chinese for 3,000 years were in real danger of being destroyed. He drew a comparison between the northwestern portion of the globe (the West) and the southeastern portion (China): "The southeast is soft and quiescent, the northwest, hard and active. Quiescent [civilizations] are adept at conserving; active ones are adept at changing. . . . Soft [civilizations] are able to maintain themselves; hard ones are able to control others. Therefore, the [countries] of the northwest have always been able to visit harm upon those of the southeast, but the [countries] of the southeast have never been able to hurt those of the northwest."[7]

Wang was prepared to grant that sometimes change could be countered by nonchange (conserving) and hardness overcome by softness. But this was at best a slow and uncertain process, and in the meantime the West could be counted on to seize every opportunity to make trouble for China. China's only sensible course of action, therefore, was to beat the West at its own game by mastering its strengths (*shi qi suo chang*). Of course, this would mean change. But it was change necessitated by circumstance, and such change, according to Wang, had always been sanctioned: "When the course of Heaven changes above, the actions of men must change below. The Yijing [Classic of changes] states: 'When the possibilities inhering in a situation have been exhausted, change must take place; when there has been a change, things will run smoothly again.'"[8]

If China had to change before she could stand firm as a nation, did this mean she must abandon her traditional customs, government, and culture and undergo a process of all-out Westernization? "No," Wang answered emphatically, "when I speak of change, I mean changing the outer, not the inner, changing what it is proper to change, not what cannot be changed. The change I have in mind, [moreover], must proceed from us. . . . If they make us change, the advantage will be reaped by them; only if we change of our own volition will we retain control over our affairs."

Wang went on to note that just as China had started out as a small country and gradually expanded, reaching its greatest extent under the Qing, a parallel development had now taken place in European history. Like a great tidal bore, in a century's time the Europeans had spread from India to Southeast Asia and from Southeast Asia to south China, their knowledge advancing all the while.

A change of so fundamental a character could not have been programmed by humans; it had to have been designed by Heaven. And since it was Heaven's will at work, it could only be for China's good, one of the deepest strains in Wang Tao's world view being the assumption that Heaven (or destiny) was on China's side: "Heaven's motive in bringing several dozen Western countries together in the single country of China is not to weaken China but to strengthen it, not to harm China but to benefit it. Consequently, if we make good use of [this opportunity], we can convert harm into benefit and change weakness into strength. I do not fear the daily arrival of the Westerners; what I fear is that we Chinese will place limits upon ourselves. We have only one alternative, and that is to undergo complete change [*yibian*]."

Earlier Wang Tao had specified that what he meant by "change" was change of the outer (*wai*), not change of the inner (*nei*). Now he called for "complete change." How was this inconsistency to be resolved? I think the inconsistency is more apparent than real. If I understand him correctly, Wang used *yibian* to signify not change of everything but change of everything that was *capable* of being changed. *Yibian* did not embrace the realm of *nei*, the inner, the essence, for *nei* (which was comparable in value to *dao*) was not subject to change. It did, on the other hand, encompass *wai*, the outer realm, the realm of the changeable, and because *wai* included everything that was not *nei*, the potential scope for change was considerable. So considerable that, without impinging on the security of *nei*, Wang was able to envision a fairly sweeping transformation of the Chinese landscape:

> In the military sphere we should make a complete changeover [*yibian*] from swords and spears to firearms; in the field of navigation we should make a complete changeover from [old-style] boats to steamboats; in the sphere of overland travel we should make a complete changeover from carriages and horses to trains; and in the realm of work we should make a complete changeover from [traditional] tools to machines. Although . . . [the old and the new means in these several areas] are alike in regard to their end results, they cannot be compared in respect to speed, precision, relative difficulty, and amount of labor required.
>
> [The Westerners] have all four of these things; we do not have a single one. If the situation were one in which we lacked them and they had them and there were no relations between us, our lack of them would not be a shortcoming and their possession of them would give them nothing to brag about. We could carry on in our accustomed fashion and it would be perfectly all right. But when they insult us in an overbearing manner and on comparison we are found to be inferior, when they constantly insist upon contending and competing with us so that there is mutual wrangling and recrimination, can we afford for a single day to be without these things? . . . We may be certain that before a hundred years are out, all four will be in China's possession, functioning as if they had always been with us and viewed [by everyone] as commonplace contrivances. It is not that I *want* this prediction to come true; it cannot help but come true. Circumstances and the times make it so. It is Heaven's wish that the eastern and western halves of the globe be joined in one.

The significance we attach to these paragraphs depends on the framework of assumptions with which we approach them. For one thing, there is a growing body of scholarly opinion that, in defining the relationship between "modern" and "traditional," rejects the implication that these are necessarily antithetical, mutually repellent conditions. As historian Michael Gasster summarized the issue:

> Most societies, Western as well as non-Western, are dualistic, in the sense that they are *mixtures* of the modern and the traditional, not *either* modern *or* traditional. They are "systems in which cultural change is taking place," and they are distinguished from each other in terms of the type of relationship between the "modern" and the "traditional" components that exists in each. . . . From this point of view, modernization is best understood as a process *leading toward* a condition of modernity but never quite reaching it; indeed, there is no final condition of modernity but only a continuing process of adjustment among many modernizing and traditional forces.[9]

To this I would only add that I see no reason we must limit ourselves to the two categories of "modern" and "traditional." Presumably, there are elements in the make-up of every society—the general human proclivity for story and storytelling, for example[10]—that do not fall neatly under either rubric.

If it is accepted that modernity is a relative concept and that all societies, however modern, still retain certain traditional features, two questions arise: How much of the Confucian order, objectively considered, had to be abandoned before substantive change could take place in nineteenth-century China, and was it necessary, as a prelude to such change, for this order to be openly challenged? These questions uncover a hornet's nest of further questions. Granting that Confucianism and the traditional order were not coterminous, where do we draw the line between the two? Did the conscious rejection of the Confucian order (however defined) necessarily immunize against continued contamination by it? Conversely, did refusal to take open issue with Confucianism have the ineluctable effect of protecting it against attrition? To put it more succinctly, what is the relationship between real change and perceived change? Between perceived change and desired change?

My object in posing these questions—and I return to them in the next chapter—is to warn against overhasty acceptance of the answers that have already been given. These are fiendishly difficult questions. Some of them may be ultimately unanswerable. None of them can be answered with finality, and therefore it is essential to keep asking them.

The tendency to deprecate the "ships-and-guns" stage of Chinese reform thought also reflects the widely held assumption that Chinese reform efforts prior to 1895 were a "failure." This assumption was fed initially by treaty port opinion, which was consistently impatient with Chinese "ineptness." In more recent times it has been reinforced by scholarly misinterpretation of the meaning of the Japanese example. Comparison of Chinese and Japanese modernization efforts can be useful. But it must be done with extreme caution. Japan defeated China in 1895 and went on to become a world power while China continued to flounder in weakness, but if we conclude that Japan's "response to the West" was rapid and successful and China's slow and unsuccessful, we ignore a fundamental fact about modern Japanese history—namely, that Japanese modernization, above all in the political realm, had begun long before the arrival of the Westerners.[11] As a corrective to such reasoning, it is useful to broaden our comparative perspective and measure the modernizing experiences of China and Japan not merely against each other but against those of the rest of the world, the impact of the West being taken as only one variable among many. When we do this, we find that both China and Japan come off relatively well.[12] China may have lagged behind Japan, but it started much later.

Words like *failure* and *success*, *rapid* and *slow* have a relative value only, and it is essential to keep this in mind when making comparisons. Perhaps the key question to ask in comparing the modernizing experiences of China and Japan is not why the two countries responded to the West with such differing rates of speed and degrees of success, but why China's modernization began in earnest only after the intrusion of a substantial outside stimulus while Japan's began long before.[13]

Partly as a result of the pervasive influence of assumptions such as those discussed in the foregoing paragraphs, there has been a general reluctance to bear down on the technological aspects of reform in nineteenth-century China. The upshot is that some of the most elementary distinctions have been obscured. Technological change as an objective fact has been confused with commitment to technological change, which is subjective and indicates a value preference. Also, there has been relatively little effort to distinguish different kinds of commitment to technological change. People may advocate limited changes in technology, or they may favor what amounts to a technological revolution. They may have warm, positive feelings toward technological change, viewing it as a natural concomitant of the "forward march of civilization," or they may see it as an unavoidable misfortune, something required by the pressure of circumstances but not desirable in itself. Finally, the commitment to technological change may be entered into for a variety of specific reasons (not all mutually exclusive): to improve living conditions, to compete more effectively with other countries, to increase state power, to preserve existing values and institutions, and so on.

Assuming it to be true that the nature of a person's commitment to technological change more or less reflects his or her orientation toward change in general, where did Wang Tao stand as of the late 1860s? Relative to what other Chinese were proposing at the time, how radical was his reform program and his proposals for the future? Although it is impossible to say exactly how far Wang was prepared to go at this juncture—he probably did not know himself—it was certainly a lot further than most of his contemporaries. Other reformers agreed on the necessity of introducing Western firearms and steamships. But leading Chinese officials were unanimous in their opposition to building railways,[14] and with the exception of a few highly Westernized treaty port types, no one in the late 1860s (as far as I know) was ready to advocate extensive mechanization of the Chinese economy.

Equally important were the specific reasons Wang gave for advocating technological change. Many late nineteenth-century reformers, identifying the West with "matter" and China with "spirit," argued that only by the adoption of Western material civilization could China's spiritual civilization be saved from extinction. This was the *ti-yong* approach, immortalized in the 1890s by a leading provincial official Zhang Zhidong in the famous phrase, "Chinese learning for the essential principles (*ti*), Western learning for the practical applications (*yong*)."

Although it would be incorrect to say that Wang Tao was completely unreceptive to the *ti-yong* approach—here as elsewhere he was capable of inconsistency—the central thrust of his thinking pointed in a different direction. Wang assumed that the essence of Chinese civilization—the core values, China's *dao*—was indestructible. In theory, therefore, he was free to take any position he wished in regard to technological change. He could reject even token technological change as being unnecessary. With equal logic, he could espouse massive technological change on the grounds that it could do no harm. If he chose the latter course, however, it would necessarily be for reasons other than the preservation of Chinese essence. In fact, this is precisely what we find to have been the case. Wang gave two justifications for technological revolution: first, that this was the only way China could compete with Western countries that had already undergone such a revolution, and second, that Heaven demanded it as the means to future world unification. In either instance, the preservation of Chinese values was viewed less as the justification of technological change than as its limiting condition.

In proposing sweeping technological change, was Wang merely advocating the inevitable, or was he to some extent using the argument of inevitability to buttress his advocacy? In other words, did he view such change as desirable because it was going to happen anyway, or did he simply say it was going to happen anyway because he felt it to be desirable? On the face of it, it would appear that Wang regarded technological revolution as a necessary evil. It was not, he insisted, that he wanted his predictions to come true; they *had* to come true as a result of "circumstances and the times." In a context like this, however, we must be wary of accepting Wang's words at face value. This was not, after all, a letter to a friend or a private diary; it was a newspaper article. Wang's object was to persuade the newspaper's readership. Since it had to be assumed that in the late 1860s this readership was largely opposed to massive technological change, it only made sense, tactically speaking, to portray such change as inevitable. Wang's personal feelings about the advent of the "machine age" were doubtless more accurately reflected in the travel diary he kept during his visit to Europe (1868–70), in which his response was one of unqualified admiration and awe.[15]

The radical quality of Wang Tao's commitment to technological change brought him quite early to the recognition that other kinds of change would also be necessary. He became one of the first proponents in the 1870s of institutional change (*bianfa*), and it was not long before his commitment to innovation widened further to embrace basic social, economic, educational, and political reforms. Inevitably, as this happened, the old sanctions for change proved increasingly inadequate and Wang was obliged to seek new ones.[16]

One such, historical in character, reflected the developmental, non-cyclical side of Wang's view of history:

> Westerners who have perused the annals of Chinese history think that for five thousand years there has been no change. When, on the contrary, has China not experienced change? First, Youchao, Suiren, Fuxi, and the Yellow Emperor cleared the wilderness and gave China governmental institutions. Then, Yao and Shun, following in their footsteps, styled China the center of the firmament and provided it with the attributes of civilization. From the Three Dynasties to the Qin there was another complete change and from the Han and Tang to the present yet another complete change.[17]

Wang's defensiveness, in the face of Western criticism of Chinese stasis, is interesting. He could, after all, have turned the criticism into a backhanded compliment—a glorification of China eternal. The fact that, instead, he chose to respond with an insistent "We too have had change" implied an emotional identification with the idea of change that was not commonly encountered in the Chinese setting of Wang's time.

The same positiveness of spirit may be seen in another of Wang's sanctions for reform, his assertion that it had always been the Way of the Sages (that is, the Confucian Way) to make proper accommodations to the times and that if Confucius were living in the nineteenth century he would certainly have lent his support to the introduction of Western technology and the general cause of reform.[18] The view of Confucius as a would-be reformer—here Wang clearly anticipated the radical late nineteenth-century thinker Kang Youwei—was potentially revolutionary. It not only provided a powerful justification for particular changes but also introduced into Confucianism a more affirmative attitude toward change in general.

Just as revolutionary, though much less obvious, were the implications of Wang's universalistic conception of *dao*.[19] The prevailing tendency among his contemporaries was to equate China with *dao* and the West with *qi* (technology). Wang's conviction that *dao* was an attribute of human civilization, and therefore the property of the West as well as of China, injected something very new into the discussion. It brought the West into a Chinese world of discourse and in the process furnished China with a rationale for borrowing more than mere *qi* from the West.

Did Wang's dynamization of Confucius and his universalization of *dao* modify the Confucian tradition to the point where it could no longer be called Confucian? In his efforts to find a basis of legitimacy for China's modernization, did Wang reinterpret Confucianism to death? When faced with such questions, it is easy to lapse into a kind of retrospective determinism that, starting from the conscious rejection of Confucianism in the May Fourth period of the early twentieth century, sees all modifications of Confucianism in the immediately preceding decades as leading inexorably to this conclusion. One antidote to such reasoning is to remind ourselves that radical changes in Confucian doctrine had taken place before without bringing an end to the tradition. It is very possible that neither Han nor Song Confucianism would have been recognizable to Confucius, but this did not keep their adherents from seeing themselves as authentic followers of the Sage. Similarly, in the case before us, there is probably no way of determining whether the liberties Wang took with Confucianism were fatal to it in any objective sense. All we can say for sure is that Wang continued to regard himself as a Confucian.

Sources of Change in Nineteenth- and Twentieth-Century China

In the final part of my book on Wang Tao, I moved away from the biographical emphasis and addressed some broader issues relating to change in nineteenth- and twentieth-century China. I revisited these issues in the preface to the paperback edition of the book, which came out in 1987. Let me briefly summarize the main themes of the book's last part and then suggest some of the modifications I later came to feel would strengthen it. The framework of interpretation that I originally advanced embodied three propositions: (1) that sweeping culture change often takes place in two phases, the first dominated by pioneers (or innovators), the second by legitimizers (or validators); (2) that Chinese history since the Opium War may be viewed as a product of the interaction between two largely distinct and self-contained cultural environments, the littoral or coast (Hong Kong, Shanghai, etc.) and the hinterland or interior; and (3) that, in the nineteenth century and for a while in the twentieth, the primary responsibility for the initiation of change in China rested with the subculture of the coast, the interior functioning mainly as a vehicle of legitimation. In an effort to clarify how the littoral served as an initiator of change in the late Qing period, I shifted in the book's final part from individual to collective biography and probed the careers of a dozen pioneer reformers, eight of them (including Wang Tao) closely associated with the culture of the littoral, four representative of the Chinese hinterland.

I openly acknowledged the tentative and exploratory nature of this framework at the time and hedged it with a fair number of qualifications.[20] It wasn't until I got deep into the writing of my next work, *Discovering History in China* (1984) and was able to put some distance between myself and the Wang Tao book that I gained a clearer sense of where the soft areas were and how I might go about firming them up. The most critical of these areas was a tendency, visible not only in the final part of *Between Tradition and Modernity* but in the earlier sections as well, to imply that the prime measure of change in late Qing China was the extent of the West's impact on Chinese institutions and on the world view of China's educated strata. In other words, change was over-identified with Western influence on Chinese life, with the threefold consequence that endogenous patterns of change were either overlooked or trivialized; that the process of institutionalizing change, referred to in the book as "legitimation," was too readily reduced to simple Sinicization (de-Westernization); and finally, that attention was diverted from social, economic, and political barriers to change to focus almost exclusively on intellectual and cultural barriers.

If I were to rewrite the final part of that book today, I would retain the polarity between coast and interior and continue to insist on the importance of distinguishing between the pioneering and legitimizing phases of culture change (using *culture* in a broadly anthropological sense). However, I would devote much more attention to patterns of internally powered change emerging in China in the latter half of the nineteenth century—commercial development,[21] growing politicization of local elites, and so on—and even more crucially, I would say something about the special problems involved in validating such change and how these problems differed from those involved in the legitimation of foreign-influenced changes. To illustrate, take the case of the influential late Qing scholar-official Feng Guifen (1809–74). Feng's far-reaching proposals for the reform of Chinese local government, first set forth in 1860–61,[22] were largely (if not entirely) endogenous in inspiration, but they encountered barriers to incorporation into the Chinese world of the 1860s, 1870s, and 1880s that were arguably no less formidable than those confronting the reform efforts of a man like Wang Tao. In Wang's case, however, because so many of his reform proposals reflected the influence of the West, the obstacles to legitimation tended to be more cultural and social in nature, whereas in Feng's case they were more political and economic.

Greater recognition of the importance of internal processes of change in the late Qing would serve as a natural corrective to overstatement of the role of the West; it would also make it more difficult to misstate this role. In rereading *Between Tradition and Modernity* some years after its original publication (1974), I noted, for example, a tendency in places to assume, almost in spite of myself, that the more radical forms of change in the latter half of the nineteenth century were generally (if not invariably) those stemming from the "Western challenge." From this later perspective, I was inclined to steer clear of the "challenge" terminology altogether, and I would make the more basic point that Chinese promotion of Western-inspired change (initially in the realm of technology but eventually in other sectors) was often justified, especially when the promoters were members of the government or the social elite, as a defensive strategy to block far more fundamental—and hence more threatening—changes of partially or wholly indigenous origin. Western-related change, in other words, in certain circumstances could be allied with forces of a relatively conservative nature in Chinese society. There was no guarantee that just because it was Western in inspiration, it would necessarily be more "radical," "fundamental," or "system-threatening" in character.

Finally—and somewhat paradoxically in light of the points I have just been making—if I were redoing the final part of that book today, I would be less hasty in writing off the littoral as a major source of innovation in the latter decades of the twentieth century. One of the main features of the Deng Xiaoping era (beginning in the late 1970s) was an opening to the outside world far exceeding anything remotely imaginable in the early 1970s when the original edition of my book on Wang Tao was completed. Although not all of the foreign influences that flowed into China in the Deng and post-Deng years were channeled through the littoral, a great majority of them were, and the contrast in terms of accessibility and receptivity to foreign-inspired innovation between such coastal entrepôts as Shanghai, Tianjin (Tientsin), and Guangzhou (Canton) and the more remote cities of the Chinese hinterland was still immense.

By the same token, the post-Mao years have also underscored the persistence of the distinctive problems of incorporation and acceptance presented by foreign-patented (especially Western-patented) changes. The suppression of the democracy movement in 1979, the campaign against "spiritual pollution" in 1983, and the sharp attack on "bourgeois liberalization" that began in the winter of 1986–87—all events that took place on Deng Xiaoping's watch—clearly suggested an ongoing resistance to the legitimation of certain kinds of foreign-linked ideas in the Chinese world. The sources of this resistance, however, were complicated and differed in important respects from those that operated in Wang Tao's day. Now it was the perception that the purity not of native cultural traditions but of a foreign-derived ideological system, Marxism-Leninism, was being threatened that provided the major justification for clampdowns on other foreign-derived ideological influences (such as democratic liberalism). Moreover, where resistance has been shown to such Western-grounded political demands as the right to demonstrate or greater freedom of expression or an independent judiciary, it seems clear that the basis for the resistance has not been confined to the Westernness of the demands; far more important has been their challenge to a tradition of political authoritarianism that is at least as intractable today as it was under the emperors.

Proprietary feelings about China's cultural distinctiveness and self-sufficiency, on the other hand, are still a force to be reckoned with. In spite of—and partly because of—all the foreign influences that have buffeted China over the past 150 years, a deep reservoir of ethnocentrism remains to be tapped, especially in the vast Chinese hinterland areas and sectors of the bureaucracy, and especially in situations of crisis. This ethnocentrism establishes an unstable standard of Chineseness that foreign ideas can negotiate with but cannot easily meet; it places people who have been profoundly influenced by such ideas (including maverick or unorthodox forms of Marxism) in a uniquely marginal, tenuous, and potentially illegitimate position in the larger Chinese world. Take the example of Liu Xiaobo (d. 2017), who in April 1993, when I was teaching a seminar at Wellesley College on "Tiananmen as History," visited my class and spoke eloquently on the part he took in the popular protest movement in Tiananmen Square in 1989 on the eve of the government crackdown.[23] Although the substantive ideas of Western-influenced individuals like Liu, who won the Nobel Peace Prize in 2010 but was serving an eleven-year prison sentence at the time because of his activities in support of greater democracy in China,[24] are very different from those of the pioneer reformers of the late Qing, the problems they encounter with respect to their legitimacy in Chinese society and the legitimacy of certain of their intellectual orientations resonate palpably with problems faced by Wang Tao and his generation. In this sense, the themes explored, however preliminarily, in the final section of *Between Tradition and Modernity* may speak not only to the late Qing but also to the more recent history of China.

I can't leave the subject of Wang Tao without sharing an experience I had toward the end of the last century that related to Wang and also perhaps said something about how much China, at least in nonpolitical areas, had changed by that point. I had been invited by East China Normal University (Hua Dong Shifan Daxue) to be a visiting professor for a few weeks in June 1996, mainly to consult with people and give a couple of talks. The chief person I was in touch with was Xin Ping, a member of the ECNU History Department. Xin was the only other person who had written a full-scale study of Wang Tao at that time.[25] During my visit, he and I hired a car one day to drive us to Fuli (about fifteen miles southeast of Suzhou in Jiangsu province), where Wang had been born. We went to a few places where Wang had lived or spent time and got a sense of his boyhood environment. Before leaving to return to Shanghai, we visited the office of a town official and told him of our interest in Wang Tao. The enterprising official, realizing that one of the town's most illustrious sons had become an object of global notice and seeing an opportunity to put Fuli on the map, suggested that perhaps it would be a good idea to organize an international conference centering on Wang, the centenary of whose death, as it happened, was in 1997, only months away. Nothing ever came of this, but it dramatically symbolized the change that had taken place in China and in its relationship to the rest of the world in the two decades since the end of the Cultural Revolution (1966–76).

CHAPTER 3

The Next Step

Discovering History in China

People who are not historians sometimes think of history as simply facts about the past. Historians are supposed to know otherwise. The facts are there, to be sure, but they are infinite in number and speak (if at all) in conflicting, sometimes unintelligible voices. The task of the historian is to reach back into this incoherent babel of facts, choose the ones that are important, and figure out what they say.

This is no easy job. Although we have rules of evidence to help keep us honest, a large subjective element necessarily enters into all historical scholarship. Which facts we choose and what meanings we invest them with are deeply influenced by the questions we ask and the assumptions we operate under, and these questions and assumptions in turn reflect the concerns that are uppermost in our minds at any given moment. As times change and concerns shift, the questions and assumptions reflecting them also change. Thus, it is often said, each generation of historians must rewrite the history written by the preceding generation.

However, the idea of generation is vague and ambiguous. In corporate terms, every historian belongs to a particular generational cohort, and there is a tendency within the historical profession to associate professional cohorts (scholars, for example, trained at Harvard in the 1950s under John King Fairbank) with particular approaches or stages in a field's evolution (the "Harvard school" of China historiography). In individual terms, all historians in the course of their productive years move through a succession of generational changes. The corporate generation to which each of us belongs is a powerful force, and it places real constraints on our capacity for intellectual movement. But these constraints are partial, not absolute. For one thing, individuals differ from the outset. People of the same age trained during the same time by the same teachers, although sharing certain assumptions, never replicate each other exactly; indeed, as will be made amply clear in this chapter, they may vary substantially in historical approach. For another thing, as we grow older and as the world changes, sometimes in quite sweeping ways, we are affected by these internal and external shifts, even those of us of stubbornly conservative bent whose bedrock assumptions appear to remain least disturbed.

Both of these generational perspectives—the corporate phases marking the development of a field and the individual phases experienced by historians as they respond to the changes going on about (and within) them—are reflected in *Discovering History in China*. The book is a critical appraisal of some of the major approaches that have shaped American writing on recent Chinese history since World War II. By *recent* I mean generally the nineteenth and twentieth centuries, a span of time often referred to as the modern era. For reasons that will become plain, I have developed serious misgivings about the application of the term *modern* to Chinese history, even for purely nominal purposes, and where possible I have used labels like "recent" or "post-1800" instead. I have found it impossible, however, to avoid using the word entirely, as so many writers I deal with in the book divide Chinese history into modern and traditional (or premodern) segments.

Apart from being an exploration of American historiography on China—and, as such, bearing directly on the intellectual dimension of Sino-American relations more broadly construed—the book also marks a point in the inner evolution of one historian. The decision to write it, made after I turned forty, was a direct outgrowth of intellectual problems I had been wrestling with for some time. These problems were partly biographical, partly historical in genesis. When my first book, *China and Christianity* (1963), came out, I had only just been launched on my career as a college teacher, and my main preoccupations were in some ways more personal and professional than intellectual. To be sure, critical developments had happened in the world in the late 1940s and early 1950s: the inception of the Cold War not long after the end of World War II, the first successful Soviet atom bomb test in August 1949, the communist victory in the Chinese civil war in the same year, and the outbreak of the Korean War in June 1950. These developments produced a crisis situation that was ripe for engendering fear, suspicion, and rampant emotionalism among Americans, which set the stage (beginning around 1950) for the charges of communist subversion brought by Senator Joseph McCarthy and others against China specialists like John Fairbank and Owen Lattimore.[1]

These developments initially had little effect on my life—I didn't graduate from high school until spring 1952—but by the time I reached my last undergraduate year at the University of Chicago (1954–55), McCarthyism, even on the wane, was still very much a force to be contended with. The U.S. government, fearful of the slightest taint of communism, was reluctant to give short-term visas to foreign scientists who were believed to be (or to have once been) sympathetic to Marxism, thus preventing some very smart people from taking part in scientific meetings in the United States and sharing their knowledge—a policy that, ironically, instead of promoting U.S. national interests, was widely felt to affect it adversely. I wrote a seminar paper on this topic in my final undergraduate year, which was awarded first prize in a political institutions essay contest.[2] How well I remember the students in my dorm in spring 1954 gathering in the common room every evening after dinner to watch the latest episode of the Army–McCarthy hearings, which enjoyed wide media coverage and contributed substantially to the decline in McCarthy's popularity and his eventual censure by the Senate in December 1954.

The next few years were quieter, and between the time of *China and Christianity*'s germination as a seminar paper in my third year of graduate school (1957–58) and its publication in 1963, nothing terribly earthshaking occurred in the world at large—at least, nothing that shook my small piece of the Earth. Unchallenged from without, the assumptions I had when I began the book were more or less the ones I had when I finished it. Coming from a nonacademic background—the only other person in my extended family who had strong intellectual interests was my cousin Arthur A. Cohen, a novelist, publisher, and serious student of Jewish theology—and not quite believing that book authors were real people, I was primarily concerned with proving to myself that I could be a historian. Which meant, in essence, producing a work of scholarship that measured up to the standards of craftsmanship set by the historical profession.[3]

My second book, *Between Tradition and Modernity*, appeared in 1974. I was surer of myself as a historian and felt that it was a good book—better than the first in terms of craft. But I worried about whether it was "right" in terms of the internal coherence of its intellectual design and the validity of the assumptions that informed it. Unlike the period from 1957 to 1963, the years from 1964 to 1973, during which I worked on this second book, were fraught, tumultuous years in the United States. What the Great Depression had done for an earlier generation, Vietnam, Cambodia, the Club of Rome report on the limits of growth, and the Watergate scandal did for mine. There was a difference, however. Where the Depression years had aroused a deep sense of concern over how wealth was distributed and society structured, the successive crises of the 1960s and early 1970s, by highlighting the contradiction between the destructive capability of American technology and the moral opaqueness of those Americans who had ultimate control over its use, raised questions about the very course of "modern" historical development.

During the U.S. military action in Vietnam, which like many Asianists I strongly opposed, I was teaching Chinese and Japanese history at Wellesley College. I regularly took part in teach-ins and was invited one July Fourth to speak on the steps of a Massachusetts town hall along with a fellow China specialist, Steve Levine. I went down to Washington, DC, for the huge antiwar demonstration of November 15, 1969, in which an estimated half a million people took part. After Vietnam, as I saw it, there could be no more easy assumptions about the goodness of U.S. power, no more easy equating of being "modern" with being "enlightened." I was hardly alone. My teacher, John Fairbank, the outgoing president of the American Historical Association, in a speech of December 29, 1968, that received coverage in the *New York Times*, asked whether, with a fuller understanding of history, Americans would have gotten themselves into the mess they were in in Vietnam—"an object lesson," as he framed it, "in historical nonthinking." With more knowledge of the complex history of the relationship between China and North Vietnam, he asked, "would we have sent our troops into Vietnam so casually in 1965? A historical appreciation of the Buddhist capacity for individual self-sacrifice, of the Confucian concern for leadership by personal prestige and moral example, even of the Communist capacity for patriotism, might also have made us hesitate to commit ourselves to bomb Hanoi into submission."[4]

Between Tradition and Modernity was about a Chinese reformer, Wang Tao, who lived on the cultural frontier between China and the West in the latter half of the nineteenth century and thought and wrote about the Sino-Western encounter extensively. The problem I faced in trying to understand Wang was that the assumptions concerning "China" and "the West," "modernity" and "tradition," I had when I started the book were severely jarred in the course of the decade it took me to complete it. I was aware of this difficulty and at a number of points in the text discussed the problematic character particularly of the tradition-modernity polarity. I even toyed with the idea of titling the book *Beyond* (rather than *Between*) *Tradition and Modernity*. But in the end, although Wang Tao may have been "beyond," I remained "between." The thrust of my thinking pushed in one direction, but the concepts that framed it were pulling me in another, with the result that the underlying intellectual framework of the book was marked by a certain tension.

After completing the Wang Tao book and gaining some distance from it, my discomfort came to a head and I realized that the only way to deal with it was to directly confront the overarching conceptual frameworks or paradigms that, it seemed, had dominated postwar American writing on nineteenth- and twentieth-century Chinese history. (As will shortly be noted, I had already made a preliminary stab in this direction in 1970.) Although in terms of motivation there was bound to be a strong personal component to such a confrontation, the end product, I hoped, would also be of use to colleagues and students. The field of recent Chinese history had been relatively free of self-critical historiographical writing until the late 1960s. Beginning around that time, in the *Bulletin of Concerned Asian Scholars* (and later in the quarterly journal *Modern China*, which began publishing in 1975), a more critical perspective gradually developed. I welcomed this critical perspective and felt that its effects on a field that had grown overly sleepy in its thinking were salutary. I did not, however, always agree with the specific criticisms leveled. Moreover, even when I wanted to agree I often found the empirical data gathered in support of the criticisms to be inadequate or the criticisms themselves to be too unqualified, simplistic, or extreme to be persuasive. Torn between uneasiness over parts of the new critical perspective and equal uneasiness over much of what the critics were criticizing, I aspired to present a historiographical overview that, if less iconoclastic than some of the critiques that had thus far been offered, would at least have the merit of clarifying the central issues involved.[5]

The Problem with "China's Response to the West"

In the first chapter of *Discovering History in China*, I took a critical look at the Western impact–Chinese response approach (closely identified with Fairbank) that played such an important part in American writing on nineteenth-century China in the immediate postwar decades. I had alluded to the problems attending this approach in the final chapter of *China and Christianity*. "Modern students of Chinese history," I wrote,

> have all too often focused on the process of Western impact and Chinese response, to the neglect of the reverse process of Chinese impact and Western response. The missionary who came to China found himself confronted with frustrations and hostilities which he could hardly have envisaged before coming and which transformed him, subtly but unmistakably, into a *foreign* missionary. His awareness (one might indeed say resentment) of this metamorphosis, together with his fundamental dissatisfaction with things as they were in China . . . greatly conditioned the missionary's response to the Chinese setting.[6]

The Western impact–Chinese response approach, in other words, oversimplified things by assuming that Chinese–Western interactions in the nineteenth century were a one-way street in which all of the traffic flowed from West to East.[7]

In 1970, several years after the appearance of *China and Christianity*, I published an essay in which I scrutinized the impact–response approach more systematically, attempting to identify some of the hidden premises on which it was based. Apart from the assumption of unidirectionality of influence just noted, I pointed to a number of problems inherent in the approach. One was "the tendency, when speaking of the 'Western impact,' to ignore the enigmatic and contradictory nature" of the West itself. This was a point that had been made with particular force by another of my teachers, Benjamin Schwartz. Although most Western historians were properly humbled, Schwartz suggested, by the superficiality of their understanding of "non-Western" societies, they viewed the West as home ground, a known quantity. Yet, he cautioned,

> when we turn our attention back to the modern West itself, this deceptive clarity disappears. We are aware that the best minds of the nineteenth and twentieth centuries have been deeply divided in their agonizing efforts to grasp the inner meaning of modern Western development. . . . We undoubtedly "know" infinitely more about the West [than about any given non-Western society], but the West remains as problematic as ever.[8]

A related source of ambiguity was that the West, even in its modern guise, had changed greatly over time. The West that China encountered during the Opium War (1839–42) and the West that exerted such great influence on Chinese intellectual and political life beginning in the last years of the nineteenth century were both the "modern West." But there were vast differences between the two—differences that Western historians of China regularly overlooked.

Other problems were that the impact–response approach tended to direct attention away from those aspects of nineteenth-century China that were unrelated or only distantly related to the Western impact; that it was inclined to assume uncritically that Western-related facets of Chinese history during this period were Chinese responses to the impact of the West when in fact they were often responses (however much Western-influenced) to indigenous forces; and finally, perhaps because of its emphasis on "conscious responses," that the approach seemed to gravitate toward intellectual, cultural, and psychological forms of historical explanation at the expense of social, political, and economic ones.[9] The upshot was that the impact–response framework, although a decided improvement over earlier approaches that ignored Chinese thought and action entirely, encouraged a picture of nineteenth-century China that was incomplete and suffered unnecessarily from imbalance and distortion.[10]

One of the strongest evocations of this imbalance and distortion was made by Ssu-yü Teng and John Fairbank in the introduction to their influential book, *China's Response to the West* (1954):

Since China is the largest unitary mass of humanity, with the oldest continuous history, its overrunning by the West in the past century was bound to create a continuing and violent intellectual revolution, the end of which we have not yet seen. . . . Throughout this century of the "unequal treaties," the ancient society of China was brought into closer and closer contact with the then dominant and expanding society of Western Europe and America. This Western contact, lent impetus by the industrial revolution, had the most disastrous effect upon the old Chinese society. In every sphere of social activity the old order was challenged, attacked, undermined, or overwhelmed by a complex series of processes—political, economic, social, ideological, cultural—which were set in motion within China as a result of this penetration of an alien and more powerful society. The massive structure of traditional China was torn apart. . . . The old order was changed within the space of three generations.[11]

Moving Beyond "Tradition and Modernity"

Another perspective that went hand in hand with the impact–response approach and exerted a strong influence on Western scholarship of the 1950s and 1960s was modernization theory, a critique of which is the main theme of chapter 2 of *Discovering History in China*. Modernization theory was a corpus of societal analysis that first assumed explicit shape in the years following World War II; against the backdrop of the Cold War, it served the ideological need of Western (primarily U.S.) social scientists to counter the Marxist-Leninist explanation of global "backwardness" or "underdevelopment." The aspect of the theory that cast the greatest spell over American historians of China was its neat division of China's long history into traditional and modern phases of evolution (*modern* generally referring to the period of significant contact with the modern West). Modernization theory also provided a coherent intellectual explanation of the processes whereby "traditional" societies became "modern"—or, as the editors of a series on the "modernization of traditional societies" phrased it, "the way quiet places have come alive."[12]

Although the proximate origins of modernization theory were the conditions of the postwar world, in its most fundamental assumptions about non-Western cultures and the nature of change in such "quiet places," it drew heavily on a constellation of ideas that had wide currency among Western intellectuals of the nineteenth century. One almost invariable ingredient in such commentary was the image of China as a stationary, unchanging society. Thus, just prior to the beginning of the nineteenth century, French mathematician-philosopher Marquis de Condorcet wrote of the "human mind . . . condemned to shameful stagnation in those vast empires whose uninterrupted existence has dishonoured Asia for so long," and the German philosopher Georg Hegel, some years later, entered the judgment, "We have before us the oldest state and yet no past . . . a state which exists today as we know it to have been in ancient times. To that extent China has no history."[13]

The view of China as unchanging was nothing new. It had enjoyed wide currency prior to the nineteenth century. What was new was the negative judgment placed on China's alleged immobility. For many writers prior to the French Revolution, the stable, changeless quality of Chinese society had been regarded as a definite mark in its favor, a condition worthy of Western admiration and respect. Beginning in the late eighteenth century, however, as the Industrial Revolution brought what appeared to be a widening gap between European and Chinese material standards and as Europeans began to identify "civilization" with a high level of material culture, China, whose technical skill and material abundance had once been the envy of the West, came to be identified as a backward society.

This new picture of China was reinforced by important intellectual shifts that were happening in Europe: in the economic sphere, a strong reaction against mercantilist constraints and an increased tendency to embrace the principles of free trade and laissez-faire; in the political realm, a growing discontent with despotic rule; and more generally, a commitment to the values of progress, dynamic movement, and change in all spheres of life. As this new world view came more and more to be equated with being "enlightened," China, with its annoying restrictions on trade, autocratic government, and apparent resistance to fundamental change, took on the aspect (for many Westerners) of an obsolescent society doomed to languish in the stagnant waters of barbarism until energized and transformed by a dynamic, cosmopolitan, and cosmopolitanizing West.

The assumptions underlying the nineteenth-century Western perception of China exerted a powerful shaping influence on American historiography in the period from World War II to the late 1960s. No one ex-
emplified this nineteenth-century drag effect more clearly than the
brilliant historian Joseph Levenson. In Levenson's perspective, modern
society, as embodied in the culture of the West, acted on Chinese culture in two ways concurrently: first, as a solvent, against which the old
culture stood defenseless; and second, as a model on which a new Chinese culture was increasingly patterned. The picture of China's transformation that emerged from this perspective was one that was shaped
from start to finish by problems posed by the modern West. It was, to use
Levenson's own language, a revolution against the West (seen as imperialism) to join the West (seen as the embodiment of modernity). There
was little room in this picture for a conception of the revolution as a response, in significant measure, to indigenous problems of long standing—
problems that might be aggravated by the West but were not its exclusive, or even always its primary, creations. Even less was there room in
Levenson's picture for the possibility that past Chinese culture might
contain significant features that, far from acting as barriers to the country's modern transformation, might actually help in this transformation
and take an important part in directing it.[14]

In his assumption that Confucianism and modernity were fundamentally incompatible and the traditional order had to be torn down
before a modern order could be established in China, Levenson was joined
by many other scholars of the 1950s and 1960s, among the more prominent being Mary C. Wright and Albert Feuerwerker.[15] Toward the end
of the 1960s, however, the reasoning behind this pattern of thinking
began to be challenged by an emerging body of scholarly opinion that
questioned the implication that "modern" and "traditional" were dichot-
omous, mutually antithetical conditions. I already noted in this regard
the views of Michael Gasster in the preceding chapter. With respect to
Chinese history in particular, in his critique of Levenson's organic or
holistic view of culture Benjamin Schwartz insisted that "areas of experience of the past may, for good or ill, continue to have an ongoing existence in the present," that "'Chinese past' and 'modernity' may not
confront each other as impenetrable wholes."[16] More broadly, Lloyd
and Susanne Rudolph, in their illuminating study of Indian political

development, *The Modernity of Tradition*, identified the problem as being rooted in the angle of vision of the observer and made the vitally
important point that when modern societies alone were the focus of investigation, there was an increased tendency to stress traditional sur-
vivals, whereas when modern societies were compared with traditional
societies, the traditional features of the former often disappeared from
view. In other words, the perspective of the inquirer had a substantial
impact on what she or he saw.[17]

Imperialism: Reality or Myth?

The third chapter of *Discovering History in China* explores an aspect of
American historiography that set itself up in express opposition to both
the impact–response and modernization approaches. In the context of the
Vietnam War, radical American students of China in the late 1960s, influenced by Maoist historiography, sometimes seemed propelled more by
the need to indict the imperialism of America and the West than by the
commitment to understand China. Indeed, for such scholars, imperialism was often seen as the key explanatory variable in the history of China
in the nineteenth century. Proponents of this view, although starting from
different premises, had an ambiguous relationship with the impact–
response and modernization approaches. This was clearly seen in the
cases of James Peck and Victor Nee, two radical scholars whose writings
attracted a good deal of attention starting in the late 1960s. Ironically,
although Peck was severely critical of the impact–response approach identified with Fairbank, as well as the closely allied approach of modernization theory, he shared much with these approaches. Like them, he believed that Chinese society prior to the full impact of Western imperialism
in the early nineteenth century was both unchanging and apparently incapable of introducing major change on its own.[18] Indeed, it was only
with the intrusion of the nineteenth-century West that true change became a genuine possibility in China. Although the West thus created the
preconditions for massive change in Chinese society, having done so, it
proceeded effectively to block any and all changes that were not in its

interests. The only way the Chinese could extricate themselves from this situation was through revolution, which Peck and Nee are explicit in describing as "a protracted and continuous historical process which grew out of the Chinese response to the impact of Western expansionism in the mid-nineteenth century."[19]

Toward a China-Centered History of China

In the final chapter of *Discovering History in China* I identified a new approach in American scholarship—it was really more a collection of discrete characteristics than a single, well-defined approach—that I labeled "China-centered." This approach had emerged around 1970 and, in my judgment, went a long way toward overcoming earlier Western-centric biases. The attack leveled by Schwartz, the Rudolphs, and a growing number of scholars against the picture of "tradition" and "modernity" as mutually exclusive, wholly incompatible systems bore enormous potential consequences for Western understanding of the recent Chinese past. The entire structure of assumptions inherited from the nineteenth century—the perception of China as barbarian and the West as civilized; of China as static (or at best cyclically changing) and the West as dynamic; of China as incapable of self-generated linear change and therefore requiring the impact of a "force from without" for its transformation; that the West alone could serve as the carrier of this force; and finally, that in the wake of the Western intrusion, "traditional" Chinese society would give way to a new and "modern" China, fashioned in the image of the West—was thoroughly shaken and a new and more complex model suggested for the relationship between past and present in a modernizing context.

One of the most influential efforts in this direction was Philip Kuhn's landmark study, *Rebellion and Its Enemies in Late Imperial China: Militarization and Social Structure, 1796–1864* (1970). In an introductory discussion of the "boundaries of modern history," Kuhn (fig. 3.1) notes that the prevailing view of China's transformation in modern times defines "modern" at least by implication as "that period in which the motion of history is governed primarily by forces exogenous to Chinese society and

3.1. Philip Kuhn.

Chinese tradition." Uncomfortable with this definition, Kuhn makes the crucial point that before we can dispense with it, we must free ourselves of the old picture of an unchanging or cyclically changing China. The central question he addresses in his introduction therefore is that of the nature of the changes taking place in Chinese society just prior to the full Western onslaught. After noting the "phenomenal population rise (from 150 to 300 million during the eighteenth century); the inflation of prices (perhaps as much as 300 percent over the same period); the increasing monetization of the economy and the aggravation of economic competition in rural society," he expresses doubt as to whether changes of such character and magnitude can be viewed as cyclical.[20]

What Kuhn began to do here was offer a sharply altered picture of the role of the past in recent Chinese history and in the process redefine the issue of what was important about the changes taking place in nineteenth-century China. The upshot of this fresh approach was that the past century and a half of Chinese history regained some of its lost autonomy and the way was paved for a less inflated, more cautious portrayal of the part taken by the West in this history. It is no coincidence that precisely as this new understanding of the relationship between "tradition" and "modernity" was taking shape (it can be dated roughly to the mid- to late 1960s), studies began to appear that clearly reflected it.

These studies were marked by a number of characteristics. Their main identifying feature was that they began with Chinese problems set in a Chinese context. These problems might be influenced or even generated by the West. Or they might have no Western connection at all. But either way they were Chinese problems, in the double sense that they were experienced in China by Chinese and that the measure of their historical importance was a Chinese (rather than a Western) measure. The conventional paradigms of the past, all of which began history in the West and incorporated a Western measure of significance, were thus explicitly or implicitly repudiated. The narrative of the most recent centuries of Chinese history did not commence in Europe with Prince Henry the Navigator and the first stirrings of Western expansionism; it began in China. As more and more scholars searched for a Chinese story line, moreover, they found magically that there really was one, and far from grinding to a halt in 1840 and being preempted or displaced by the West, it continued to be of central, paramount importance right through the nineteenth century and beyond.

Frederic Wakeman Jr. provided the classic statement of this pattern of change. "Gradually," he wrote:

> social historians began to realize that the entire period from the 1550s to the 1930s constituted a coherent whole. Instead of seeing the Ch'ing [Qing] as a replication of the past, or 1644 and 1911 as critical terminals, scholars detected processes which stretched across the last four centuries of Chinese history into the republican period. The urbanization of the lower Yangtze region, the commutation of labor services into money payments, the development of certain kinds of regional trade, the growth of mass literacy and the increase in the size of the gentry, the commercialization of local managerial activities—all these phenomena of the late Ming set in motion administrative and political changes that continued to develop over the course of the Ch'ing [Qing] and in some ways culminated in the social history of the early twentieth century.[21]

A second identifying characteristic of the China-centered approach was that it attempted to cope with the size and complexity of the Chinese world by breaking it down into smaller, more manageable spatial units. The core assumption on which this strategy rested was that because China encompassed a vast range of regional and local variation, the content and extent of this variation needed to be delineated if we were to gain a more differentiated, more contoured understanding of the whole— an understanding of the whole that did more than blandly reflect the least common denominator among its several parts. One result of this new development was a mushrooming of province-level—and even some county-level—studies by Western historians, which enriched our appreciation of the diversity of China.[22] Sensitivity to China's diversity was also a great strength of G. William Skinner's regional systems approach, which drew attention to critical variation within the vast Chinese hinterland.[23]

A third feature of the China-centered approach that became increasingly common in the 1970s and 1980s was that it envisioned Chinese society as being arranged hierarchically in several different levels. To the spatial or "horizontal" differentiation just noted, a "vertical" axis of differentiation was added. Where American research on China prior to the

1970s often tended to focus on the view from the top—the policies and actions of the central government and powerful provincial officials, events of national moment (such as the Opium War, Boxer Rebellion, and other wars fought with foreign countries), intellectual and cultural figures of more than local or regional prominence (such as Kang Youwei and Liang Qichao), and so forth—the new approach concentrated on the lower reaches of Chinese society (merchants, religious leaders and followers, lower gentry, militarists, and even bandits and bullies). Thus, among other things, it opened the door to a richer understanding of the previously neglected popular history of China in the nineteenth century.[24]

A fourth facet of the China-centered approach, although in itself hardly "China-centered," was the high degree of openness its practitioners showed to the techniques and strategies of other disciplines, particularly the social sciences, and their serious commitment to incorporating these techniques and strategies into historical analysis. The desirability of applying social science analysis to the study of Chinese history had long been recognized. For years, however, the insights applied were linked, explicitly or implicitly, to modernization theory, with its heavy burden of Western-centric assumptions; this resulted, as we have seen, in an understanding of China that was seriously flawed. In the 1960s, two developments took place that significantly altered the context for cross-fertilization between the social sciences and the data of Chinese history. One was the awakening to the importance of social history—an awakening that, once it occurred, uncovered a wide spectrum of previously unrealized possibilities for fruitful collaboration between history and the social sciences.[25] The second development was the emergence, however limited and halting, of a more critical awareness among Western and more particularly U.S. social scientists of the degree to which social science theory was parochially grounded and in need of radical restructuring. Not surprisingly, it was the field of anthropology, accustomed to the investigation of non-Western societies and more sensitive than most social science disciplines to the perils of ethnocentric bias, that led the way.[26]

The China-centered approach outlined here resulted in a very different understanding of Chinese history in the nineteenth century. The consensus of earlier American scholarship had been that the great divide between the modern period of Chinese history (presumptively a time of far-reaching change) and the traditional period (a time, it was once thought, of little or no real change) was the Opium War. The growing consensus in more recent years has been that the true watershed event of nineteenth-century Chinese history was the Taiping Rebellion (1850–64). Kuhn described the rebellion as "in many respects the hinge between China's pre-modern and modern histories." William Rowe, after summarizing the physical and human devastation wrought by the Taiping Rebellion, judges it, along with the Nian and Muslim rebellions that arose in its wake, to have been "unquestionably much more of a watershed event for the Qing population" than the Opium War.[27]

Broader Perspectives on the China-Centered Approach

The emergence of the China-centered approach to Chinese history was part of a broader shift in American historical scholarship, also visible in recent work on Africa, the Muslim Middle East, and other non-Western areas. Details of timing and circumstance have varied from case to case, but in each instance the general direction of movement has been the same: away from an external—often "colonial history"—perspective toward a more internal approach characterized by a vigorous effort to see the history of any given non-Western society in its own terms and from its own point of view rather than as an extension—actual or conceptual—of Western history.[28]

In the case of China, as noted earlier, this shift began to occur around 1970 or just before, precisely when some members of the profession were reviving the old imperialism paradigm, with its pronounced Western-centric bias, to attack the influence of modernization theory on American scholarship. This irony reflects a fundamental contradiction that came to light during the Vietnam War and has been confirmed and reconfirmed since. From one perspective, Vietnam represented the apotheosis of U.S. imperialism—unleashing enormous destructive power against a nation far smaller, poorer, and weaker. It was natural for many U.S. historians, appalled and ashamed by their country's behavior in the war, to see imperialism with new eyes, as key to the problems experienced by China and other Asian countries over the preceding century.

Vietnam also took Americans beyond imperialism. Like the Arab oil embargo of 1973 and the Iran hostage crisis of 1979–81, it confronted us with the limits of our power, the very real constraints on our capacity to bend the world to U.S. purposes. This second meaning of Vietnam also had a profound impact on American historians of China. By exposing the mythology surrounding U.S. global supremacy—political, moral, cultural—it freed American historians, perhaps for the first time, to abandon Western norms and measures of significance and to move toward a more genuinely other-centered historiography, a historiography rooted in the historical experience not of the West but of China.[29]

CHAPTER 4

Discovering History in China

The Backstory

In the previous chapter, I briefly summarized the contents of *Discovering History in China* and touched on aspects of the political and intellectual environment of the 1950s, 1960s, and early 1970s that prompted me to write the book and helped shape the final product. Here I relate the remarkable backstory of how my manuscript eventually appeared in print—an aspect of the publishing industry that many readers are likely to know little or nothing about unless they happen to be authors themselves.

Once published, *Discovering History in China* turned out to be a very successful work by most measures. It received strong reviews; was translated into Chinese (twice), Japanese, and Korean; and has been widely read among students of Chinese history in North America, Europe, and East Asia. It was also named a *Choice* Outstanding Academic Book (1984–85). And it has been highly praised for its pedagogical value, one historian, Sherman Cochran of Cornell University, judging that the book "teaches beautifully." Cochran wrote me that in the fall of 1986 he used *Discovering History in China* as a final assignment in a graduate course in historiography and "had the students write reviews of it in light of what they'd read all semester. Then they read each other's reviews as a basis for discussion in the last meeting of the course. The result was the best finale I've ever had for a seminar—all thanks to your book."[1]

As an indication of the singular place *Discovering History in China* has occupied in North American China scholarship, a special roundtable was organized at the 2014 annual meeting of the Association for Asian Studies (AAS) to mark the thirtieth anniversary of the book's publication—an event (I've been told) with little or no precedent in the annals of AAS meetings.[2] The book has also been unusually influential in recent years among Chinese historians. According to Li Huaiyin, one of the participants in the 2014 roundtable, the database CNKI (China National Knowledge Infrastructure) shows that, compared with 116 Chinese journal articles that cited *Discovering History in China* from 1986 to 1999 (8 citations a year on average), from 2000 to 2013, there were 774 citations in all (some 55 per year). This dramatic extension of familiarity with the book was partly a reflection of the increased use of digitization and the Internet in China. But it is surely no coincidence that at the turn of the twenty-first century, as Li points out, the revolution paradigm, previously dominant in the history field in the People's Republic, was eclipsed among a younger generation of mainland historians who evinced a growing interest in social and cultural history at the local and regional level—a shift in direction that resonated strongly with the China-centered perspectives discussed in the concluding chapter of my book.[3]

In an illuminating comment on *Discovering History in China*, Hanchao Lu also takes note of the influence of the book among historians in China. But this might never have come about (or at least not nearly as quickly) had it not been for a fortuitous encounter I had more than thirty years ago with Lin Tongqi (fig. 4.1). Lin had only recently arrived from China and I had not previously met him when he came to my office at the Fairbank Center in early 1985, saying that he had read *Discovering History in China* and thought it should be made available to Chinese historians. He was well connected in China and had already corresponded with the distinguished Beijing publishing house Zhonghua shuju, which was interested in bringing out a Chinese translation. Lin's English was excellent—he had been teaching it at the Beijing Foreign Languages College for several decades—and he said he would like to do the translation himself. At first, I found it difficult to take this offer seriously, since in the mid-1980s very little American scholarly work on Chinese history had been made available in Chinese translation. But Lin was confident that there was no obstacle to this happening, and so we began.

4.1. With Lin Tongqi.

This was still before the age of ubiquitous computers. So our working procedures were fairly primitive from today's perspective. Using the old-style Chinese writing paper that was divided into squares (*yuangaozhi*) and writing out his translation by hand, Lin would translate a chapter, then give it to me to check against the original. I would make a list of corrections, queries, suggested alternative phrasings, and so on, after which we would meet for several hours to discuss each item, and he would produce a revised draft of that chapter. What a learning experience it was for me! After the book's publication, any number of Chinese colleagues told me how fortunate I was to have been blessed with Lin Tongqi as the translator. The main point is that this providential accident—a good example of what I later referred to as "outcome blindness"—radically changed the history of a book that had been written initially for a Western (and particularly American) readership. The Chinese translation appeared in July 1989, only weeks after the June 4 massacre of prodemocracy demonstrators in Tiananmen Square.[4]

By that point the mutual involvement of Chinese and American scholars in the study of their historical relationship was developing at a fairly brisk pace, and, according to my good friend Wang Xi (see chapter 7), there was considerable interest in my book even before the appearance of the Chinese translation. In a letter to me of May 1986, Wang took note of some of the reviews that had already been published and quipped that it seemed to him that the Chinese historical profession had "discovered" me through my "discovering" of history in China. Lin Tongqi, then in the process of translating *Discovering History in China*, wrote an English-language review of the book, which he playfully titled "Discovering Historiography in America." I showed Lin the relevant part of Wang Xi's letter and he was much amused.

The Book's Prepublication History

In a perfect world one must assume that publishers would be delighted to bring to light a book like the one I've been describing. But of course, the book's ultimate success was not a foregone conclusion, and in any case the world is something less than perfect. A draft of the book was completed in early 1981. Since my first two books had been published by Harvard University Press and had been well received, I submitted the manuscript to Harvard. This proved an unfortunate decision, one that in the end resulted in a fair amount of pain. I met with Aida Donald, the executive editor of the press, in March 1981. Harvard then sent the manuscript to two outside readers, and in early June, after receiving the readers' reports, I wrote Donald responding to them. Here is the substance of what I wrote:[5]

The Press has received two reports on my manuscript. One of the reports is stridently negative and not terribly helpful; the other is strongly positive, with a number of constructive suggestions for improvement. I will assume, for the sake of argument, that the two reports really do refer to the same book and author, though I must admit to feeling something of the disorientation that the Chinese philosopher, Zhuang Zhou, felt when, after dreaming that he was a butterfly, he awoke and didn't quite know whether he was Zhuang Zhou who had dreamed that he was a butterfly or a butterfly dreaming that he was Zhuang Zhou.

It is not easy to respond to the negative report with detachment and even-handedness. It is suffused with emotionalism and strangely (perhaps not so strangely, given the nature of the charges leveled) devoid of the empirical support one expects of serious scholarly assessment. The author of the report has either a very low opinion of his own powers of persuasiveness or an exaggeratedly high opinion of mine, for evidence of which one need go no further than the report's cover letter, where it is stated that despite "a very negative review" and a firm recommendation against publication, "I fully expect that Professor Cohen's book will be published, probably by Harvard University Press." . . .

The key issue, it seems to me, is the persistent failure of the author of the negative report to understand what it is I'm up to in the book (something I would worry about were it not for the fact that the other Press reader and the half-dozen or so scholar-colleagues who have read the manuscript at my request understand perfectly what the book is about, whether or not they agree with all of my analysis and conclusions). The aim of the book is not to write a comprehensive study of the historiography of the Chinese past. It is, as plainly stated in the manuscript, "to identify and analyze critically the assumptions that have pervaded *American* historiography." . . .

I don't know how to answer the charge that my reasoning is "feeble" and "weak," since, again, the author does not support his accusations with any real evidence drawn from the text. Chapter 2, which he feels is the "weakest in the book" and in which he finds the reasoning "embarrassingly muddled" is assessed by the other Press reader as "a masterly introduction to the historiography." The other reader even lavishes the term "brilliant" upon my analysis of Joseph Levenson, which takes up approximately half of the chapter.

The author of the negative report feels it would be a waste of his time to point out more specifically the "errors and faults" in the book, because if I were capable of correcting these errors and faults, I would never have written the book in the first place. All I can say in reply to this is that I have some sense now what it must have been like to be hauled before the House Un-American Activities Committee during the 1950s.

I can see that I'm running out of good humor. But there is one other charge made by the author that merits brief comment. This is his view that the book is marred by a "Harvard-centered, coterie-centered, American-centered" parochialism. I'm not sure what the author means by "Harvard-centered." If it is a reference to the fact that I did my graduate work at Harvard, am affiliated with the Fairbank Center, and have had two books published by the Harvard University Press, I plead guilty. If it refers to the fact that well over fifty percent of the scholars dealt with in the book have at some point had a significant Harvard connection, I plead guilty again, but would immediately add (1) that as of 1981, when I submitted my manuscript, Harvard . . . [under the guidance of] John Fairbank in particular had trained far more modern China historians than any other American institution in the postwar years, making it virtually inevitable that any review of American China historiography in these years would reflect a strong Harvard influence; (2) that the Harvard scholars dealt with in the book represent the widest possible range of ideological commitments and scholarly approaches; and (3) that in the book a number of the Harvard people (including Fairbank, Mary Wright, and above all Joseph Levenson) are brought under fairly sharp critical scrutiny. The book may, in short, be Harvard-centered; but it is most certainly not an apology for a nonexistent "Harvard School."

As for "coterie-centered," this presumably refers to the "very narrow segment of friends and fellow-spirits" to whom, the author says, I confine my discussion, especially my favorable comments. Again, I'm afraid, our friend is tilting at windmills. I have the greatest admiration for Fairbank, Wright, and Levenson, and have long counted Fairbank as a friend, as well as a colleague and mentor. Yet, as just indicated, the approaches of all three are dealt with critically in the manuscript. On the other hand, Joseph Esherick, a Berkeley-trained scholar whom I scarcely know, and Sherman Cochran, a Yale-trained scholar whom I also scarcely know, are both richly praised in the book.

The American-centered aspect of my parochialism I assume refers to my concentration on American historiography [the justification for which I've already discussed]. . . .

In turning briefly to the second report, I feel like an astronaut who has been circling around in space for many days and has finally returned to Earth. Not because the report has some nice words of praise—though that is naturally gratifying—but because it represents the sort of serious, responsible, sensitive, and constructive reading of a manuscript that every scholar hopes to get. I won't comment on the reader's detailed suggestions, except to note that I find them extremely penetrating and will probably end up incorporating a goodly number of them one way or another in the final text. . . .

I've had to spend a lot more time in this letter rebutting the charges contained in the first report than responding thoughtfully to the suggestions put forward in the second. This is regrettable. But I'm afraid it is also inevitable, as my immediate priority must be to persuade you that the negative evaluation is, in this instance, a fluke. It is not a real evaluation at all. It misses the point of the book entirely. The charges leveled in it are unrelievedly negative, yet wholly lacking in empirical substantiation and therefore impossible to assess on their merits. To top it all off, the author [of the report] has the conceit to be so pleased with what he has written that he hopes to publish it, "more or less in the form in which it now stands," as a review when the book comes out. All I can say is, I hope, for more reasons than one, that he has his way, the sooner the better!

I was informed that after receiving my response to the outside readers' reports, the Syndics, the governing body of the Harvard University Press, was at sixes and sevens as to what to do and asked one of their number, a social scientist, to read the manuscript and make a recommendation at their next meeting. After hearing over the grapevine that the recommendation was going to be negative, I decided (on Aida Donald's advice) to withdraw the manuscript.

My next stop was Yale. I had gotten to know Charles ("Chuck") Grench, one of the Yale University Press editors. He knew about the difficulties I was having with Harvard University Press and encouraged me to submit the manuscript to Yale if Harvard didn't work out. Rather than make a formal submission, I asked him if he would have a look at the work and give his opinion. After a preliminary phone conversation, I wrote him, in a letter dated July 10, 1981, indicating that I had sent him under separate cover two copies of the manuscript. In the letter I tried to point out the distinctive character of my book:

It is not a monograph in the usual sense. What it is, basically, is a critical history of the field of modern Chinese historical studies in the United States from World War II to the present. As such, it inevitably reflects one histo-rian's perception of where we've been and where we're headed. I wouldn't expect everyone to agree with me. But I do make my own intellectual pref-erences clear and try to be fair in my treatment of those who don't share them. No one in the field has tried to write this sort of book before. I think that most historians of China—and some historians of other non-Western societies as well—will find it a useful and important endeavor.

In my letter I mentioned the positive responses of individuals to whom I had already shown the manuscript and noted that although none of them had advised major structural revisions, they had made sugges-tions for improvement, most of which I had already incorporated. "As for the book's prospective audience," I wrote (perhaps a bit too optimistically), "I can imagine its being required reading for any beginning student in the field of Chinese studies—undergraduate majors as well as beginning graduate students."

Chuck looked the manuscript over and said he enjoyed it. "The key question," he wrote me after consulting with a few of his colleagues, "was whether it really added up to enough in the end to justify book publica-tion." The people he spoke to felt that perhaps the best way to get the issues I discuss before my main audience would be to place the essays in a journal. In a telling aside, he added: "It is tough to deal with historio-graphic questions when the principals in the action are still living and when some raw spots still exist; you've done a judicious job, but we had the uneasy feeling that more was bubbling below the surface than would be useful or politic to deal with at this time." I wrote Chuck back saying I was sorry things hadn't worked out with Yale and thanked him for the unusual speed with which he had given me his views and commending him for his candor.

By this point (summer 1981) I was beginning to get a clearer sense of some of the obstacles in my path. One, which had been hinted at by Harvard and made somewhat more explicit by Yale, was that the book was about historiography, a topic a number of presses habitually shied away from. This was especially true when the historians dealt with—and this was a second obstacle—were still alive and active (with the excep-tion of Levenson in my case). It was okay in a book review in a scholarly journal to adopt a critical stance toward a living colleague, although untenured young faculty members (of which I was not one) were well advised to proceed with caution; a book, on the other hand, was a different story. A closely related impediment, at least to publication with Harvard, was that I spent a good part of the first chapter pointing out what seemed to be shortcomings in the Western impact–Chinese response approach long identified with John Fairbank. Was this an instance, some people might wonder, of hidden agendas bubbling beneath the surface? More than that, Fairbank had enjoyed a close and extremely productive relationship with the Harvard University Press for years, so publishing my book could easily be seen as putting the press in an awkward position.

I hasten to add that such thinking did not at all characterize Fairbank himself. Years earlier, after reading my initial critique of the Western impact–Chinese response approach in a volume edited by James Crowley,[6] he sent me the following handwritten note (undated and with typically Fairbankian abbreviations): "Yr. chap. in the Crowley vol. is very neat and stimulating. China's center of gravity lies so far within that for. influence or contact is a more marginal (or opportune) factor than foreigners cd. imagine. Needham[7] builds up data to support the idea of 'W. learning originated in Ch.' The world-history perspective is rapidly changing."

Teacher and Student: The Inimitable Approach of John Fairbank

This is as good a place as any to pause briefly and call attention to one of the more remarkable things about John Fairbank: his unique style as a mentor. As noted earlier, whenever I sent him something I had written I could count on receiving a prompt reply with detailed comments laced (generally) with comforting praise. Then, a few weeks or months or even years later, I would often receive a copy of a letter he had written to someone else drawing that person's attention, in the most flattering language, to my work. This was ego-enhancing, creative letter-writing at its best, reflecting the thoughtfulness and generosity of spirit of a man who experienced his student's achievements as extensions of his own. Which brings me to a facet of Fairbank's mentorship that was especially important to me: his tolerance of viewpoints and approaches that differed from his. He was as stubborn as the next person and did not easily change positions, and in print he could be devastating in his dismissal of theoretical constructs that he thought were silly or worse. Fairbank understood that even in the sublime world of the intellect, there was bound to be a certain amount of pushing and shoving. ("How can mankind move upward," he once wrote with characteristic pithiness, "except by standing on the shoulders and faces of the older generation?"[8]) But when his students didn't see things the way he did, he never cut off the conversation (or, as was more often the case, stopped the flow of letters) because he didn't want to listen anymore. Until the very end of his life, Fairbank was in regular communication with people who had for years disagreed with him in the sharpest terms.

Another example of Fairbank's generosity came soon after Yale's less than encouraging response to my book. After much debate with myself, I decided that in my next effort to find a publisher, it might not be a bad idea to steer clear of the university press route. The publisher that immediately came to mind was the Free Press, which specialized in serious nonfiction and had a series titled "The Transformation of Modern China," under the general editorship of James Sheridan, who taught Chinese history at Northwestern University. I wrote Sheridan explaining in general terms what the book was about and sending him, under separate cover, the preface, introduction, and table of contents. He phoned me in early November and said he liked what he had seen and would like to read the complete manuscript, which I promptly sent him. Sheridan called in early December saying he thought the book was "splendid," incisively and lucidly argued, and would be a real commercial success once in paperback, ideal for use in a course in the company of other books. He also mentioned that he did not think I had been unfair to anyone in the book. He said he had already spoken to the people at the Free Press, who would send the manuscript to one of the outside readers whose names he had given them.

By this point (late 1981), I had long since shown Fairbank a copy of my manuscript and filled him in on the difficulties I was having finding a publisher. On his own initiative, Fairbank wrote Sheridan just before Christmas and sent me a copy of his letter. "I have only now seen Paul Cohen's MS on American Historiography on Modern China," he wrote:

> I find it extremely well done—clear-cut in analysis and judicious in style. China specialists may well have read all the books mentioned, and students will be interested in most of them. The point is that Paul has put them all into a related framework, without prejudice except as he has stated his own views, and the reader is given a rapid initiation into three major areas of historical interpretation. No one else has done this so well. It gives us historiographical substance, a history of the modern China field such as every member of it needs as part of his/her own self-identification.
>
> In other words, this MS advances our sophistication as historians by laying out the alternatives available in major approaches. For the older generation it provides an opportunity to put these questions more firmly in perspective. For the younger generation it fills in the blind area in the recent past that is too recent to be historically recorded and yet too far past to be recalled from the personal experience of young people. Either way, the reader is informed and also stimulated to find his own stance.

Fairbank concluded his letter by expressing the hope that the book could be published in the Free Press series, adding that the overview then being planned for the introductory chapter to volume 13 of *The Cambridge History of China* (which he was coediting with Albert Feuerwerker) "will want to quote it."

Volume 13 (titled *Republican China 1912–1949*, part 2) of the *Cambridge History* was published in 1986. The overview chapter Fairbank referred to ("Introduction: Perspectives on Modern China's History") was coauthored by Fairbank, Feuerwerker, and independent scholar Mary B. Rankin. True to his word, in March 1984, after *Discovering History in China* was finally published, Fairbank wrote me that too many people had eventually become involved in the framing of the aforementioned introductory chapter and they were having a hard time creating a text they could all agree on. "Obviously we need the help of a Master Historiographer," he wrote me, "so we hope you can help us. Please give us a reading. It would be much appreciated." After carefully scrutinizing the essay in question, I wrote to John that it had "all the makings of one of those superintroductions that . . . go so far beyond merely introducing, are so studded with new material and interesting ideas, that they threaten to overwhelm the rest of the volume. It is really an incredible document. The problem is how to make it all cohere." I sent him a long letter with suggestions, for which he thanked me warmly.

On two other occasions, Fairbank asked me for help. In December 1981, a few days after writing Jim Sheridan, he invited me to his home for lunch. He and Edwin O. Reischauer, the original authors of the widely used two-volume textbook, *A History of East Asian Civilization* (Houghton Mifflin, 1958, 1960), felt that the time had come for a thorough redo of that text, which had been substantially based on 1950s scholarship and was in need of updating. Would I be willing, he wanted to know, to rework the parts of the text for which he had borne responsibility, covering China from the Ming to the present? The tentative plan was for Albert Craig, who taught Japanese history at Harvard, to do the same for the Japan portions of the original text, and Ying-shih Yu, then teaching at Yale (he had been a colleague of mine at Michigan in 1962–63), to take on the parts dealing with Chinese history from earliest times up to the Ming. I had a number of misgivings about this proposal. I didn't see myself as a textbook writer, and after having spent a good part of the 1970s working on *Discovering History in China* and a workshop volume on nineteenth-century Chinese reform coedited with John Schrecker,[9] I very much wanted to return to basic research. Also I resisted strongly the idea of redoing someone else's work. After I voiced my conflicts, Fairbank said that an immediate decision was not necessary and that I should take as much time as I needed to think it over. After nearly three deeply conflicted months, I finally decided that it was a no go for me and on March 20 wrote Fairbank telling him so. A week later I got a note back: "I can well see your point. We shall miss you, but you are doing the better thing." I don't know exactly what happened after that, except that the reworked East Asian textbook never materialized, and Fairbank went ahead with a book of his own (see below).

This brings me to the second occasion. On the morning of May 20, 1991, John, who was about to turn eighty-four, phoned me at home. He said he was at the Mount Auburn Hospital in Cambridge, was having a lot of difficulty with his heart arrhythmia, and that having always been "a prudential sort of fellow" he wanted to make sure there would be someone to oversee the completion and production of his new history of China if his health worsened. Since I had already given the manuscript two careful readings at his request—most recently in response to a letter he wrote me several months prior to his phone call[10]—and had been generally supportive, he wondered if I would be willing to take on this role. We chatted a bit. I alluded to the fact that I was experiencing a little anxiety myself (for what reason I don't now recall) as I was approaching my sixtieth birthday (I was about to turn fifty-seven). Sighing, John countered wistfully with what he wouldn't give to be sixty again. That clinched it. On a number of occasions in the past I had turned him down. In this instance, with some trepidation, I told him "yes."

The apprehension I felt over my agreement with John didn't have to do with the work that might be involved. Although I had long taken to heart the rule for indebted students he had laid down on the occasion of his sixtieth birthday—"Don't feel you should try to pay it back. Instead, pass it on"—I welcomed the opportunity to express some part of my gratitude to him in this more direct way. What I felt uneasy about was the prospect of having to assume his voice, so different from my own, and drape myself in his interpretive positions, some of which I was on record as being not entirely in agreement with. In the event, my worries proved unnecessary. John held on for several more months, during which time, even when hospitalized, he pressed ahead with revisions, drafting an epilogue, and filling in gaps in the text, in addition to orchestrating the efforts of what seemed (by my standards) a small army of people involved in one way or another in the book's creation. On the morning of September 12, 1991, he went with his wife to Harvard University Press to deliver the completed typescript of *China: A New History*, only hours before suffering the heart attack that two days later claimed his life. Wilma Fairbank phoned me the following day. She mentioned that John's death was good for him (alluding to the great stress he had been under trying to finish the manuscript before his heart gave out) but "bad for us" and marveled at his exquisite sense of timing.

During the months between the May phone call and his death in September, Fairbank and I were in frequent touch concerning the book. Sometimes he would phone because he wanted to talk about what he had been reading, get my reactions (since he was always way ahead of me in his reading schedule, I was usually at a loss to give any reactions), and also bounce his thoughts off me. At other times I would tell him about something I'd recently read and suggest he have a look at it. When we next talked, he not only had perused the item in question but, if he was persuaded by the author's points, had found a way to shoehorn them into the manuscript.

Several days before John's final heart attack, I stopped by his office after lunch to give him my thoughts on the latest version of a chapter in the book that had proved especially troublesome. (As it turned out, he had already drafted a later version, which effectively addressed the difficulties and no longer needed my comments. When he was in a hurry, you had to work really fast to keep up.) When I knocked on his door, which was slightly ajar, there was at first no answer. Then I heard his voice: "Come in." I had interrupted one of the legendary Fairbankian postprandial naps. But he sat straight up and started talking about the book, as if he'd been lying there thinking (or dreaming?) about it. He said the manuscript was scheduled to go into galleys in a few weeks and he was worried about being unable to incorporate the findings of "the seventeen new books" that were sure to come out between the galley stage and publication. My mind traveled back to all those stories about the stratagems John Fairbank had deployed over the years to pry manuscripts away from sticky-fingered authors, and before I knew it I was Fairbanking Fairbank with a small lecture on how there were always going to be new books, the unreasonableness of expecting to take into account scholarship that hadn't yet appeared, the necessity of knowing when to stop revising and accept the finality of being done, and so on. He smiled one of his complex Fairbank smiles. He knew I was right. But he knew that, in some more fundamental sense, he was right, too, that this was his last book, he probably wouldn't be around to look after it during its passage into the world, and he really wanted to make sure it was safe before finally letting go.[11]

Aside from being in regular communication with John in the last months of his life, at the request of Aida Donald, then assistant director and editor-in-chief of the Harvard University Press, I served as an outside reader for the manuscript;[12] moreover, after Fairbank's death, I took an active part in the editorial tasks involved in the book's production. I consulted with Wilma about the illustrative material that was to go in the work. I read through the proofs carefully, doing my best to make the book as error-free as possible. I even rewrote one paragraph dealing with the implications of China's unfavorable population–land balance for the late imperial agrarian economy. In the end, I felt good about my involvement in the production process, a clear expression of my indebtedness to a man to whom I owed much.

Ongoing Efforts to Get a Publisher for My Book

In the end, things didn't work out with the Free Press. Right around the time Fairbank sent his letter to Sheridan (December 1981), the latter wrote me a long, thoughtful critique of the manuscript, pointing out a number of soft spots that he felt needed strengthening. I agreed with some of his points and wrote back that I would definitely do something about them. I don't know what the outside reader's views were, if indeed there was an outside reader. In February I received a phone call from Joyce Seltzer, the history editor at the Free Press, informing me that the press was rejecting the book on the grounds that it wasn't a work they thought would result in "large text adoption" for classroom use. She said I wrote very well but felt—how familiar it sounded!—that books on historiography tended to be of interest mainly to other historians and that I would probably be better off with a university press. In a brief follow-up letter she reiterated her view that the book would not have "a large enough reading audience to make it a commercially viable project" for the Free Press. A few days later, Jim Sheridan phoned expressing his anger and disappointment over the press's decision, claiming that he still thought it was a super book and had argued vigorously in favor of publishing it.

It had been a full year since I had first submitted my book to a publisher, and it was not any closer to being accepted. I still believed in the book, feeling it had something valuable to contribute to the Chinese history field in North America. But for reasons I only dimly understood, two university presses and a trade press with strong scholarly leanings had all responded to it with something less than enthusiasm, despite a number of supportive letters attesting to its worth. My experience was nothing like what had happened with my two previous books, which had been accepted by Harvard only months after being submitted. I was not quite ready to jump off the Brooklyn Bridge in despair. But I was definitely hurting.

There was one other non–university-press publisher I thought might be worth contacting. This was Pantheon Books, which in the past had evinced a particular interest not only in books about Asia but also in books that attempted to develop a critical perspective on how Americans thought about Asia. My book, though focused only on part of Asia, clearly fell into the latter category. I had a passing acquaintance with Tom Engelhardt, who had become the main editor of Asia-related books at Pantheon. So I sent him a letter (in August 1982), along with the preface, introduction, and table of contents of the manuscript. I got a brief letter back, saying that he couldn't really tell enough from the introduction and would have to look at the entire manuscript to have a firmer reaction. At the same time he made it clear that on the basis of the introduction, he was "left with the feeling that the book may prove a more likely candidate for a university press than for a trade house like Pantheon." Pantheon, it now seemed clear, would be a long shot. I wrote Engelhardt that while I appreciated his willingness to look at the entire work and would like to keep that option open for the future, my sense was that prospects might be brighter, as he himself suggested, with a university press and I wanted to give that route another go first.

One reason for not pursuing Pantheon more aggressively was that by this point (late September 1982) something unexpected and unrelated had happened that eventually led to a resolution of my problem. The key person involved was Dorothy Borg, author of a number of important books on United States–East Asian relations, including *The United States and the Far Eastern Crisis, 1933–1938* (Harvard University Press, 1964), for which Columbia awarded her its Bancroft Prize in American History in 1965.[13] Dr. Borg had spent two years in China in the 1940s as a staff member of the American Council of the Institute of Pacific Relations. A few years later, when the institute became a target of a campaign by Senator Joseph R. McCarthy to find out "who lost China" to the communists, she set aside her career for some time to help defend Owen Lattimore and other colleagues who had come under fire.[14]

Borg came into my life in the summer of 1982. At the time she was a senior research associate at Columbia's East Asian Institute. Larry Sullivan, a China political scientist and friend of mine who was well acquainted with the book I was trying to get published, had recently moved to the New York area. After getting to know Borg, he mentioned my manuscript to her. Since she had been putting some thoughts together for a short volume on American historiography relating to China and more broadly East Asia, she phoned me in July. In the long conversation that ensued—I think it lasted over an hour—I was predictably nervous and on guard. But I was also flattered at the idea of being interviewed (which is really what it was—I could hear her reporter's pencil working hard on the other end). Since Borg was coming up to Boston for a conference soon thereafter, we met for a long lunch on August 6 and I sent her my manuscript later on the same day with a note telling her that she should feel free to show it to her Columbia colleague, China politics scholar Andrew Nathan, who I thought would find it of interest.

In late August I received a letter from Dorothy (after our lunch we were on a first-name basis), written in a thin, bony, almost printed form of handwriting with which I'm sure many of her friends were familiar. She wrote that the manuscript had "proved very disturbing" to her, as it covered much of what she had been covering, and that if she had first encountered it in published form, "it would have come as a real bombshell." Then she thanked me profusely for "the very friendly and generous way" in which I had handled the situation, which "meant an immense amount" to her. I of course wrote her back immediately, assuring her that whatever similarities she and I might have in terms of overall point of view, there was no way I could write a book that would be anything like one that she might write. Her book would be addressed to a readership of Americanists, which mine was not, and hers would focus on the history of American–East Asian relations, a subject hardly mentioned in my manuscript.

After her return to New York, Dorothy shared my manuscript with Andy Nathan, who in late September sent me a long letter commenting on it. Having some years earlier been commissioned to write a state-of-the-field piece on twentieth-century Chinese politics, Andy had an insider's view of the problems attending such a challenge. "All these problems," he wrote somewhat self-deprecatingly, "you have solved with real distinction, and so gracefully that only people like me who have tried and failed can appreciate the magnitude of the achievement." He had two main concerns about my manuscript. One was the by now familiar one of audience. How widely would a book like mine be bought and read?

He said he wasn't sure of the answer but felt that "any press considering publication would worry about this a lot and would ask its outside reader for a judgment." He then made a number of thoughtful and sensible suggestions as to how I might broaden its appeal without changing the overall thrust of my book. His second major concern dealt with the matter of fairness. Had I, in support of my own argument, dealt with figures like Fairbank and Levenson too schematically? The points he made here were exceptionally thoughtful. They were also cogent and persuasive and led me to rewrite the part of the book's preface that dealt with the fairness issue. It now read as follows:

> I take the matter of unfairness very seriously and have worried about it a good deal in the writing of these pages. I have tried to be balanced in my judgments and, in pointing out deficiencies in an individual's work or an overall approach, have spelled out as clearly as possible the premises on which my criticism is based. Still, a certain amount of distortion is inevitable when one attempts to present someone else's writing as confirmation of one's own analytical perspective. Something of the ebb and flow of people's ideas in time is bound to get lost; the contrapuntal themes and qualifications, even the redeeming inconsistencies, that texture any scholar's work are apt to recede from view. Thus, in portraying John Fairbank and Joseph Levenson as leading exponents of the dominant approaches of American historiography in the 1950s and 1960s, it is easily forgotten that Fairbank, in the course of a career spanning more than fifty years, has approached China from a number of different perspectives—he never, in any case, was remiss in welcoming scholarship rooted in premises other than his own—and that Levenson, although prevented by a tragic death in 1969 from responding to the new currents of interpretation just then emerging, had a mind that was far too searching and subtle to be permanently confined by any one framework of assumptions.[15]

A Strange Conjunction

Before returning to Andy Nathan's letter, let me add here a word or two on Joseph Levenson, who drowned in a canoeing accident in the Russian River in California on April 6, 1969. I had gotten to know Levenson somewhat during the six or seven years before his death. I admired him greatly as a scholar and as a human being, and I was deeply affected by his death. His death was also inextricably linked in my mind to another event that took place at the same time. In early April 1969 I received a letter (dated March 29, 1969) from the renowned historian Arnold Toynbee inviting me to write one of the essays in a book he was editing on East Asia. (The final title of the book was *Half the World: The History and Culture of China and Japan* [London: Thames and Hudson, 1973].) Mark Elvin of the University of Glasgow had suggested that I might be interested in doing the chapter in question. Still a youngster (I was in my mid-thirties at the time), I was awed and wrote Dr. Toynbee that I would be honored to write the chapter—it was titled "Europe Goes East: The First Impact of the West on China and Japan." In my letter (dated April 8) I provided some details concerning how I would be inclined to frame the chapter. Toynbee (in a letter dated May 14) indicated that he was delighted with my response and assured me that I would be free to interpret things as I saw them. He added that the particular points I mentioned would, in his view, "add greatly to the value and significance" of my chapter. He enclosed a list of the contributors to the book. Then he mentioned the news of Levenson's untimely death and wondered whether, in addition to the chapter I had agreed to write, I might possibly consider writing the chapter that Levenson had signed on to do, which dealt with "the second impact of the West." I wrote back (in a letter dated May 21) that that was not something I felt I could take on at the time since I was busily engaged finishing a book (the one on Wang Tao) and had other commitments as well. I took the liberty of recommending a few scholars who I was confident would do a first-rate job with the Levenson chapter. Toynbee (June 2) wrote back that he understood my situation completely and expressed his gratitude for the suggestions I had given him.

Good News from Columbia

After also pointing out in his letter of late September 1982 a few comparatively minor matters that I might give further consideration to, Andy Nathan said he was happy to join Dorothy Borg in recommending that the Columbia University Press consider my book "carefully and sympathetically," although he did think they should retain a reader of their own before arriving at a decision. I wrote back thanking Andy for his reactions to the manuscript and for his help in smoothing its way to the press. In the meantime, Dorothy had sent the manuscript to Bernard Gronert, the executive editor of the press, who called me on October 6 to say that he'd spent an hour with the manuscript and liked the writing and the direct, personal way I introduced the work. He mentioned a forthcoming Columbia book of historiographical pieces written in honor of Dorothy Borg and edited by Warren Cohen, which he thought would make a nice companion volume to mine.[16] He queried me about the reasons for Harvard's less-than-enthusiastic reception of the book, especially in light of the fact that I'd already published two books with them. I was completely candid, conjecturing that especially after the sharply divergent reader reports, the strong identification of Harvard with Fairbank may have caused the Syndics to back off. Gronert said the manuscript would be sent out to a reader immediately.

By now Dorothy Borg had put aside whatever personal stake she may have had initially and was prepared to lend any and all support necessary to the publication of my manuscript. Aside from the letter of praise she wrote accompanying the book's submission to the press, in early November she sent me a note asking me to let her know as soon as I heard anything. "I feel sure all will go well," she added in her typically encouraging way, "but I hope it will do so quickly."

On Thanksgiving weekend, Dorothy was thoughtful enough to phone me at home and excitedly read me excerpts from the outside reader's report, which she'd gotten a copy of but I hadn't yet received. A day or two later, I received my own copy of the report, along with a handwritten note from Gronert, in which he described it as "glowing." "Given this and Andy & Dorothy's supportive letters," Gronert added, "I will be putting the project to the Faculty Publications meeting on December 15. I have all confidence in its favorable approval."

The external reader's report started by addressing the concern that from the start had been uppermost in the minds of prospective publishers: was there an audience for my book? Here is what the writer of the report (who I later discovered was John Israel) said:

Would this book, you ask, "be required reading for China Specialists?" My answer is an emphatic "Yes." It will be the point of departure for colloquia, historiography courses, and upper-level surveys of China's "recent past" (after Cohen, who will dare speak of "modern China"?). "Modern Chinese History" courses will begin with lectures entitled, "The Problem of 'Modern China'"—which will, in effect, be summaries of Cohen. Cohen's work will be required reading for graduate students preparing for Ph.D. orals, and these students may correctly anticipate that their professors will confront them with one or more "Cohenian" questions, if not an entire Cohenian examination.

The report went on to identify areas in the manuscript that could benefit from further attention. One in particular had to do with the book's title, which over the previous few years had undergone at least a dozen reformulations:

Cohen's lucid, flowing style is a splendid vehicle for his analysis. In his title, however, he becomes a victim of his own critique. Having dismissed "Modern China" as a meaningful descriptive term, he cannot very well entitle his volume, "American Historians and Modern China." As a title, "American Historical Writing on the Recent Chinese Past" [the title of the manuscript as sent to the outside reader] does not snap, crackle, or pop, but simply lies in the bowl sopping up milk. It does, however, tell us what the book is about and it should therefore be retained—as a subtitle. The title for the book should be identical to that of Chapter 4: "Toward a China-Centered History of China."

I adopted the first part of the reader's suggestion but not the second. The main title of the book, which felt right to me at the time and, more than thirty years on, still seems right, became *Discovering History in China*, the perfect riposte to Hegel's complaint, "We have before us the oldest state and yet no past . . . a state which exists today as we know it to have been in ancient times. To that extent China has no history."

The book was accepted not long after this, and the next note I received from Dorothy in connection with it came in April 1984, just after its publication. She began by wishing the book well: "May it have excellent sailing—good reviews, good sales and all that all of us want." Then she thanked me for the way I had thanked her in the book's preface: "I often think that among the happenings that have given me most pleasure," she wrote, "are the messages people send in their forewords. They seem so genuine and unperfunctory." If I look back on the actual phrasing I used to acknowledge Dorothy's help, it really was quite ordinary-sounding. But sometimes, messages that are intended to convey deep feeling are masked in conventional language. I knew from Dorothy's response to my thanks that she understood how truly grateful I was and, equally important, she knew I understood the range of feelings that had inspired her support of the book in the first place.

When I reflect on my unusual friendship with Dorothy Borg, what I always come back to is the behavior she demonstrated in connection with my book. Many other people, faced with similar circumstances, would have played it close to the vest, as indeed I myself had when first approached by her. Dorothy's instinctive response was to put her own feelings aside and embrace ideas she believed in, without dwelling overly much on pettier concerns of authorial patrimony and pride. She was by no means an entirely selfless person; she was much too interesting for that. But she had a bigheartedness that was rare and that, along with her other exceptional qualities, made one feel truly privileged to be counted among her friends.

CHAPTER 5

Limits of the China-Centered Approach

I n the previous two chapters, I discussed the contents and the prepublication history of *Discovering History in China*. The first three chapters of that book probe the Western-centric biases of three leading conceptual frameworks adopted by American historians of China in the 1950s and 1960s: the impact–response approach, the modernization (or tradition–modernity) approach, and the imperialism (or perhaps more aptly, imperialism–revolution) approach. In the final chapter of *Discovering History in China*, I identified a new departure in American writing that I labeled the China-centered approach. The core attribute of this approach is that its practitioners make a serious effort to understand Chinese history in its own terms—paying close attention to Chinese historical trajectories and Chinese perceptions of their own problems—rather than in terms of a set of expectations derived from Western history.[1] This does not mean that the approach gives short shrift to exogenous influences; nor does it preclude—on the contrary, it warmly embraces—the application to Chinese realities of theoretical insights and methodological strategies of non-Chinese provenance (often developed in disciplines other than history), as long as these insights and strategies are sensitive to the perils of parochial (typically Western-centric) bias.

I would not change any part of this formulation today. There are countless issues in the recent period of Chinese history for the probing of which a China-centered approach is both appropriate and desirable. A very partial listing of works with a China-centered perspective that appeared around the time of the original publication of *Discovering History in China* (1984) or shortly thereafter might include Madeleine Zelin's book (1984) on the indigenous evolution of the eighteenth-century Chinese state, with particular attention to fiscal reform; William Rowe's study (1984) of the remarkable development of commerce in Hankow (Hankou) in the nineteenth century; Benjamin Elman's work (1984) on the critical changes in Chinese intellectual discourse that took place in the eighteenth century in the Lower Yangzi region; Philip Huang's book (1985) on long-term patterns of agrarian change in north China in the late imperial and Republican eras; Mary Rankin's study (1986) of the growing mobilization and politicization of late Qing social elites, focusing on Zhejiang; Prasenjit Duara's inquiry (1988) into the impact of state-making on the social history of rural north China in the first half of the twentieth century; James Polachek's reconfiguration of the Opium War (1992), seen from the perspective of the internal Chinese political setting of the day; and Kathryn Bernhardt's analysis (1992) of the weakening of the landlord class in the Lower Yangzi area during the late imperial and republican periods as a result of the increasing intrusiveness of state power coupled with China's growing commercialization.[2]

There are other issues, however, where the use of a China-centered approach is manifestly less appropriate. I have in mind a number of areas of recent scholarly interest that, although unquestionably relating to Chinese history, are best identified in other ways, either because they raise questions (for instance, in addressing world-historical issues) that are broadly comparative in nature, because they examine China as part of an East Asian or Asian regional system, because even while dealing with the subject matter of Chinese history they are principally concerned with matters that transcend it, because they focus on the behavior and thinking (including self-perception) of non-Han ethnic groups within the Chinese realm, or because their paramount interest is in the migration of Chinese to other parts of the world. Each of these issues—and doubtless many others—raises questions about the boundaries of "Chinese history" and, indeed, in some cases the very meaning of the word *China*. Inevitably, therefore, each challenges the adequacy of the China-centered approach.

For historians of China, and surely others as well, one of the most interesting and deservedly influential exercises in comparative history in recent years has been the work of R. Bin Wong and Kenneth Pomeranz—I refer specifically to the former's *China Transformed* (1997) and the latter's *The Great Divergence* (2000)—grappling with the thorny issue of the West's ascendancy in the world during the past two centuries or so.[3] There are significant differences between these scholars. Pomeranz is more exclusively interested in questions pertaining to economic development, whereas Wong devotes much space to issues of state formation and popular protest.[4] Moreover, as he himself notes, Pomeranz places greater emphasis on "global conjunctures and reciprocal influences and bring[s] more places besides Europe and China into the discussion,"[5] whereas Wong is more consistently and exclusively concerned with Europe–China comparisons. What these scholars share is, however, far more important than what separates them. Most noteworthy is their agreement that in the past Westerners venturing comparisons between Europe and other parts of the world have posed the wrong sorts of questions. Tightly bound by the Eurocentrism of nineteenth-century social theory, they have assumed that the trajectories of change that occurred in Europe were the norm and that if something like the Industrial Revolution took place in Europe but not in China, the proper line of inquiry was to ask what went awry in the Chinese case.

Contesting this approach, Wong and Pomeranz insist on the need to engage in two-way comparisons, Wong using the phrase "symmetric perspectives" and Pomeranz "reciprocal comparisons."[6] Freed from Eurocentric presuppositions about normative trajectories of change, when they look at the economic situations of Europe and China (or, in Pomeranz's case, parts of Europe, parts of China, and parts of India and Japan) in the latter half of the eighteenth century both scholars find a remarkable degree of parallelism. "In key ways," Wong states, "eighteenth-century Europe shared more with China of the same period than it did with the Europe of the nineteenth and twentieth centuries." Pomeranz makes a similar point in more nuanced spatial terms, observing that in the middle of the eighteenth century "various core regions scattered around the Old World—the Yangzi Delta, the Kantō plain, Britain and the Netherlands, Gujarat—shared some crucial features with each other, which they did not share with the rest of the continent or subcontinent around them (e.g., relatively free markets, extensive handicraft industries, highly commercialized agriculture)."[7] Given the largely common economic circumstances prevailing between parts of Europe and parts of Asia at this time, the key question for Wong and Pomeranz shifts from what went wrong in Asia to what made possible the radically discontinuous economic change that occurred in Europe after 1800—first in England and then in other European core areas—and did not occur even in the most highly developed regions of the Asian continent. In responding to this question, both scholars agree that technological innovation along with the shift to new sources of energy (coal) in England were of critical importance. Wong also emphasizes the liberating function of certain structural features of the evolving European political economy (states, for example, that stood in a competitive relationship with one another), while Pomeranz develops an explanation that lays greater stress on factors external to Europe, particularly its involvement in a new kind of trading system and the windfall the New World and its resources provided.[8]

Although Wong asserts that his work "is primarily a book about Chinese history and secondarily a book about European history,"[9] and although he is exquisitely sensitive to the need to approach China's history without blinders carried over from the history of Europe, my distinct sense is that "China" is not what the book is principally about. The supreme value of Wong's book, for me, is its careful construction and elaboration of a fresh and more even-handed way of doing comparative history, one that does not privilege the historical path followed in one part of the world over those followed in other parts and therefore frees us to ask questions of any part's history that are not preloaded, as it were. In Pomeranz's study, the overall approach places less exclusive emphasis on comparison (even though the spatial field of comparison is wider than Wong's) and is more single-mindedly focused on the issue of the divergent economic trajectories taken by Europe and East Asia after the mid-eighteenth century. Although seriously concerned with showing "how different Chinese development looks once we free it from its role as the presumed opposite of Europe and . . . how different European history looks once we see the *similarities* between its economy and one with which it has most often been contrasted,"[10] his paramount objective is to shed light on the substantive question of how the modern world economy came into being. Therefore, Pomeranz, like Wong, although devoting much space to China and caring a great deal about getting his China stories right, is ultimately interested in matters that transcend Chinese history.

Application of the designation "China-centered" to scholarship, such as that of Wong and Pomeranz, that so clearly pertains to world history (regardless of whether this scholarship is primarily comparative or also pays serious notice to conjunctures and influences) seems obviously inappropriate. The same may be argued with respect to studies that look at China as part of a broader regional system in Asia. As intermediate categories between individual states and the world, regions have their own historical dynamic and must therefore (we are told by those who study them) be scrutinized from a region-centered perspective. Takeshi Hamashita,[11] for example, wants us "to understand East Asia as a historically constituted region with its own hegemonic structure"—a region that "entered modern times not because of the coming of European powers but because of the dynamism inherent in the traditional, Sinocentric tributary system."[12] The tributary system, inaugurated by China many centuries ago, formed a loose system of political integration embracing East and Southeast Asia. More than just a relationship between two states, China and the tribute-bearing country, at times it also encompassed satellite tributary relationships—at various points, Vietnam required tribute from Laos; Korea, while tributary to China, also sent tribute missions to Japan; and the kings of the Liuqiu (Ryūkyū) Islands during the Qing/Tokugawa had tributary relations with both Edo and Beijing—thus forming a complex web of relationships throughout the region.

The other key feature of the Asian regional system, according to Hamashita, was economic. A network of commercial relations (often multilateral), operating symbiotically with the tribute system, developed in East and Southeast Asia, closely intertwined with the commercial penetration of Chinese merchants into Southeast Asia and the emigration there of workers from south China. "The relationship between tribute goods and 'gifts' was substantially one of selling and purchasing." Prices of commodities "were determined, albeit loosely, by market prices in Peking." In fact, Hamashita argues, from the late Ming on, "it can be shown that the foundation for the whole complex tribute-trade formation was determined by the price structure of China and that the tribute-trade zone formed an integrated 'silver zone' in which silver was used as the medium of trade settlement. The key to the functioning of the tribute trade as a system was the huge 'demand' for commodities outside China and the difference between prices inside and outside China."[13] The importance Hamashita attaches to regional economic integration, it may be noted, is one of the more salient ways his analysis departs from earlier accounts of the "tributary system" by John Fairbank and others.[14]

Although China is an absolutely fundamental part of Hamashita's region-centered perspective (indeed, he frequently uses the word *Sinocentric* to describe it), it should be evident that a China-centered approach would be inadequate for understanding the Asian regional system he elaborates.[15] This becomes even clearer in another part of his analysis, in which he advances the notion that the sea was as important a locus and determinant of historical activity as the land in Asia. Although we are accustomed to viewing the Asian region as a collection of landed territorial units, it may also be seen as a series of interconnected "maritime regions" stretching from Northeast Asia all the way to Oceania. Once we adopt this sea-centered geographical perspective, Hamashita shrewdly suggests, it is easier to understand why intra-Asian political relationships developed as they did over the centuries: "The states, regions, and cities located along the periphery of each sea zone . . . [were] close enough to influence one another but too far apart to be assimilated into a larger entity. Autonomy in this sense formed a major condition for the establishment of the looser form of political integration known as the tributary system."[16]

Research on non-Han ethnic groups[17] points to another arena of historical scholarship that is not especially well served by China-centered analysis. Such research has taken a variety of forms. A small but unusually talented coterie of historians has injected new life into the question of the Manchuness of the Qing empire, looking at such topics as the evolution of Manchu identity (cultural and/or ethnic), the special character of the Qing frontier, the multiform nature of Manchu rulership and its contributions to the functioning of the Qing imperium, important Manchu institutions (most notably the Eight Banners), the contribution of the Manchus to twentieth-century nationalism, and so on.[18] Often supplementing Chinese sources with those in the Manchu language and sharply contesting the old view that the Manchus were largely absorbed or assimilated into a "Chinese world order," these scholars are in broad agreement that, as one of them has phrased it, "the notion of Manchu difference mattered throughout the Qing dynasty."[19] Indeed, several of them have used such phrases as "Qing-centered" and "Manchu-centered" to highlight this very difference.[20] The argument is not that the Manchus weren't a part of Chinese history in important ways but that Chinese history during the final centuries of the imperial era looks very different when seen through Manchu eyes. To view the parts taken by the Manchus in this history from a Han Chinese perspective—the conventional assimilation or Sinicization model—is to invite the same kinds of distortions that result when Chinese history is depicted in Eurocentric terms.

If Manchu difference mattered throughout the Qing, a major (although not the only) reason for its mattering was that the Qing was a conquest dynasty that brought China and eventually Inner Asia under the Manchu sway during this period.[21] It was a different story in the case of other non-Han groups, such as (to cite one of the more important examples) Muslim Chinese. Muslims in China also raise questions concerning the aptness of the China-centered approach, but because their experience over the centuries has been very different from that of the Manchus, the sorts of questions they raise also are different. One difference from the Manchus is that although Muslims (above all, during the Yuan dynasty) served as high officials at various points, they never ruled China as a group, in the sense that the Manchus (and Mongols) did. Another difference is that Muslims were and continue to be linked to varying degrees and in widely different ways to a religion—Islam—that is of non-Chinese origin and worldwide embrace.

As Dru Gladney and Jonathan Lipman have insisted,[22] Muslims in different parts of China (even in some cases in a single province) also tend to be very different from each other. Some Muslims (for example, many of the Uighurs in present-day Xinjiang, an area that until its subjugation by the Qing in the eighteenth century had been situated outside the Chinese realm), although inhabiting a space that is politically part of China, do not speak Chinese and tend to identify culturally and religiously more closely with their counterparts in the Central Asian states to the north than with Han Chinese. Other Muslims, scattered in various places throughout the Chinese realm, are descended from families that have lived in China for generations, speak one or another form of Chinese, and are indistinguishable in many aspects of their lives from non-Muslim Chinese. In recent centuries, in short, people in China could be both Chinese and Muslim in a range of different ways, making it hard to claim (as was done in the People's Republic in the 1950s) a "unified 'ethnic consciousness'" for Sino-Muslims.[23]

Given the heterogeneous character of the Muslim population of China, the argument could be made, at least in theory, that while a China-centered approach would be clearly misguided if applied to the Turkic-speaking Uighur population of Xinjiang,[24] it ought to be perfectly appropriate in the case of more acculturated Muslim Chinese. A key feature of the approach, after all, is that it seeks to cope with the immense variety and complexity of the Chinese world by breaking it down into smaller, more manageable spatial units, thereby facilitating close scrutiny of the whole range of local variations, including religious, ethnic, and social differences.[25] As it turns out, however, even in the case of Chinese-speaking Muslims, China-centered analysis can present problems. Lipman provides a fascinating illustration of the potential complications in his discussion of Muslims in a subprovincial part of Gansu in the nineteenth and twentieth centuries. The political center of Gansu and the center of Chinese-oriented economic life in this period was Lanzhou, the provincial capital. But Lanzhou was situated on the edges of two distinct Muslim spheres—one around Ningxia, the other centering on Hezhou—and from a Muslim perspective would be considered a peripheral area. Conversely, Hezhou, some sixty miles southwest of Lanzhou, was for Muslims (who constituted 50 percent of its population in the nineteenth century) a major commercial and religious center, but "would be the periphery of the periphery in any China-centered mapping." In other words, a China-centered mapping would be insufficiently sensitive to aspects of social, economic, and religious existence that were of vital importance to the Muslims of Gansu. Beyond this, it would more than likely have the drawback of presenting an undifferentiated picture of the province's Muslim community, flattening out its members' diversity, when, as Lipman clearly demonstrates, Muslims in different parts of the province in fact occupied a wide range of different social and occupational niches (and assumed different roles vis-à-vis the state), sometimes engaged in violence against each other, and were anything but unified in the nature and degree of their religious commitments.[26]

The new work on Manchus and Muslims relates to a much broader scholarly concern in recent years with the whole *minzu* ("nationality" or "ethnic group") question in China. Energized in part by Han–minority tensions on China's peripheries, in part by growing interest in and sensitivity to multicultural and multiethnic issues globally, this concern has been discernible in writing on the Uighurs, Mongols, Tibetans, Yi, and other groups.[27] Insofar as it challenges the notion of a transparent, unproblematic "Chineseness," complicating this category and forcing us continually to rethink its meaning, it has understandably not been very hospitable to China-centered analysis.

If a China-centered approach is not especially well-equipped to address the distinctive perspectives and experiences of non-Han communities within China, it also poses problems in regard to Han Chinese who have migrated to places outside the country—another phenomenon that has lately attracted wide interest in the scholarly world. Chinese migration abroad is an enormously complicated subject, which scholars have only recently begun to conceptualize anew.[28] Certain of its characteristic features derive from broader (and prior) patterns of migration within China, and insofar as the focus is on the "push" part of the process—the factors that favored decisions to migrate internally or overseas from a specific part of the country—the sensitivity of China-centered analysis to local particularity and variation is of potential value. But even at this stage we begin to encounter problems. Although local conditions of impoverishment or social unrest were fairly widespread in both north and south China in the nineteenth and early twentieth centuries, migration overseas originated largely from specific locales in the southern provinces of Fujian and Guangdong, rather than the northern part of the country. A major reason had to do with the access these places had to highly developed networks in a few southern treaty ports and above all the British colony of Hong Kong. These "in-between places," to use Elizabeth Sinn's apt phrase, served as points of transit or hubs, enabling people, goods, remittances, and even the bones of the dead to move in one direction or another between villages in south China and destinations all over the world. Migration, using such networks, became for families in certain parts of the south—and even in some cases entire villages and lineages—a prime economic strategy.[29] It was manifestly part of the regional and global systems discussed earlier.

At this point in the migration process, the utility of the China-centered approach as an exclusive—or even a primary—avenue to understanding becomes seriously diminished. The most obvious reason is the fact that China had important links with external locales. Once Chinese settled temporarily or permanently in Java or California or Lima or Pretoria, even if they remained in important ways embedded in Chinese social and historical narratives, they also became integrated into Indonesian, North American, Peruvian, and South African histories. Their adaptations to a range of environments that varied not only from place to place but also over time—Philip Kuhn uses the phrase "historical ecology" to characterize the process—can hardly be comprehended in terms of a single national or cultural perspective.[30] But the complication created for China-centered analysis by the need to factor in multiple place-based understandings is only part of the problem. Beyond this, Adam McKeown argues persuasively, if we are to gain a fuller comprehension of Chinese migration, nation-based perspectives as such (China- or North America- or Indonesia-centered, and the like) must be complemented by approaches that put special emphasis on mobility and dispersion, "drawing attention to global connections, networks, activities, and consciousness that bridge these more localized anchors of reference."[31] In other words, migration is not just a matter of push factors and pull factors, a sending place and a receiving place. It must also be understood as a process—one that involves constant movement back and forth along well-established, highly articulated corridors; for this very reason, it is profoundly subversive of conventional national boundaries.[32]

The adequacy of the "China-centered" approach may, in certain instances, be called into question in regard to scholarship that is directly and extensively concerned with Chinese history. A good illustration would be my book, *History in Three Keys: The Boxers as Event, Experience, and Myth* (1997) (discussed in detail in the next two chapters). For one who had been identified as a strong advocate of moving away from the Western-centric understandings of late imperial China that had dominated U.S. scholarship of the 1950s and 1960s toward a more China-centered approach, *History in Three Keys* represented a fairly radical shift in the direction of my work. Certainly, in large portions of the book I make a sustained effort to get inside the world of the Boxers and other Chinese inhabiting the north China plain in the spring and summer of 1900, and in this respect the approach may be viewed as China-centered. But I'm also interested, to a lesser degree, in the thoughts, feelings, and behavior of the non-Chinese participants in the events of the time and frequently point out commonalities between the Chinese and foreign sides, suggesting an approach that, at least at certain junctures, is more generally human- than specifically China-centered.

Finally and most important, as I make clear throughout *History in Three Keys*, my main purpose there is to explore a wide range of issues pertaining to writing history in general, "the Boxers functioning as a kind of handmaiden to this larger enterprise."[33] This is rather different from the usual procedure in historical studies. It is not at all uncommon in such studies (not just in the China field) for authors to conclude by situating their findings in a broader frame of reference in the hope of enhancing the significance and importance of their work. In *History in Three Keys*, I start right off with a set of broader questions and never really let go of them. Although I use the Boxers as an extended case study, I make it clear especially in the concluding chapter that there is no necessary or exclusive connection between the Boxers and the larger points I am interested in exploring. Many other episodes of world history could serve equally as well.[34] The main object of the book is to say something not about Chinese history but about writing history generally. There's nothing especially China-centered about that.

The research themes treated here all raise problems of some sort for the China-centered approach, in some instances requiring that it be abandoned, but more often that it be used in nuanced conjunction with a variety of other approaches. More than thirty years ago, when I first described the China-centered approach—and I hasten to emphasize that, from my perspective at the time, all I was doing was giving articulation (and a name) to a set of research strategies that others had already begun to use and that seemed to me an appropriate and salutary direction for American China scholarship to be moving in—I expressly linked it to the study of the Chinese past. Indeed, the chapter in *Discovering History in China* in which I introduce the approach bears the title "Toward a China-Centered History of China." As long as the topics historians choose to study are centrally and more or less unambiguously situated within a Chinese context (political, social, economic, intellectual, cultural, religious)—and despite the new scholarly developments of recent years this remains true of a substantial portion of historical work on China—the China-centered approach remains, in my judgment, eminently useful. The difficulty arises when we move into research areas, such as the ones I've been discussing, that either decenter China by linking it to transnational processes (migration, the emergence of the modern world economy, the evolution of an Asian regional system) or general intellectual issues (multiple ways of addressing the past, the conduct of comparative history), or transform China from a physical space into something else (the currently fashionable word is *deterritorialization*)[35] or in some other way problematize its meaning (the self-perceptions of non-Han ethnic groups within China and of Han Chinese migrants abroad).[36]

Such research directions, although presenting problems for a narrowly conceived China-centered approach, make vitally important contributions to the study of Chinese history more broadly considered. Among the several ways they do this are the following: they remove some of the artificial walls that have been erected around "China" over the centuries (as much by Chinese as by Westerners); they subvert parochial readings of the Chinese past (fostered, again, no less by Chinese than by Western historians); they complicate our understandings of what it has meant in different places and at various points in time to be "Chinese"; they enable more even-handed (less loaded) comparisons between China and other parts of the world; and in general they weaken the West's long-standing perception of China as the quintessential "other" by breaking down arbitrary and misleading distinctions between "East" and "West" and making it possible to see China—its peoples and their cultures—less as prototypically exotic and more as plausibly human.

Problems with the East–West Contrast: The Overemphasis of Culture

I want to elaborate on this last point, as it has become an increasingly important concern in my work. I refer specifically to my skepticism concerning exaggerated Western claims of Chinese and Western cultural difference—claims frequently (though not invariably) rooted in Western-centric perspectives. I take culture seriously in almost everything I've written[37] and would not for a moment deny that there are important differences between the cultural traditions of China and the West. But at the same time, I believe that historical approaches that place excessive emphasis on such differences are apt to generate unfortunate distortions, even caricatures, of one sort or another. One such distortion takes the form of cultural essentialization—the radical reduction of a culture to a particular set of values or traits that other cultures are believed not to embody or to embody much less prominently. The stereotypes of the authoritarian East and the liberal and tolerant West, for example, do not readily allow for the possibility, brilliantly argued by Amartya Sen, that the histories of India or China might include traditions of tolerance or freedom, or that authoritarianism might be a significant strain in the West's own past. Yet the actual historical record flies right in the face of such conventional understandings. Indeed, "when it comes to liberty and tolerance," Sen suggests, it might make more sense, giving priority to the substance of ideas rather than to culture or region, "to classify Aristotle and Ashoka on one side, and, on the other, Plato, Augustine, and Kautilya."[38]

Overemphasis on Chinese–Western cultural contrast also—and this was generally true of American historical scholarship until not too many decades ago—has had a tendency to desensitize Western historians to China's capacity for change and encourage a timeless conception of the Chinese past. When I initially advanced the notion of a China-centered approach, I observed that one of the approach's more important concomitants was a gradual shift away from culture and toward history as the dominant mode of structuring problems of the recent Chinese past (by which I meant chiefly the nineteenth and twentieth centuries). During the 1950s and 1960s, when the impact–response and tradition–modernity paradigms held sway in U.S. scholarship, enormous explanatory power was invested in the nature of China's "traditional" society or culture—and, of course, in how this society/culture differed from that of the West (or Japan). Studies of clash between China and the West—Fairbank's *Trade and Diplomacy on the China Coast*, my own *China and Christianity*—although devoting much space to political, economic, social, institutional, and other factors, tended to view cultural difference and misunderstanding (as expressed above all in the realm of attitudes and values) as the ultimate ground of conflict.[39] Similarly, influential treatments of such themes as China's failure to industrialize in the late Qing (Feuerwerker), the ineffectiveness of China's response to the West compared with Japan's (Fairbank, Reischauer, and Craig), the fruitless efforts of the Confucian state to modernize (Wright), and the inability of Chinese society to develop on its own into a "society with a scientific temper" (Levenson) all attached fundamental importance to the special nature of Chinese society and culture.[40]

This emphasis on the social or cultural factor was a natural by-product of intellectual paradigms built around the notion of sociocultural contrast that sought to explain China principally in terms of its social and cultural differences from the West. The reason, I argued, the China-centered approach lent itself to a structuring of the Chinese past more in historical than in cultural terms was that its locus of comparison was not the differences between one culture and another (China and the West) but the differences between earlier and later points in time within a single culture (China). The former kind of comparison, by drawing attention to the more stable, ongoing properties of a culture—a culture's "intrinsic nature"—encouraged a relatively static sense of the past. The latter, by stressing variation over time within one culture, fostered a more dynamic, more change-oriented sense of the past, one where culture as an explanatory factor receded into the background and history—or a heightened sensitivity to historical process—moved to the fore.[41]

When historians seek to understand the people of another culture, an exaggerated attention to cultural difference, aside from making it more difficult to apprehend the complex, often contradictory elements in that culture's make-up or to appreciate the changes it has undergone over time, can also conceal from view aspects of the thought and behavior of its people that, reflecting supracultural, inherently human characteristics, overlap or resonate with the thought and behavior of peoples elsewhere in the world. This was a central concern of Benjamin Schwartz in his writing. From Schwartz's perspective, the value of China as an object of study did not rest in any qualities of exotic uniqueness it might possess, nor was it of value as the West's "other" in some absolute sense. Rather, China was valuable as an alternative repository of human experience, a vast laboratory (with its own distinctive furnishings) for the exploration of universal human dilemmas.[42] This universal human dimension must be addressed along with cultural difference, if we are to gain a fuller, more shaded, less parochial understanding of the Chinese past.[43] Addressing it is also, as I hope to demonstrate in the following chapters on the Boxers, one of the more effective ways of crossing the boundaries that Western and Chinese historians both (albeit in different ways and for different reasons) have too often inscribed around China and its history.

CHAPTER 6

A Multiplicity of Pasts

History in Three Keys

Philosophers have written lengthy theoretical treatises on what historians do. In my book *History in Three Keys: The Boxers as Event, Experience, and Myth* (1997), I explore the issue through an actual historical
case, the Boxer uprising in China at the turn of the twentieth century.[1]
Before going any further, I need to say something about the origins of
that book. I had been interested in the Boxers ever since my dissertation
and first book, where I wrote about the political problems resulting from
the intrusion of foreign missionaries into Chinese society in the 1860s.
Very similar political problems, I suggested in the book's final chapter,
were posed for the Qing government by the Boxer uprising of 1900: "To
support the virulently antiforeign Boxers meant to risk war with all the
foreign powers. But to suppress them was to run the equal danger of alien-
ating the more xenophobic elements at the Chinese court."[2] I began to
read about the Boxers seriously in the mid-1980s after finishing *Discovering History in China*. During the decade I'd spent thinking about and
writing the latter book, I had also become deeply interested in issues of
what I referred to as "historical epistemology"—what we know about the
past and how we know it—and this led to the tripartite framework I developed for my work on the Boxers.[3]

When I first began to study history, my idea of what historians "did"
was very different from what it later became. I used to think of the past
as, in some sense, a fixed body of factual material, and it was the histo-

rian's job to unearth and elucidate it. I still think of the historian as a person whose main object is to understand and explain the past. But I now have a far less innocent view of the processes—and problems—involved. I now see the reconstructive work of the historian as in constant tension with two other ways of "knowing" the past—experience and myth—that tend to be far more pervasive and influential in terms of their bearing on people's lives.

Three Ways of Knowing the Past

Plotted at a certain level of abstraction, the Boxer uprising formed a major chapter in the narrative structure of the final years of the Qing dynasty. It was the largest-scale armed conflict to occur between the rebellions of the mid-nineteenth century and the 1911 revolution, and as such reflected the increasingly tenuous political position of the dynasty. Seen as a social movement, the Boxers, many of them young farm boys made destitute by the successive natural disasters that had battered north China since the early 1890s, were a striking expression of the more general breakdown of the agrarian order in China. This breakdown, characterized in many parts of the empire by high levels of popular unrest, was also reflected in the religious beliefs of the Boxers, in particular their practice of spirit possession and frequent recourse to magic. The antiforeign dimension of the Boxer phenomenon, expressed most dramatically in the attacks on native Christians and foreign missionaries, created a profound crisis in Sino–foreign relations and eventually led to direct foreign military intervention and a Chinese declaration of war against all the powers. Finally, the lifting of the siege of the legations in Beijing in August 1900, the flight of the court to Xi'an in the northwest, the foreign occupation of the capital, and the diplomatic settlement (including a huge indemnity) imposed on China by the victorious powers brought about a decisive shift in Qing government policy, which in the first years of the twentieth century became increasingly (if reluctantly) wedded to far-reaching reform. It is little wonder, taking all of these different aspects of the Boxer episode together, that Mary Wright should have begun her widely read essay on the background of the 1911 revolution with the ring-ing pronouncement: "Rarely in history has a single year marked as dra-matic a watershed as did 1900 in China."[4]

In addition to being tightly woven into the larger tapestry of events comprising this period of Chinese history, the Boxers also gave rise to a potent set of myths in the popular imaginations of both Chinese and Westerners. In the West in the early decades of the twentieth century, the Boxers were widely viewed as "the Yellow Peril personified[,] . . . the very word Boxerism conjur[ing] up visions of danger, xenophobia, irra-tionality and barbarism."[5] Chinese intellectuals prior to the early 1920s—people like Lu Xun, Hu Shi, and the early Chen Duxiu—often shared this negative perception of the Boxers, adding "superstitiousness" and "backwardness." Then, during the period of heightened nationalism and antiforeignism that marked the 1920s, while many Westerners sought to discredit Chinese nationalism by branding it a revival of Boxerism, Chi-nese revolutionaries began to rework the Boxers into a more positive myth, centering on the qualities of patriotism and anti-imperialism. This more affirmative vision of the Boxers as heroic soldiers against foreign aggres-sion reached a high-water mark among Chinese on the mainland (and some people of Chinese ancestry abroad) in the Cultural Revolution years (1966–76),[6] at the very moment that Chinese on Taiwan (and many West-erners) were resurrecting the more lurid image of the Boxers as fanatical, uncivilized xenophobes and pinning it on the Red Guards.[7] During the Cultural Revolution, under the spirited oversight of Mao Zedong's wife Jiang Qing, praise was also lavished on the Boxers' female counterparts, the Red Lanterns, particularly for their alleged rebellion against the sub-ordinate status of women in the old society.[8]

The Boxers as event represent a particular reading of the past, whereas the Boxers as myth represent pressing the past into the service of a par-ticular reading of the present. Either way, a dynamic interaction is set up between present and past, in which the past is continually reshaped, either consciously or unconsciously, in accordance with the diverse and shift-ing preoccupations of people in the present. What happens to the past—or, to be more exact, the lived or experienced past—when we perform this feat of redefinition? What happens to the experiential world of the original creators of the past when, for purposes of clarity and exposition, historians structure it in the form of "events," or mythologizers, for altogether different reasons, distill from it a particular symbolic message? If it is true, to paraphrase French philosopher Paul Veyne, that events never coincide with the perceptions of their participants and witnesses and that the historian carves out of the evidence and documents the event he or she has chosen to make,[9] what are the implications of this for historical understanding? Are historians, too, ultimately fashioners of myth? Finally, if we were to unravel an event, break it down into smaller, more discrete mini-events or units of human experience—the tedium and physical wretchedness of life in the trenches rather than the grand order of battle—what would we be left with? Just a messy and meaningless pile of data? Or, on a more optimistic note, a closer approximation of what the past was actually like and what exactly happens to this "real past" when historians attempt to explain it or mythologizers try to exploit it for its symbolic content?

These questions illustrate but do not exhaust the range of issues I am concerned with in *History in Three Keys*. The first part of the book tells the "story" of the Boxer uprising, as later narrated by historians—people with foreknowledge of how things turned out, a wide-angle picture of the entire event (that is, the capacity to discern how the experiences of different people in the past related to one another and how a profusion of small-scale events widely distributed in space interconnected to form event structures of broader compass), and the goal of explaining not only the Boxer phenomenon itself but how it fit into a mosaic of prior and subsequent historical developments. The second part probes the thought, feelings, and behavior of those directly involved in different phases of the Boxer experience—rural Chinese youth who joined Boxer units in their villages, anxious missionaries scattered across the drought-parched north China plain at the height of the uprising, Chinese and foreign inhabitants of Tianjin trapped during the battle that raged there in the early summer of 1900—in short, individuals who didn't know whether they would emerge from their respective ordeals dead or alive, who did not have the entire "event" preinscribed in their heads, and who therefore conceptualized what was happening to them in ways that differed most fundamentally from the retrospective, backward-reading constructions of historians. The third part of the book explores the myths surrounding the Boxers and "Boxerism" that were fashioned in twentieth-century China—symbolic images designed less to throw light on the Boxer past than to draw energy from it, often (though not always) for the purpose of advancing political or overtly propagandistic agendas, in the post-Boxer present.

My aim in distinguishing—and carefully scrutinizing—these three zones of consciousness is to impart something of the complexity of the historical enterprise in general, to illuminate the tension between the history that people make, which is indeed in some sense fixed, and the histories that historians write and mythologizers use, which seem to be forever changing. This is really quite different from the well-known Rashomon effect (referring to the famous Kurosawa film about a rape-murder in eleventh-century Japan and the different accounts the four people who witnessed it supplied of what happened).[10] "Rashomon," as it has come to be used in English, refers to the different points of view different people have of an event (different versions of the truth) depending on where they are situated, either literally or figuratively, in relationship to that event. The different ways of knowing the past that I'm interested in certainly encompass differences in perspective. But they also go beyond this and address differences of a more substantive nature. Experiencers of the past are incapable of knowing the past that historians know, and mythologizers of the past, although sharing with historians the advantage of afterknowledge, are uninterested in knowing the past as its makers experienced it. In other words, although the lines separating these ways of knowing the past are not always clear (as we are well aware, historians engage in mythologization, and the makers of the past are entirely capable of turning their own experiences into history after the fact), as ways of knowing they are analytically distinct.

The Issue of Representativeness: Do the Boxers Make the Cut?

There are a number of issues raised implicitly in *History in Three Keys* that I address explicitly in the book's conclusion. One has to do with the matter of representativeness. In an effort to gain a clearer picture of what historians do, I examine the distinctive characteristics of event, experience, and myth in reference to a single—and in many ways quite singular—episode out of the past, the Boxer movement and uprising at the turn of the twentieth century in China. I assume that buried in the particularity of the Boxers are universals that are applicable to other historical events. This assumption needs to be looked at more closely.

Let me begin with a clarification. In the book I am not interested in all aspects of the past, only in those directly engaging the consciousness not only of the historian but also of the experiencer and mythmaker. This leaves out a whole category of historical writing focused on long-term, impersonal developments (frequently but not necessarily social or economic) that, however important, are generally too incremental to be noticed and thus rarely engage people's passions. The writing that encompasses such developments assumes, like all historical writing, a narrative form,[11] expressing the consciousness of the historian-narrator (historians never lose *their* consciousness). But it leaves little or no room for the consciousness of the agents of history, the people who make and experience the past, and it is doubtful anyone would ever set out to mythologize price inflation in eighteenth-century China or agricultural change in northern Europe during the late feudal era.

If we omit those aspects of the past that, whatever their cumulative effect on people's lives, are so slow-changing as to go undetected and train our attention instead exclusively on the aspects that individual human beings experience on a conscious level, there is still a lot left. In fact, virtually everything is left that people ordinarily think of when they contemplate the past as an arena in which "things happened." The real question for us, then, is whether the Boxers, for all their distinctiveness, may still be taken as illustrative of the consciously apprehended past in general. My answer to this question is strongly in the affirmative.

When viewed as an event, reconstructed after the fact by historians, with the goal of understanding and elucidating what happened and why, the Boxers, I would argue, are as appropriate for illustrative purposes as any other phase of the past. Indeed, since the focus in all such reconstructive effort is on the consciousness of the historian, rather than that of the direct participant or mythologizer, there is no reason historical reconstructions of even the more impersonal parts of the past—as opposed to "events" and "individuals"—cannot be used to exemplify what historians do. The contents of every historical event are unique. Moreover, some events, like the Boxer movement, are complex, occurring over great stretches of time and space, whereas others, such as the first performance of a Broadway play or the death of a national political leader, are relatively simple (although their ramifications may not be). But the historian's structuring of these events—the narratives we tell about them—operates according to a fairly distinctive set of principles regardless. One of these principles, which is absolutely fundamental, is that, unlike the mythologizer, the historian seeks to understand and explain the past in accordance with a socially agreed-on and enforced set of professional guidelines. Although we are subject to the same spectrum of emotional requirements as anyone else, in our capacity as historians our efforts to understand the past are guided by a conscious commitment (never fully realized in practice) to accuracy and truth. This commitment defines us as historians. If the other commitments to which we also owe allegiance—say, a feminist historian's desire to give voice to women who have previously been silent and thus contribute to the empowerment and liberation of women in the present and future—take precedence over the goal of understanding and explaining what happened in the past in accordance with generally accepted standards, we abdicate our responsibility as historians and move in the direction of mythologization.[12] Another principle, no less important (though admittedly far less controversial), is that in contrast to the participant/experiencer, historians know in advance the outcomes of the events they seek to reconstruct. Like Merlin the magician, we know what is coming next; indeed, it is precisely this knowledge, J. H. Hexter observes, that enables us to "adapt the proportions" of the stories we tell "to the actual historical tempo."[13] A third principle, again distinguishing the historian from the immediate participant, is the former's freedom from the constraint of spatial location; that is, unlike the original agents of history, the historian is endowed with what I earlier alluded to as wide-angle vision.

The suitability of the Boxers as an illustrative case when the past is viewed as experience is somewhat less straightforward. Here the spotlight is trained not on the consciousness of the historian-reconstructor but on that of the historical agent, and although we may argue with confidence that historians always do more or less the same thing, surely the same cannot be said of the people who made the past in the first place and directly experienced it. Wars, election campaigns, baseball games, first loves, and final exams all refer to intrinsically different kinds of experience. The number of different kinds is infinite, and the individual experience is always unique. How, then, can an event like the Boxer episode—in which the key areas of experience included such things as drought, spirit possession, magic, rumor, and death—be taken as illustrative of the experienced past in general? Indeed, isn't the very notion of experience "in general" a contradiction in terms?

The answer, like that to the question of the representativeness of the Boxers *qua* event, has several levels. At its most concrete and particular, the experience of those involved in the Boxer summer was, like the experience of participants in any phase of the past, unique and nonreplicable. Here, for example, are two wish rumors (one of them incorporating Boxer magical claims) that circulated in Tianjin at the time of the fighting in the early summer of 1900, along with my analysis of their meaning for Chinese contemporaries. The Boxers were said to have told people in Tianjin on July 4 that their teacher, after rendering himself invisible, had entered the foreign concession area (Zizhulin), where he came upon a tall building that was vacant. Making himself visible again, he went inside. The building had four stories. There was nothing on the first two floors. But the third floor was filled with gold, silver, pearls, and precious gems, and on the fourth floor he encountered an elderly foreign couple seated facing each other. The couple performed the *koutou* (a ubiquitous Chinese ritual denoting respect for a superior) before the teacher. They said that they were husband and wife and were over 100 years of age. Suddenly bursting into tears, they said they knew that the teacher's magic was very powerful and that he was to come on that day. They were waiting for him. They said that the foreign countries had only firearms to rely on. Today the foreigners were to be destroyed. Heavenly soldiers had come into the world. The firearms would not fire. The foreign countries had therefore resigned themselves to being extinguished. They invited the teacher to go to the lower floor and help himself to the gold, silver, pearls, and jewels. Then they announced they were going to die. When they had finished talking, they both seized pistols and shot themselves in the chests.

"The Boxers," we are told by a contemporary chronicler, "took much pleasure in telling this story and the people of Tianjin were convinced it was true. Suddenly, they spread the word that the government forces and Boxers had repulsed the foreign armies and that the Chinese had taken

Zizhulin. . . . The news circulated noisily through the streets of the city. Only after a long time had passed did people discover that it had no basis in fact."

A related rumor that circulated at the same time asserted that the foreigners had fled Zizhulin, that the government forces and Boxers had entered the area and quartered themselves there, and that within the concession they had found forty crates, each containing 280,000 ounces of gold. Neither the government troops nor the Boxers took the gold; instead they presented it to the governor-general's *yamen* (office) to be used for relief purposes.[14]

There were a number of wishes symbolized in these rumors, and they had to do with people's deepest and most pressing concerns. On the most obvious level, of course, there was the wish, shared by both Boxers and the larger population, that the Chinese side would be victorious in the Battle of Tianjin and the foreigners go down in defeat. (This wish was also given expression in the woodcut art of the day, which frequently showed the foreigners being overwhelmed by the Chinese in military encounters or humiliated by them in some other way; see fig. 6.1.) In an area suffering from the effects of protracted drought, there was also the wish, expressed in the second rumor (and implying a possible divergence of interest between the Boxers and the general population), that ordinary people (not the Boxers or the government soldiers) would be the beneficiaries of the windfall discovered in the foreign concession. Finally, and perhaps least obvious, the first rumor incorporated the fantasy that the foreigners (as represented by the truth-telling elderly couple) accepted the efficacy of Boxer magical claims and had bought into the master narrative of the heavenly nature of the Boxer movement and its mission, thereby confirming in the most powerful way the validity of the Boxer cause.

Experience on this level of particularity, while enormously helpful in advancing our understanding of the psychological climate prevailing during the spring and summer of 1900 in Tianjin, doesn't tell us much about events occurring in other places and other historical eras. On a somewhat more general level, on the other hand, world history is full of popular movements in which, as with the Boxers, religion and magical rituals played a key part, antiforeign feeling was a driving force, rumor and incredulity were pervasive, and war, bloodshed, and dying predominated. And on the most general (or abstract) level, there are a number of

6.1. Battle of Tianjin. Detail from a larger patriotic print depicting the use of a variety of weapons (including explosives) by glowering Chinese troops in a victory over the foreigners. *Source:* C. P. Fitzgerald, *The Horizon History of China* (New York: American Heritage, 1969). By permission of the British Library.

phenomena that appear to characterize all human experience, regardless of the specific, concrete forms in which it is expressed. I have in mind here such things as indeterminacy (or outcome-blindness), emotional engagement, multiple motivation, cultural construction, and biographical consciousness (as distinct from historical consciousness).[15]

The kinds of historical data available for reconstructing different experiential worlds will, of course, vary according to the idiosyncrasies of historical circumstance. Except at the most superficial level, for example, it is impossible to explore the consciousness of individual Boxers because very few were literate and, although we have a good deal of oral history material collected from former Boxers more than a half-century later, at the time none left detailed accounts of their experience.[16] On the other hand, there is a profusion of documentation relating to such facets of the Boxer experience as the high levels of anxiety occasioned by the uncertainties attending prolonged drought and premature death and the pervasive tendency of Chinese and foreigners alike to interpret their experiences in terms of prior cultural patterning.[17] Although we obviously cannot reconstruct the Boxer experience in its entirety, therefore, we can certainly gain access to significant portions of it and, at a certain level of generality, gain insight into the experienced past more broadly considered.

The problem of the Boxers' representativeness as myth is different, but not fundamentally so. The main difference is that many parts of the past—here I refer expressly to the consciously experienced past—do not survive, in any significant way, as myth. To live on as myth, an event or person must embody characteristics or themes that seem especially pertinent to the concerns of particular groups of people and/or governments in later times. Christopher Columbus is important to Italian Americans because when viewed as the discoverer of North America he is emblematic of the contribution people of Italian ancestry have made to American life. In a different way, Columbus is also important to African Americans and Native Americans, who, focusing on his involvement in the slave trade and his brutal treatment of the Indian populations of the Caribbean, have refashioned him into a powerful symbol of the oppression and racist exploitation these groups have suffered throughout their history at the hands of Americans of European ancestry.[18]

On the Chinese side, to take an example very different from the Boxers, the anti-Manchu, Christian-influenced Taiping Rebellion of 1850–64 has been mythologized in a variety of ways. In the last years of the Qing, the radical journal *Minbao* hailed the Taiping founder, Hong Xiuquan, as one of China's great Nationalist revolutionaries (along with the first emperor of the Ming dynasty and Sun Yat-sen).[19] The Guomindang in the early 1920s and the Chinese Communists throughout the period of Maoist dominance also identified with and saw themselves as carrying on the Taiping revolutionary tradition.[20] Individual Taiping leaders, in heavily mythologized form, have figured centrally in Chinese Communist political wars. After being sumptuously praised in the historiography of the 1950s, for example, the able commander Li Xiucheng, because he confessed (following torture) to Zeng Guofan after the Taipings' defeat, was reviled during the 1960s as a traitor to his class and regularly deployed as a negative symbol in Cultural Revolution attacks on revisionists.[21] Chinese historians in the late 1970s and early 1980s, in their attacks on feudal despotism in general and (more guardedly) the "patriarchal despotism" of Mao Zedong in particular, regularly drew parallels between Mao's slide into increasingly autocratic leadership after 1958 and that of such past political leaders as Hong Xiuquan.[22]

The Taipings have also been a favorite source of local-level mythmaking, especially in the area of their origin, the Pearl River delta. Sun Yat-sen, who came from the same part of southern Guangdong as Hong Xiuquan, is said to have admired and identified with the Taiping leader ever since his childhood days.[23] Refugees in Hong Kong reported that in the mid-1950s Guangdong peasants, viewing Hong as an all-purpose spokesman for popular resistance to the coercive power of the state, looked for him to return from the dead and lead them in opposing the forced cooperativation of their land.[24] Recent work on the Hakka minority of southern China shows how Christian members of this ethnic group have integrated a positive vision of the Taiping movement (whose founders were Christian-influenced Hakkas) into the invented traditions that form part of their definition of themselves as a community.[25]

The Boxers, too, as we have seen, have been mythologized by later Chinese in sharply conflicting ways over the years, depending on which aspect of modern Chinese cultural identity—condemnation of foreign imperialist aggression or emulation of foreign-inspired models of modernity—has been uppermost in the mind of the mythologizer. Although the particularities of one or another example of mythologization will differ greatly (the Taiping experience does not, for example, like that of the Boxers, resonate in a special way with the issue of modern cultural identity), the underlying processes involved do not. Whether it is the Boxers or Columbus or the Taipings or the French Revolution or Martin Luther King Jr., in mythologization of the past, the emphasis is less on what actually happened than on how what happened is transformed and recast by later people for their own purposes. Invariably particular themes from the past are identified, simplified, magnified, and highlighted, to the point that they become sources of energy in the present, making it possible for present and past to affirm and validate one another, sometimes in extremely powerful ways. The themes may or may not be part of the actual historical past—it isn't clear, for example, that real Red Lanterns ever saw themselves as rebelling against the Confucian social conventions that hobbled Chinese women at the end of the nineteenth century (as alleged by Cultural Revolution mythmakers)—but if they are to work effectively as myths, they must possess at least a degree of plausibility. They must be believable, even if not true.

On the matter of the Boxers' representativeness, to summarize, I would draw essentially the same conclusion with respect to the three alternative avenues of access to the past I explore in *History in Three Keys*. At the most concrete and specific level, the Boxers, whether viewed as event, experience, or myth, are undeniably unique. This uniqueness, however, has embedded within it broad recurrent patterns encountered in all phases of the consciously experienced past, making it perfectly feasible, at a more general level, to appropriate the Boxers (or for that matter, any other historical episode) for illustrative purposes. We don't study lions to learn about giraffes, but we can study either lions or giraffes to enrich our understanding of the animal kingdom.

The Comparative Validity of Event, Experience, and Myth as Ways of Knowing the Past

Another issue that invites further comment has to do with the comparative validity of event, experience, and myth as ways of knowing the past. Are we to understand the experienced past as being privileged over the historically reconstructed one because it is more real? Or the historically reconstructed past as preferable to the mythologized one because it is truer, a more accurate reflection of what happened? At one point in my career as a historian I would not have hesitated to answer "yes" to both of these questions, but my growing conviction is that each approach, despite manifest tensions among them, possesses a solid kind of legitimacy within its sphere.

The case is perhaps hardest to make with respect to the polarity between the experienced and the historically reconstructed pasts. Although we see how they differ, the value we attach to the one is difficult to cordon off and keep from being affected by the value we attach to the other. For example, in certain circumstances we may delight in confronting, for the first time, the historical recounting of a part of the past—a war, say, or a political campaign or a social movement—in which we ourselves have directly participated, marveling at the new information and perspectives it supplies. But in other circumstances, our earlier participatory role may, in the light of later historical understanding, become a source of far greater pain or guilt or emotional conflict than we originally experienced. Reading about the history we ourselves have lived, in other words, invariably touches it, affecting for better or worse our memory of the actions we engaged in and the thoughts and feelings we had at the time. A good example of this is the new insight into gender inequality and male entitlement that I gained from the reconstruction of my experiences in Taipei in the early 1960s a half century later (see chapter 1).[26]

The situation with respect to the value of myth is also complicated and potentially problematic, although perhaps less so in regard to the relationship between myth and experience than that between myth and history. Experience does not take place in a cultural void. As people encounter "life" they "process" it in terms of the myths—or cultural assumptions—that have formed a vital part of their socialization. Boxers do not hesitate to identify the gods who possess them as the historical and literary figures they learned about from early childhood or to understand the failure of their magic in battle situations in terms of deep-seated cultural beliefs about female pollution. Christian missionaries almost instinctively interpret the Boxer movement as the work of Satan, and their own actions (and fate) as reflections of God's will. Such mythic constructions are ubiquitous in the world of experience and form an inseparable part of it. But as merged as they seem—and perhaps are—at the moment an experience is first registered (the immediate past) they remain analytically distinct. This distinctness, moreover, becomes a lot clearer (at least to others) when we review the personally experienced past from a more remote point in time and inadvertently mythologize it. The process of constantly reworking one's own experienced past, which I call autobiographical mythologization, obviously does violence to the "purity" (not to mention the accurate remembering) of the original experience. "However honest we try to be in our recollections," a character in Robertson Davies's *World of Wonders* cautions, "we cannot help falsifying them in terms of later knowledge."[27] At the same time, as a number of writers have argued compellingly, autobiographical mythmaking has a clear value, in that it helps preserve a sense of psychological coherence and personal integrity over time.[28]

The value of myth in the context of the relationship between myth and history is still more complicated. Most professional historians see it as part of their responsibility to distance their reconstructions of the past from the relatively crude, mythologized understandings of the general population. For example, we shrink from accepting a simple, idealized vision of Abraham Lincoln as "the great emancipator" and feel duty bound to point out that despite his personal conviction that slavery was wrong, Lincoln's priority was not to free the slaves but to save the Union.[29] Similarly, historians today (although not always in the past) challenge the simple American view of World War II as "the good war" and insist on pointing out that although many Americans believed the war was waged at least partly to vanquish an ideology based on racial difference, the U.S. government, in addition to fielding a military force segregated along racial lines, in the name of wartime exigency systematically incarcerated well over 100,000 people for no other reason than their Japanese ancestry.[30] Nevertheless, despite our best efforts, the mythic power of Abraham Lincoln or of World War II—the emotional investment in an essentialized understanding of certain individuals and events that isolates out one strand from a complex picture and emphasizes it to the exclusion of all else—remains serenely intact. This is true even for historians when we're not behaving as historians. The most disciplined purists among us will perhaps do their utmost to substitute empirically demonstrated truths for long-cherished myths. But I think it's fair to say that the majority of historians are happiest when laying siege to other people's mythologized understandings, not their own.

Indeed, the very notion that the truth about the past—what historians seek to attain[31]—is necessarily and always of greater value than what people want to believe is true about the past may itself be little more than a myth. Gabriel García Márquez's fictional portrayal of Simón Bolívar as a foul-mouthed, flatulent hypochondriac "capable of crossing the Andes barefooted, naked, and unprotected, just to go to bed with a woman" threatened to deprive Latin Americans of one of their few genuine heroes. Although García Márquez insisted that *The General in His Labyrinth* captured "the way Bolívar really was," Belisario Betancur, the former president of Colombia, said the book left him feeling "an immense desolation" as well as "an impression of anguish and infinite sadness" that would force readers to "rethink the world, amidst sobs."[32] In short, as García Márquez's account and Betancur's reaction plainly suggest, there are several different kinds of value—moral, intellectual, emotional, political, aesthetic—and an assertion about the past that ranks high in respect to one of them may not rank high at all in respect to the others.

My Role as Author in the Several Parts of History in Three Keys

One last issue, related to but distinct from the one just discussed, bears scrutiny. This concerns my role as author in the different parts of *History in Three Keys*. Each part, after all, explores a different realm of consciousness: the consciousness of the historian in the first part, that of the participant experiencer (or historical agent) in the second, and that of the mythologizer in the third. Yet in all three parts my own consciousness as historian-narrator is also at work. This presents no problem in the first part of the book, since the consciousness of the author and that of the historian-reconstructor of the Boxer episode are one and the same. But what about the second and third parts, where this is not so?

In the experience portion of the book, I, as historian-author, select the specific themes to be presented: drought, spirit possession, magic, and so forth. I also explore analytical issues that it would never have occurred to the Boxers to raise—issues such as the role of youth and hunger (and hunger anxiety) in the rapid spread of the Boxers' possession ritual in the spring and summer of 1900, or of prepubescence in the collective fantasies that existed concerning the exceptional magical powers of the Red

Lanterns. Similarly, in the myth section, in addition to identifying how the Boxers were mythologized in different time periods, I analyze the process or dynamic of mythologization in ways the mythologizers themselves would likely resist. In both parts, in the course of playing the conventional historian's role of reconstructor of the past—in this case the experienced and mythologized pasts—I introduce a consciousness, my own, that is certainly different from and may well run counter to that of the people whose consciousness I am probing.

It would be foolish to maintain that this is not a problem. The question is: how debilitating a problem is it? The answer hinges partly on what as a historian one is capable of doing and partly on what one aspires to do. Although it is clearly not within the bounds of the historian's capability to resurrect the experienced past in its pristine form (if, indeed, such a thing ever existed), it is certainly possible, in the case of both the experienced and the mythologized pasts, to reproduce live voices from those pasts (although not necessarily the voices one might ideally wish to reproduce), and this is as good a way as we have of evoking what the people we are studying (whether experiencers or mythmakers) thought and felt. I do this repeatedly in the second and third parts of the book. But to do only this would have been to do only a portion of what I initially set out to accomplish. From the outset it was my hope not merely to present examples of event, experience, and myth but to analytically scrutinize their distinctiveness as ways of knowing the past, so it was essential to introduce my intelligence as a historian into the scrutinizing process. It may well be that I created a situation in which different consciousnesses, the scrutinizer's and the scrutinized's, are in a state of tension with one another. But apart from being unavoidable, it occurs to me that there is a palpable benefit, in terms of greater historical understanding, to be derived from this very tension.

The Outsideness of the Historian

Essentially, the problem I am addressing here is that of the historian's "outsideness." This outsideness can take a variety of specific forms: European or American (or Japanese or Southeast Asian) historians writing about the Chinese past, male historians reconstructing the experience of women, white historians probing black history. It can also—indeed, must always—take the more general form of people in the present attempting to elucidate the experience of people in the (sometimes remote) past. In all of these cases, the historian's outsideness, precisely because it is outside, has the potential to misconstrue and distort, to introduce meanings alien to the material under examination. In this respect, clearly, outsideness can be a problem.[33]

But the historian's outsideness can also be an asset. It is an essential part of what makes us different from the immediate experiencers of the past and from the past's mythologizers, enabling us, in our capacity as historians, to render the past intelligible and meaningful in ways unavailable to either. In addition to attempting, with all the attendant risks, to re-create the consciousness of the experiencer and/or the mythologizer of the past, we also seek to form a bridge between those worlds and the world of the people of our own day, making possible some degree of useful communication between the two. Akin to the translator, whose job is to render a text not only faithfully but also meaningfully from one language into another, historians act as mediators between present and past. In the complex process of negotiation that ensues, we must curb our outsideness as we try to understand the consciousness of the people we are studying (in the past). But we cannot curb it—on the contrary we must capitalize on it—in the effort to explain this consciousness meaningfully to the people for whom we are writing (in the present). In short, historians, not unlike translators, must be acquainted with two languages—those of the present and the past—and the need to navigate back and forth between these two different realms, incessantly, sensitively, and with as much honesty as possible, is the ultimate source of the tension in our work.

CHAPTER 7

History in Three Keys

Research, Writing, and Publishing History

This chapter has three parts, all of which relate to *History in Three Keys* to different degrees and in different ways. The first part deals with the intellectual access of U.S. scholars to the People's Republic of China. The second and longest part, although revisiting some of the historiographical themes touched on in chapter 6, raises the lid on an aspect of historical writing that is seldom addressed openly: the hidden strategies of the author. The third part treats the backstory of the book's prepublication history.

The Opening of China to American Scholarly Research

Politics determines who can go to China and do research there; what kinds of archives are accessible (and to what degree); what sorts of contact, if you are a foreigner, you can have with Chinese scholars with whom you might wish to exchange information and ideas or perhaps collaborate; whether, as a foreigner, you are invited to take part in scholarly conferences; and so on. As I noted in chapter 1, when I earned my doctorate (in 1961), it was impossible for Americans to go to China at all, although you could go to Taiwan to do research, and there were other places that had archival materials pertaining to China, such as missionary papers at Harvard's Houghton Library or Yale's Divinity School Library or the Toyo Bunko ("Oriental Library") in Tokyo or government and church archives in Paris, London, Rome, and elsewhere.

China's closed-door policy, at least for U.S. scholars, began to change toward the end of the 1970s. For his pathbreaking work on the Boxers,[1] to take an example, Joseph Esherick was able to spend a year in China beginning in fall 1979 and carry out extensive research in the oral history interviews (unpublished) of former Boxers done by students and faculty of the Shandong University History Department in the early 1960s. I went to China for the first time myself in 1977 as the China specialist accompanying a delegation of young U.S. political leaders sponsored by the National Committee on United States–China Relations.[2] This was more than two decades after I had begun to study the country. It is hard to convey today the sense of excitement I felt on receiving the National Committee's invitation, a little like a medievalist being told out of the blue that he could go back to the thirteenth century for a visit. The sheer sensory experience of actually being in China—the sights, the smells, the sounds—was exhilarating.

I went to China again in the winter of 1979–80 as part of a delegation of thirteen U.S. China scholars drawn from different academic disciplines and representing the Joint Committee on Contemporary China (of the American Council of Learned Societies [ACLS] and the Social Science Research Council) and the Committee on Studies of Chinese Civilization (of the ACLS). A major purpose of the visit was to exchange information with Chinese colleagues in five cities (Beijing, Chengdu, Nanjing, Shanghai, and Guangzhou). The information we obtained was published after our return to the United States. As the representatives of modern Chinese history on the delegation, Merle Goldman and I (both members of the Joint Committee on Contemporary China) wrote the report on that topic.[3] Although it was clear from our exchanges that Chinese scholars had not fully broken out of the political straitjacket created by the Cultural Revolution, there was a definite sense of excitement about progress in the modern history field. One scholar I met in Shanghai, economic historian Wang Xi of Fudan University, had read my book on Wang Tao (in English) and at our meeting (in the presence of Chinese colleagues) dutifully supplied an ideologically edged critique of the book.

I had a further conversation with Wang before our delegation's departure from Shanghai and was much taken by him.

After my return to the States, Al Craig, the director of the Harvard Yenching Institute, told me over lunch that the institute was then accepting applications for the Harvard-Yenching Fellowship Program for the 1981–82 academic year. He said that for the first time, scholars from China were being invited to apply and asked me whether I had met anyone on my recent trip I thought would profit from spending a year at Harvard. I told him that one scholar in particular had greatly impressed me and that I would write him to see if he might be interested. Craig mentioned that aside from English-language competence, there was an age restriction. The usual age limit for applicants was forty, but because of the unusual circumstances pertaining to China, Chinese scholars not over the age of forty-five would be eligible to apply. I wrote Wang Xi describing the program and told him that if he was interested he should seek further details from the president of Fudan (one of the Chinese university presidents invited to nominate suitable scholars from their institutions). Wang wrote back that in theory of course he would be interested. He had studied in the United States in the late 1940s and had fond memories of the time spent there. But, he added, much to his chagrin, he was about to turn sixty that year.

The fellowship opportunity fell through, but Wang and I became fast friends (fig. 7.1). Some years later, knowing that I was not married at the time (my marriage to Andrea had ended in divorce in 1968 and a second marriage also ended in divorce some eight years after), he even tried to fix me up with, as he sometimes playfully put it, "a nice Jewish girl." Although disappointed when his matchmaking efforts came to naught— he believed he had just the right woman for me and used the Chinese expression describing unrequited love (*luohua you yi, liushui wu qing* [the flower by the water pining for love sheds its petals, while the heartless stream flows on])[4]—we saw each other frequently over time. In 2003, when I was in Shanghai to give a talk (fig. 7.2), Elizabeth Sinn, neither Jewish nor unrequited in her love, accompanied me. After the visit, Wang Xi emailed me some photos taken during our visit and remarked that he was "very impressed with her intelligence, elegance, and candor."[5] Prior to that visit, in early March 2001, I had written Wang Xi introducing Elizabeth (and incidentally clarifying the Jewish issue):

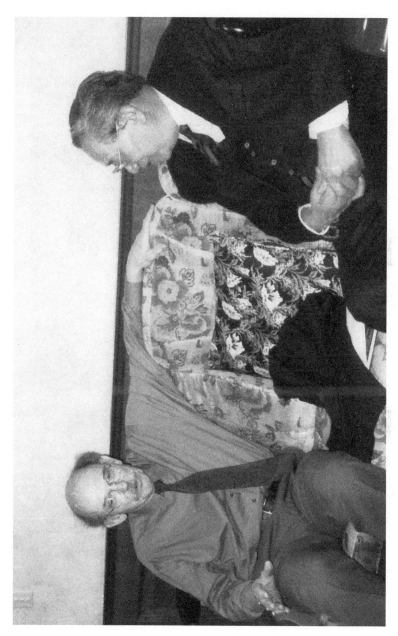

7.1. With Wang Xi, Shanghai, November 2003.

7.2. Giving a talk in Shanghai, November 2003.

She is a historian of Hong Kong, and she is deputy director of the Centre of Asian Studies at the University of Hong Kong. Although she is of Cantonese background, she speaks perfect English, so I haven't had to learn Cantonese. I teach her a few Yiddish words and expressions from time to time and actually went with her to the Yom Kippur services at the synagogue in Hong Kong last October. But I don't think I can convert her. (Actually, not being a very observant Jew myself, it never occurred to me to try.) So life is good.[6]

As recently as October 2014, when I gave a talk on my latest book at Fudan, Wang Xi invited me to dinner at his home afterward. He was then in his mid-nineties but insisted on sitting next to me at dinner and toasting me periodically with a glass of good red wine. This was the last time I saw my old friend. After a long and very productive life, he died in December 2016 at age ninety-seven.

Serious intellectual engagement with Chinese scholars only began in my case in August 1981 when I attended the conference "Chinese Society during the Late Qing and Early Republican Periods," hosted by Fudan University. Wang Xi, in late November 1980, wrote me informally about the plans for the conference and expressed the hope that I would attend. Although it was a sizable gathering, very few foreigners were invited; in the end, Al Feuerwerker and I were the only U.S. participants. Since this was my first scholarly conference in China and in 1981 conferences attended by both Chinese and American scholars were just starting to take place, I'd like to say a bit about my experience.[7]

When I left the United States, I literally did not know what to expect. I had no idea who was going to be at the conference or what was going to happen. I had the usual anxieties over my Chinese failing me at some crucial moment. I had spent a considerable amount of time preparing for the meeting: reducing my paper to a manageable length, having it translated into Chinese, revising the translation, having it copied over and photocopied, and then practicing reading the Chinese text out loud, in the event I should be called on to perform this heroic feat. (The final text came to eighty-one pages, which, if I had indeed been prevailed on to read it, would have taken the better part of three hours.) The more I invested in preparing for the meeting, the more fearful I became that I had made a huge mistake in accepting the invitation in the first place.

Fortunately, all of these ruminations proved to be phantoms in the end. The conference turned out to be a substantial success. I arrived in Shanghai a few days before it started and had time to go over the papers beforehand (they had not been circulated in advance). Mercifully, one only had to read with care those papers that were to be discussed in one's own subgroup, which for me came to about a dozen. Also, I did not have to present my entire paper, but I did have to make a twenty-minute summary of its main themes—a statement that, to be on the safe side, I wrote out in Chinese beforehand. Most important, the atmosphere in the small group I was assigned to (intellectual history) was extremely animated, serious, and productive (a tone that Feuerwerker later told me also prevailed in his small group on economic history). There were some very sharp people in my group. Discussion of each paper was thorough and critical. (Another of my phantoms that proved baseless was that Chinese colleagues would be timid and retiring in the presence of a foreigner.) Some papers were torn to shreds, yet their authors did not seem mortally wounded when the battle was over—a lesson in ego-object differentiation from which we Westerners could certainly profit. An example was Cai Shangsi, at the time seventy-four years old, vice president of Fudan, and a well-known intellectual historian. Cai sat in his undershirt, in the steaming August heat, while his colleagues, many of them thirty years his junior, demolished his contribution. However painful for me, the ego-involved outsider, to watch, the criticism was largely constructive, and from start to finish Cai maintained his good humor.

Generally speaking, the papers ranged all the way from tiresome rehashes of work done years ago to fresh and incisive analyses of controversial topics (such as the question of Liang Qichao's revolutionary commitment in the early years of the twentieth century) to substantial pieces based on extensive archival research (Wang Xi's paper on Zheng Guanying, built on the Sheng Xuanhuai archives in Shanghai, in the editing and publication of which Wang had been a principal). In two cases—a paper on the great translator Yan Fu and one on Zhu Zhixin's socialist thought—there was either a lack of knowledge of work done in the West (Benjamin Schwartz on Yan Fu, Martin Bernal on early Chinese socialism) or an inability or unwillingness to make reference to it. (Which of the two it was I don't know, as neither of the authors was able to participate personally in the conference, although their papers were discussed.)

I was quite unrelenting in bringing this sort of thing to the notice of the Chinese, whenever an instance arose, because if the Chinese really meant it when they talked about exchanging views with foreign friends, they were going to have to become more knowledgeable about what their colleagues abroad had been doing all these years.

This brings me to my own contribution. I would say that it could be viewed on several different levels. The mere presence of two U.S. historians at the conference was, I believe, important. It forced consideration of certain issues, certain points of view, that otherwise might have gone unnoted. Yet as already suggested, it did nothing to constrain our Chinese colleagues from articulating their own ideas and positions freely. In my small group, my participation was pretty much like that of other group members. There were a number of papers on which I had a degree of real expertise—Gu Changsheng's piece on the propaganda activities of the Guangxuehui (Society for the Diffusion of Christian and General Knowledge among the Chinese) at the time of the 1898 reform movement, Wang Xi's contribution on Zheng Guanying—and in these cases my comments and criticisms were substantive and possibly even appreciated. In other cases, I gave my general reactions, in some instances pointing out foreign (and occasionally Taiwan) scholarship on the topic in question, of which the authors seemed ignorant.

My own paper, drawn from chapters 3 and 4 of my still-unpublished book *Discovering History in China*, was an interpretive overview of some of the new tendencies in U.S. historical scholarship on late Qing–early Republican China. I noted the increasing dissatisfaction with such old Western-centric paradigms as impact–response and tradition–modernity, and the growing emphasis, particularly marked from about 1970, on internal determinants of Chinese history in the nineteenth and twentieth centuries. I concluded by pointing out some of the implications of these new trends, in particular the gravitation away from 1840 as the most important time division in the last few centuries of Chinese history.

My paper was discussed at great length. Different participants agreed or disagreed with different parts. I received some very constructive criticism from a number of Chinese colleagues and got into a lively argument with another. The latter, Ding Shouhe of the Institute of Modern History, Chinese Academy of Social Sciences (CASS), maintained that in his view, it was unthinkable to deemphasize 1840 as a general time marker, for it was as a result of the Opium War that China lost its independence and became a semicolonial, semifeudal society. I replied that it was possible to argue that in a sense China had already lost its independence in 1644 when an alien dynasty assumed power, and that if he were to ask such early Qing thinkers as Huang Zongxi or Wang Fuzhi or Gu Yanwu, or more recently the leaders of the Taiping movement, whether they thought China under the Qing was an independent country, he might have gotten a somewhat different picture. Ding countered by arguing that the Manchus weren't really foreign, they were one of the races included in the larger Chinese nation. I replied that this was a noble concept, but a relatively recent one in point of origin and that in reconstructing past history one ought to free oneself, as far as possible, from presentist conceptions and strive to understand the past in its own terms.[8] Ding's remarks on the final day of the conference, when individual conference members were invited to come up to the microphone and speak their minds, clearly indicated that I had not budged him from his position, and that ended our exchange for the time being.

Ding Shouhe was one of the ideologues—fortunately there were not too many of them—at the conference. He made the wrap-up statement on the final day, attacking both Feuerwerker and myself and exhorting his Chinese colleagues to study their Marxism-Leninism more assiduously. I had the distinct sense that however Ding intended his remarks, many of those present took them as ritualistic and did not pay them much heed. A number of people privately took my side in the controversy, maintaining that Chinese historians had indeed laid too much emphasis on external determinants, and one man in particular, Shen Weibin of Fudan, said so publicly, arguing that in his view 1840 was not as important as 1911 as a watershed in recent Chinese history.

On the final day I took the opportunity, in my concluding statement, to praise the members of the conference for their liveliness, their fearless criticism, and the truly impressive learning many of them displayed. At the same time, I noted a number of characteristics of Chinese historiography that caused me some discomfort. One was the failure to distinguish adequately between Marxism-Leninism as a hypothesis to be confirmed, modified, or abandoned on confrontation with the data of the past and Marxism-Leninism as absolute theory, as dogma, which because it could not be abandoned, tended to be superimposed on past reality whether it fit or not. A second point I made was that Chinese historians—although I had Ding Shouhe uppermost in my mind, there were other examples—tended to be overly present-minded in their efforts to reconstruct the past. I acknowledged that all historians suffered from some degree of present-mindedness and what it really boiled down to was whether one surrendered to this predilection or strove to combat it. My complaint with many Chinese colleagues was that they surrendered to it too easily. The final point I made was that, while recent U.S. scholarship had perhaps gone too far in emphasizing internal determinants of late Qing–early Republican history, Chinese scholarship had for some time overemphasized external determinants. Originally I had it in mind to lament Chinese ignorance of foreign scholarship. But I decided it would be far more appropriate (and certainly more diplomatic) if this point were made by Chinese scholars themselves. I was delighted when a number of speakers did precisely this, one in particular (Jiang Yihua of Fudan) contending that Chinese neglect of Japanese scholarship and of Meiji history was inexcusable if Chinese really wanted to understand the history of the 1911 revolution in general and that of the Tongmenghui (the Revolutionary Alliance of Sun Yat-sen) in particular.

What interested me most was that as I made my remarks, different heads nodded in different directions. Obviously some Chinese present found my criticism hard to swallow. Just as obviously, others in the audience warmly supported at least portions of what I had to say. The most important confirmation of this came when the editor of the *Fudan xuebao* invited me to publish an abridged version of my conference paper in their December issue.[9] I was flattered. But more important by far, if my reading of the signals was accurate, I saw this as an effort on the part of some Chinese scholars to get certain ideas, which they didn't yet feel free to articulate in print themselves, into the public domain so they could be discussed and debated.

My first experience doing actual research in China came in fall 1987, when, as part of my own work on the Boxers, I spent several fruitful days at Shandong University in Ji'nan, Shandong, reading oral history documentation relating to the uprising. On the same visit I went to Nankai University in Tianjin, where I was able to make copies of a sizable quantity of unpublished oral history materials dealing with the Boxers in Tianjin and elsewhere in Hebei province. On my visit to Ji'nan I spent almost

7.3. With Lu Yao in Ji'nan, October 2011.

a full day talking with Lu Yao (see fig. 7.3), one of China's foremost Boxer historians and the prime mover behind the Shandong oral history surveys. I had previously corresponded with Lu and sent him a photocopy of a book on the Franciscan hierarchy in China (*Hierarchia Franciscana in Sinis*, 1929), which he needed for his research but couldn't get in China. During our conversation he spoke with candor about the limitations on the interviewing process carried on years earlier by the Shandong History Department students.

Before my departure from China, I took the train from Ji'nan to Shanghai, where in mid-September I gave a talk (arranged by Wang Xi) at the Shanghai Academy of Social Sciences (Shanghai shehui kexue yuan). By this point, as my 1987 visit to China made clear, it was possible to maintain regular and useful communication with Chinese scholars. And it only got better as the twentieth century wound to a close. In 1992 Zi Zhongyun, who had been director of the Institute of American Studies at the Chinese Academy of Social Sciences, interviewed me at the Fairbank Center in connection with a study she was conducting on the interactions between Chinese intellectuals and U.S. China scholars. She was particularly interested in the efforts on both sides to build "a cross-cultural bridge" and saw herself as "one of the bridge-builders." A few years later Zi sent me several articles she had written, asking for my comments. One of the articles dealt with her views on Chinese nationalism. I wrote her a long letter with my thoughts and mentioned that I was going to be attending a conference in Taipei in March 1998 on the subject of nationalism and Chinese national identity. Since I planned to go to the mainland at that time, she invited me to visit her and her husband (a Europeanist) at their home in Beijing. She also noted that, having read my newly published work, *History in Three Keys* (1997), and being much impressed by it, she had drafted a review article dealing with Esherick's and my books on the Boxers. The review, which focused on the differences between the two U.S. approaches, on one hand, and traditional Chinese views of the Boxer uprising, on the other, was titled "A Fresh Look at an Old Subject" (*Lao wenti xin shijiao*); it was published in the well-known magazine *Dushu* (Reading) in 1998.[10]

By the last years of the century, aside from the rapidly developing personal contacts between American and Chinese scholars, American students of China had much greater access to Chinese documentation than had been the case earlier. In addition to carrying on research in the collections of the First Historical Archives in Beijing and the Second Historical Archives in Nanjing, we were now often able to use the provincial and county archives in various parts of China. The Chinese, moreover, had begun to publish substantial collections of documents from their archival holdings, which people outside China had ready access to. Of course, the explosion of data on China that now became available— unimaginable from the perspective of the 1950s, when I began my study of Chinese history—was given a huge push by the growing development and availability of the Internet.

To be sure, there were still problems. Chinese government authorities, for political reasons, have occasionally denied visas to foreigners and people of Chinese extraction living abroad in response to publications or publicly aired criticism that gave Beijing offense. For similar reasons, it has not been uncommon for ethnic Chinese residents or citizens of foreign countries, visiting or carrying on research in China, to be detained there, creating tensions over their legal rights.[11] Chinese authorities have periodically imposed limitations on access to specific archives, and it continues to be relatively difficult to conduct research on politically sensitive topics in the country. Still, on the whole, access to people and documentation has changed for the better in recent decades. The same is true in regard to conducting interviews with people who have had important parts in China's recent history or, to take a different kind of example, are able to shed light on what life was like at various levels of Chinese society at specific points during the years of Mao Zedong's rule. Here again, although plenty of obstacles remain, conditions have improved over time. Certainly, as will be made clear in the following section, my research on the Boxers benefited tangibly from the new state of affairs.

Silences in Historical Writing

Books are strange things, and one of the strangest things about them is that the form in which readers encounter them often conceals as much as it reveals.[12] This is especially true, I think, in regard to the working procedures of the book's maker. These procedures, which reflect a range of unconscious and conscious forces operating in and on the author's mind, are sometimes shared with the reader, sometimes not. For example, books are generally presented to readers as linear constructions: when you pick up a book and start to read it, although you need not begin at the beginning and read through to the end, the sequential numbering of the pages and chapters signals that that is what the author expects you to do. But for reasons of a very practical and material nature, books often are not *constructed* in a linear way at all. In the case of *History in Three Keys*, I wrote the final part, dealing with mythologization, first, partly because I was fairly clear about what I meant by myth and the issues I wanted to raise, and partly because the sources for the mythologization of the Boxers were relatively easy to identify and bring under control. On the other hand, I wrote the first part, containing a spare reconstruction of the Boxer phenomenon as a sequence of interconnected events, last, mainly because—and to my dismay, this was picked up on by one reviewer—frankly it was the part that least captured my interest.

The nonlinear process by which *History in Three Keys* was written was concealed from the reader. Also hidden from view to varying degrees were a number of private concerns that I had been wrestling with for years in my work as a historian. At several points, I do allude to the goals of the historian. "The historian's objective," I state, "is, first and foremost, to understand what happened in the past, and, then, to explain it to his or her readership." The historian's account of the past, I also note, must be "as accurate and truthful . . . as possible." But while "truth-seeking, as a *goal*, may be an absolute," I recognize that "insofar as the questions historians ask and the concepts they use to organize the data of the past are profoundly shaped by such variables as gender, class, country, ethnicity, and time, the *act* of seeking the truth tends to be highly relative."[13]

Notably absent from this catalog of variables influencing the historian's work are private issues—the author's personal agenda. Although we may or may not be aware of them, all historians have such agendas. Certainly I did in writing *History in Three Keys*. Moreover, although these unspoken—or softly spoken—agendas need not and hopefully do not compromise the ultimate goal of understanding and explaining the past in as truthful a manner as possible, it is undeniable that they exert an important influence on our work. In my discussion here, I'd like to say something about the shaping role of two such concerns in the conception and construction of my book.

One is the sense of relative isolation I experience in what I do. In my work as a historian and especially as a historian of China in the United States, I have often found it difficult to make my way into the general conversation in the way that doctors, lawyers, psychologists, or fiction writers seem to find so easy. History, the kind of history we teach and write, just isn't something many people feel is intimately related to their day-to-day lives. And Chinese history, at least for most Americans, seems particularly esoteric and remote. This was an especially painful problem in the early stages of my career, when I was heavily invested in proving myself as a historian. Since I was intent on gaining the approval and respect of my peers, I tended to write in a safely specialized vein, and this only intensified the problem. Gradually, as I gained more confidence and self-assurance, I began to tackle the issue of isolation head-on, partly by raising questions of broader concern that a wider readership might find interesting, and partly by adopting strategies in my writing and in the manner in which I approached and framed my subject matter that were designed to make my work less exotic, more accessible.

In *History in Three Keys* I dealt with this problem in several ways. First, I tried to emphasize the "everydayness" of history—even the history of the Boxers in China—by drawing on literature, sports, theater, even the news in the daily *New York Times*, to make my points. I underscored the growing anxiety of farmers facing drought conditions in north China in spring and summer 1900 by noting the panic of the newly unemployed in California in the early stages of the recession that hit the United States in late 1990. To dramatize the divergent ways people mythologized the past—an important issue in the case of the Boxers—I made reference to the emotional battles fought in the early 1990s over how to mark the 500th anniversary of Christopher Columbus's arrival in North America.[14] To highlight the question of whether the reconstructive work of historians was a simple gathering together and re-presentation of things that had already happened in the past or was in important ways a new production, lacking some elements that existed in the past and incorporating others that did not, I alluded to the ruling of the Tony Awards committee in 1989 that the musical *Jerome Robbins' Broadway*, although consisting almost entirely of elements that had already been presented on Broadway, was to be classified as a "new musical" rather than a "revival," since the show as a whole had never before been staged.[15]

To cite one more example, I illuminated the degree to which the meaning of the past is hostage to an as-yet-undefined future by recalling an event no Boston Red Sox or New York Mets baseball fan will ever forget: the night Red Sox first baseman Bill Buckner allowed a ground ball hit by Mookie Wilson of the Mets to scoot through his legs in the tenth inning of the sixth game of the 1986 World Series, allowing the Mets to score the winning run. There was no way for Buckner (or anyone else) to know at the time whether his error would be relegated to the status of a footnote, of little significance historically, quickly to be deleted from the consciousness of players and fans alike, or become the one thing about him that, when everything else had been forgotten, would remain etched in people's memories. Everything depended on the outcome of the seventh game, which, unfortunately for Buckner's place in history, the Red Sox lost.[16]

Another strategy I used to counter the sense of distance I'd felt between my work and an imagined more general readership was cross-cultural comparison. I resorted to this strategy at a number of points. In Boxer notices that were widely circulated in the first half of 1900, the pervasive drought then gripping the north China plain was consistently portrayed as resulting from the anger of the gods over the growing influence of the foreigner, in particular of the foreign religion Christianity. Rain would again fall and the drought lift, the notices explicitly stated, only after all foreigners had been killed and foreign influence in China completely eradicated. The establishment of a supernatural connection between lack of rainfall and some form of improper human action—the intrusion of a foreign religious rival in this case—reflected a pattern of thinking that had been ingrained in Chinese cultural behavior for centuries. What was fascinating for me was the discovery that the same pattern had also been widely displayed in other cultures (especially agrarian ones) in many different historical eras.

There is a classic statement of the logic informing this pattern in the Hebrew Bible, where God announces to the Jews that if they heed His commandments and love and serve Him faithfully, He will favor their land with "rain at the proper season," ensuring ample harvests and an abundance of grain for their cattle. But if they are "tempted to forsake God and turn to false gods in worship," His wrath will be directed against them, and "He will close the heavens and hold back the rain."[17] Other examples abound. In Nigeria in 1973, Muslims interpreted the drought as a sign of "the wrath of Allah against mankind." For Christians in late Elizabethan England, the famine of the 1590s "showed that God was angry with the people."[18] In Botswana in the nineteenth century, it was widely believed that a prolonged drought was caused by the incursions of Christianity, especially after a renowned rainmaker, upon being baptized, abandoned his rainmaking practices.[19]

It is now widely accepted that the core religious practice of the Box-ers as they fanned out across the north China plain in 1900 was spirit possession—a transformative religious experience in which a god (or spirit) descends and enters the body of a person who then becomes the possessing god's instrument. The anthropological literature on spirit pos-session, within China and in many other parts of the world, is extensive, and reading in it helped me place Boxer possession in a wider context, thereby clarifying its meaning and functions within the movement. An-thropologist Erika Bourguignon, for example, examining possession trance globally, distinguishes between societies such as Palau (in the west-ern Pacific), in which possession trance plays a predominantly public role serving the needs of the community, and societies like the Shakers of St. Vincent in the West Indies or the Maya Apostolics of Yucatán, in which the function of trance is mainly private, focusing on its importance for the individual, "who believes himself 'saved' as a result of the experi-ence and . . . derives euphoria and personal strength from it." Bourgui-gnon sees these ideal-typical functions of trance, the public and the pri-vate, as endpoints of a continuum, and she recognizes that in some societies, possession appears to serve both roles simultaneously.[20] Cer-tainly this was the case with the Boxers, among whom possession was closely tied to invulnerability beliefs affording protection in combat. In fact, it would not be far off the mark to argue that the broad range of individual (or private) needs that spirit possession satisfied in the Boxer movement constituted a major reason for the ease with which possession developed into a mass (or public) phenomenon in the last years of the nineteenth century. Self-preservation, in an immediate sense, and national preservation, on a more abstract level, were mutually reinforcing.

The population of north China was in a nervous and jittery state in the spring and summer of 1900, and rumors flourished in this setting. By far the most widely circulated rumor was one that charged foreigners and Christians with contaminating the water supply by putting poison in village wells. The well-poisoning charge, according to a contemporary, was "practically universal" and "accounted for much of the . . . fury" di-rected by ordinary Chinese against Christians.[21] An interesting question has to do with the content of the hysteria in this instance. Why mass poi-soning? And why, in particular, the poisoning of public water sources? If one accepts the view that rumors convey messages and that rumor

epidemics supply important symbolic information concerning the collective worries of societies in crisis, one approach to answering such
questions is to try to identify the match or fit between a rumor panic
and its immediate context. In the case of kidnapping panics (which have
a long history in China and many other societies) the focus of collective
concern is the safety of children, who (as the term *kidnap* seems to imply)
are almost always seen as the primary victims. Rumors of mass poisoning, on the other hand, are far more appropriate as a symbolic response
to a crisis, such as war or natural disaster or epidemic, in which all of the
members of society are potentially at risk.

Such is, in fact, exactly what we find to be the case. Charges of well
poisoning and similar crimes were brought against the early Christians
in Rome and the Jews in the Middle Ages at the time of the Black Plague
(1348). During the cholera epidemic in Paris in 1832, a rumor circulated
that poison powder had been scattered in the bread, vegetables, milk, and
water. In the early stages of World War I, rumors were spread in all bel-
ligerent countries that enemy agents were busy poisoning the water supplies. Newspaper accounts at the onset of the Sino-Japanese War in 1937
accused Chinese traitors of poisoning Shanghai's drinking water.[22] Within
hours of the great Tokyo earthquake of September 1, 1923, which was accompanied by raging fires, rumors began to circulate charging ethnic
Koreans and socialists not only with having set the fires but also with plot-
ting rebellion and poisoning the wells.[23] Rumors of mass poisoning pro-
liferated in Biafra during the Nigerian civil conflict of the late 1960s.[24]

In many of these instances, the rumors targeted outsiders (or their
internal agents), who were accused (symbolically if not literally) of seeking the total destruction of the society in which the rumors circulated.
This closely approximates the situation prevailing in China at the time
of the Boxer uprising. Like the charge that the foreigners were the ones
ultimately responsible for the lack of rain in early 1900, rumors accusing
foreigners and their native surrogates of poisoning north China's water
supplies portrayed outsiders symbolically as depriving Chinese of what
was most essential for sustaining life. The well-poisoning rumor epidemic
spoke directly to the collective fear of death that was uppermost in the
minds of ordinary people at the time.

A third strategy I use in *History in Three Keys* to make the subject
matter more accessible is what anthropologist Paul Rabinow has called

the "anthropologization of the West."[25] The ultimate objective of anthropologizing the West is the creation, as far as is humanly possible, of a level playing field between the Western inquirer and the non-Western object of his or her inquiry. Rabinow calls on anthropologists to accomplish this by showing how culturally specific and exotic the West's own understanding of reality has been. I basically turn Rabinow on his head. I fully share his objective, but I seek to achieve it in my book by emphasizing how unexotic, even universally human, was the understanding of the Boxers. In my development of various aspects of the experiential world of the Boxers, I make it a point wherever possible to counteract their exceptionalism, to remove them from the realm of the strange and exotic. In part I do this by paying close attention to the extraordinary emotional climate that characterized north China in 1900—the unusual levels of excitement, anger, and above all fear and anxiety that prevailed among all groups, Chinese and foreign. Emotions are a great leveler. In part, I show that in important respects the Boxers' responses to the problems they faced were not all that different from the responses of people in other cultures, including Europe and America, when faced with comparable difficulties.

We have already seen how common it is all over the world to view drought as supernatural in origin. Predictably, among people who hold to such a view, a characteristic response to drought is direct propitiation of the gods through prayer or other rain-inducing ceremonial practices. Our intuition, however, prompts us to identify such a response with "backward" societies with low educational levels; it is not something we would anticipate encountering, say, in modern secular America, with its general trust in scientific explanation of the physical world and extraordinary technological capability. How surprising, then, to discover that when a serious drought hit the Midwest in the summer of 1988, Jesse Jackson, then campaigning for the Democratic nomination for president, prayed for rain in the middle of an Iowa cornfield, and an Ohio florist flew in a Sioux medicine man from one of the Dakotas to perform a rainmaking ceremony, which thousands came to watch.[26]

Another example has to do with magic and how people in different cultures respond when magic doesn't work. Chinese and foreigners who have written on the Boxer movement, either as contemporary witnesses or latter-day scholars, have consistently ridiculed the movement's vaunted magical powers, above all the claims to invulnerability to foreign bullets. In my book I make a number of points in this regard. First, we have compelling evidence that the Christian antagonists of the Boxers operated from a perspective, with respect to magicoreligious protection, that was broadly similar to that of the Boxers themselves: Chinese Catholic survivors in southeastern Zhili province apparently believed that the appearance of the Virgin Mary above their church was instrumental in safeguarding them from a number of Boxer attacks between December 1899 and July 1900, and foreign missionaries (Protestant and Catholic), when threatened by fire (see fig. 7.4), regularly attributed life-saving shifts in the wind to the hand of God.[27]

Second, I would argue that the empirical-efficacy test applied by all critics of Boxer magical beliefs, generally leading to the conclusion that these beliefs were ineffective, largely misses the point. When the rites of medieval Catholics failed to result in miracles, people didn't stop performing them. When Protestant prayers for deliverance in 1900 went unanswered, the Christian faith of those who survived often became even stronger. Prayers and other ceremonies designed to induce rain sometimes "work" and sometimes don't, yet it seems an invariable rule the world over that when drought conditions prevail, the popularity of rainmakers goes up. Empirical efficacy as a test of magicoreligious validity has been universally used to discredit other people's beliefs. Yet even those who view themselves as culturally advanced continue to believe. They continue to make, as hardheaded psychologists who study superstition are apt to put it, "false correlations between a particular act and a particular result."[28] Why?

This is a difficult question, and it is answered differently in various religious settings. One answer questions the very premise on which the challenge to magicoreligious ritual is often founded—that such ritual must be immediately and discernibly effective. Thus, anthropologist Mary Douglas writes of the Dinka herdspeople of southern Sudan: "Of course Dinka hope that their rites will suspend the natural course of events. Of course they hope that rain rituals will cause rain, healing rituals avert death, harvest rituals produce crops. But instrumental efficacy is not the only kind of efficacy to be derived from their symbolic action. The other kind is achieved in the action itself, in the assertions it makes and the

7.4. Boxers setting fire to a church. *Source: Quanfei jilüe* (Shanghai: Shangyang Shuju, 1903).

experience which bears its imprinting." "So far from being meaningless," she adds, "it is primitive magic which gives meaning to existence."[29]

In responding to the same question, Christian missionaries at the turn of the twentieth century would certainly have put the emphasis elsewhere. For Christians, prayer might indeed inform existence with subjective meaning. But the inner logic of events in objective terms was knowable only to God. God could be counted on to "bring forth the good to the *greatest number*," and one could be certain that whatever happened, in the end it would be for the furtherance of His Kingdom. But in the daily workings of human life, His plan was often beyond comprehension, and all Christians could do in the face of this was trust in it absolutely, even when their prayers were of no avail.[30]

The Boxers had yet other ways of accounting for the inefficacy of their rituals without threatening the belief system on which they were based. Sometimes, when their rituals failed to work properly, it was explained in terms of the insincerity, spiritual inadequacy, or insufficient training of the person performing them. More often the Boxers pointed to sources of pollution in the external environment (the most powerful of which were things relating to women, particularly uncleanness in women)— countervailing magical forces that had the power to destroy the efficacy of the Boxers' magic.[31]

For all that separated the Dinka, the Christians, and the Boxers, in the ways they dealt with the issue of ritual efficacy, there was one thing that drew them—and perhaps all other religious practitioners—tightly together. Their religious and magical practices had the paramount goal of affording protection and emotional security in the face of a future that was indeterminate and full of danger. Through their rituals, they sought to exercise some degree of control over the uncertainty—in my book I call it outcome-blindness—that is one of the defining marks of human experience.

The strategies I have been discussing for bridging the distance between the subject matter of my work and the people who read it are not risk-free. In striving to present the Boxers as flesh-and-blood humans— whose practices, beliefs, emotions, and responses to their world are not entirely out of line with those of people in other places and times—there is the danger that I give inadequate attention to what makes the Boxers different and unique. There is also the danger that in lacing my prose with references to literature I happen to have read, events that have taken place in my place and time, and personal interests (such as baseball) that not all of my readers share, I might make the story I want to tell too idiosyncratic, less rather than more accessible to my readership. One reviewer of *History in Three Keys*, who confessed to knowing "more about the Boxers than about baseball," found my occasional references to baseball history "jarring." How much more jarring will the unfamiliarity of many of my examples and comparisons be for Chinese readers of the translated edition of the book, which came out in 2000?[32] I don't know how to respond to these concerns, other than to say that a risk is a risk. You try to protect yourself as much as possible, craft your rhetoric in such a way as to make the contents of what you're saying maximally clear and plausible and interesting. But ultimately, the achievement of certain goals in historical writing does involve risks, and if the goals are important enough to us as individuals, we must be prepared to take these risks.

The personal concern I've been discussing up to this point is a social/psychological one, pertaining to my relationship as a historian with the society within which and for which I write. The second concern I want to address is more epistemological in nature, having to do with the elusive character of historical truth. In a sense there's nothing hidden about this concern at all in *History in Three Keys*. Indeed, the whole book may be seen as an exploration of the epistemology of historical knowledge, how we know what we claim to know about the past. What I'd like to do here is briefly indicate how this concern evolved in my mind and then speak about the difficulties I had constructing the part of the book—the longest by far—that deals with the experienced past.

My journey from a fairly simple, positivistic understanding of the past to the more complicated conception I now have was anticipated by a new understanding of science I was introduced to in my undergraduate days. When I began college, I thought of scientific knowledge as a collection of facts about the physical world, and the scientist's job was to amass these facts. I had little or no conception of the role of theory in scientific understanding or of the possibility that scientific knowledge might be not merely cumulative but also shifting in nature. When I first encountered these ideas, it was frankly quite unsettling. Something I had thought of as solid and certain had suddenly become slippery, unstable, and problematic. It was hard to find a footing and get traction in the new scientific world I had been ushered into.

It wasn't until some years later that I found myself face to face with a similar problem in regard to history. As noted in the previous chapter, I had started out thinking about the past as, in some sense, a fixed body of factual material, which it was the historian's job to unearth and elucidate. Over time, I developed a much less innocent view of the processes—and problems—involved and came to see the reconstructive work of the historian as in perpetual tension with two other ways of "knowing" the past—experience and myth—that were far more powerful in terms of their bearing on people's lives.

I will, as suggested already, touch on the first of these tensions only. The historian, it seems to me, faces two problems that are absolutely key and affect just about everything we do in our work. One pertains to the very small part of the experienced past actually retrievable in the present; the other has to do with "the culture of the inquirer"—the world of the historian him or herself—and how it shapes and reshapes even that very small part. Inevitably, these problems result in a tension between the past as actually experienced and the past as historically reconstructed. This tension—and its bearing on the issue of historical truth—was an important theme in *Discovering History in China*, where I was particularly interested in how historians' subjective motives (the ideas in our heads) drove the questions we asked about the past and how these questions, when built into broad conceptual approaches, shape the histories we write.

These issues became even more central in *History in Three Keys*, although the framework within which I address them there is very different. In 1985, when I wrote my first grant application for the research that eventually became *History in Three Keys*, I already knew that I wanted to use the Boxer uprising to explore event, experience, and myth as three ways of engaging the past. But I had little sense of how I would go about it. I had a pretty good idea what I wanted to do with the myth part of the book; I also knew how I wanted to handle the part dealing with historical reconstruction of the past seen as a succession of interconnected events. The experience part, however, proved a major headache.

In the prologue to this part, I catalog and briefly discuss some of the main properties of the experienced past: its grounding in the senses; the full range of emotions it encompasses; its incorporation of unmemorable, forgettable occurrences as well as memorable ones; its outcome-blindness (or indeterminacy); its boundedness culturally, socially, and spatially; and its complex, multiple-motivational character. I also distinguish between biographical consciousness, the consciousness of the individual experiencer or historical agent, on one hand, and historical consciousness—the consciousness of the historian—on the other.

My initial plan was to follow the prologue with individual chapters analytically centered on these several aspects of the experienced past. There would be a chapter, for example, on outcome-blindness, in which I would collect examples of the indeterminate character of individual experience—the fact that we don't know where things are headed or how they're going to turn out—and the enormous impact this indeterminacy has on our consciousness. I was not comfortable with this arrangement, however, because it seemed overly analytical and abstract—too bloodless to convey a sense of what human experience was really like. If I had been writing about the Red Guards in the Cultural Revolution or British soldiers in the trenches in World War I, I would have known what to do, since the participants in these cases left firsthand accounts in the form of journals, memoirs, letters, and poems that afford the historian direct access to their most intimate experiences. Unfortunately, there was nothing of this sort from the Boxer episode, in which almost all of the immediate participants on the Chinese side were illiterate. On the foreign side, there was an abundant supply of wonderful source material, which I was most anxious to use. But since my focus was on the Chinese end of things—the Boxers themselves and other Chinese involved in the events of 1900—I couldn't very well use it as my main source.

As those of you who have gotten seriously stuck in something you're writing will immediately appreciate, the impasse in which I found myself was fairly painful. The more insoluble my problems seemed, the more envious I became of every book a friend or colleague published, every successful attainment of closure. I was in a real funk. Then, one summer, I began to go through the dozens of chronicles and diaries kept by elite Chinese who had lived through and personally witnessed the Boxer events. The more I read, the more excited I became. Source after source provided the most concrete and fascinating detail on the impact of the drought in early 1900, the religious and female pollution beliefs of the Boxers, the

rumors that were swirling in north China, and the horrors of the violence and death so pervasive at the time. I immediately saw the potential
of this material for digging myself out of the hole I had gotten into: instead of organizing the experience part of the book around the general
properties of the experienced past, I would structure it around such concrete and tangible phases of contemporary experience as drought, rumor,
death, and the religious beliefs and practices of participants in the Boxer
summer, both Chinese and foreign.

This approach also carried a risk. Much of the material I now planned
to use was derived from sources—contemporary foreign and elite Chinese accounts—that were openly hostile to the Boxers. To what extent,
I wondered, could I depend on such sources to provide information, especially on Boxer beliefs and practices, that was tolerably accurate and un-
distorted? Would I be able to adjust for the biases? To extract from prose
filled with scorn and ridicule a reliable stratum of truth? I was pretty sure
I was going to be all right: some of the Chinese chronicles had been written with extreme care, and many of the details found in Chinese sources
were supported by the contents of foreign sources, although the two sets
of sources were produced independently. Still, I was a touch uneasy and
would be much reassured if I could find some form of corroboration.

The corroboration came at a later point in my research, when I read
the transcripts of oral history interviews of former Boxers conducted
mainly in the 1950s and 1960s. Although such testimony is perhaps of
questionable value when it presents information that is fully consistent
with the ideological mind-set of the communist historians soliciting it
(e.g., graphic depictions of the outrageous behavior of foreign missionaries and Chinese Christians), it may be assumed to be somewhat more reliable when it describes Boxer magicoreligious beliefs that fly in the face of
communist values. To illustrate, a former Boxer from the Tianjin area,
who was captain of a rifle squad under the command of Liu Shijiu in early
summer 1900, described the harangues Liu would deliver to his Boxer
charges before they entered combat: "When you've reached the field of
combat," he shouted, "as soon as the gods have entered your bodies you'll
go up to heaven, and the devils [the foreigners] will have no way to attack
you."[33] One of the top leaders in Tianjin, Cao Futian, is said to have announced to his men, as they were advancing toward the Tianjin railway
station to attack the Russians: "All of you who are empty-handed, with

7.5. Boxer leader Cao Futian in the Battle of Tianjin. *Source: Jing-Jin quanfei jilüe* (Hong Kong: Xianggang Shuju, 1901).

no weapon, take a stalk of *gaoliang* and continue your forward advance. When you get to the front lines, it will turn into a real gun."[34] (See fig. 7.5.) These examples, and others like them, confirmed for me that although there was unquestionably an element of exaggeration and caricature in Chinese elite and foreign accounts of the Boxer experience, the basic story the accounts told was reasonably trustworthy if used with care.

The problems I encountered figuring out how to cut into the material I had on the Boxers to illustrate and elucidate the more general properties of the experienced past were, of course, not the sum total of the troubles I faced in this section of the book. There was also the huge problem—much discussed within the historical profession—of whether historians with their historians' consciousness can write anything at all about the experienced past without massively distorting it, whether, indeed, the experienced past as such is even knowable. This is a problem I take up quite explicitly at a number of places in the book. I won't say more about it here, except to state my conviction that there is a middle ground between the knowable past of the thoroughgoing empiricist and the unknowable past of the radical postmodernist. This middle ground, which allows for the existence of a past that is real and in some sense knowable but is also sensitive to the difficulties involved in reconstructing it, is the ground I feel most comfortable occupying.

Let me raise one further question. It has to do with the "silences" in historical reconstruction that I've been talking about. Some of these silences involve the unspoken concerns or agendas of the historian, others the twists and turns, the approaches tried and later abandoned, that characterize our work but remain hidden from view in the final product. It's probably just as well that in general the second kind of silence, having to do with the historian's working procedures, not be placed on open display for the reader. This is, after all, mainly a matter of craft, and for an author to share with his or her readership the messier and more agonizing aspects of a book's creation would be like a carpenter insisting that all of the false starts made in his or her work be fully exposed. I think it's sometimes useful for this sort of information to be shared. But for readers in general it can be a distraction.

The first sort of silence, on the other hand, presents a real problem that can't be so easily disposed of. If all of the personal concerns that moved us and shaped our work were benign, it wouldn't be an issue. But the fact is, they're *not* always benign. And when they're not, the transparency of our work—the congruence between what we think we're up to and what others think—is placed in some jeopardy. A policy of maximum disclosure of unspoken agendas is therefore clearly desirable. The trouble is this goal is more easily stated than carried out. Sometimes historians, while aware of their personal concerns, are reluctant to divulge them. At other times we aren't aware of them at all. In either case, we ourselves aren't necessarily the best judges of the nature and seriousness of the bearing these concerns have on our work. So, in the end, it falls to fellow historians and other readers to identify as best they can the silences embedded in our writing and to assess their importance. Every work of history, like it or not, becomes an arena in which author and reader do battle over the work's multiple meanings. Yet, to conclude on an ironic note, it is the strangest sort of contest in that the two sides don't often get to square off against one another: with publication the author's capacity to define the meaning of his or her work generally ends, after which, with occasional exceptions, it is the reader's job to tell us what the work is really about.

The Fate of History in Three Keys

As things turned out, although the risks taken in writing *History in Three Keys* proved to be a matter of some controversy prior to publication (to be discussed shortly), in the end the book proved to be a winner. The overall reaction to it was exceptionally positive and afforded me tremendous satisfaction. Indeed, *History in Three Keys* is the book I am most proud of having written. It received two major awards in 1997: the American Historical Association's John K. Fairbank Prize in East Asian History and the New England Historical Association's Best Book Award. It was chosen as an alternate selection by the History Book Club. Aside from selling well (just shy of 11,000 copies by the end of 2017), the reviews were exceptionally strong, one reviewer pairing the book with Jonathan Spence's *God's Chinese Son* as "perhaps the most adventurous writing on modern Chinese history currently available."[35] Being paired with *God's Chinese Son* had special meaning for me for two reasons: first, I loved that book and had sent its author a note after reading it telling him so, and second, the range, ingenuity, and abundance of Spence's writing on Chinese history are unique among U.S. historians, making him (with the possible exception of John Fairbank) better known among general readers than any other American writer on China.

Because of its concern with history in general, *History in Three Keys* has attracted a good deal of attention from historians who are not China specialists. One such, Australian historian Greg Dening, said: "[The author] wants to find a way in which historians cross the boundaries of their topical histories. His constant message is that historians can and should be polyglot. Asianists can talk with medievalists, Americanists with Europeanists. His book is full of examples of how time and culture aren't confining to any historian trying to understand and explain the past."[36] The distinguished Americanist Michael Kammen assigned *History in Three Keys* in his graduate colloquium in American history at Cornell University (spring 1999) and out of the blue (I had never met him) was thoughtful enough to send me a note that he had scribbled on the course syllabus: "I admire your book *very* much, and it inspired a wonderful discussion. My son, who teaches Chinese politics at Christchurch, New Zealand, also loves your book and is using it in his Honours course right now. All the best, MK."

History in Three Keys has also been widely influential in China. The first Chinese rendering of the book was published in 2000 by the Jiangsu Renmin Chubanshe (Nanjing). Despite some shortcomings in the translation,[37] it was a rousing success and attracted much attention. It was widely reviewed in Chinese journals and numerous universities made it required reading for their history students. A graduate student at Shanghai's Fudan University told me that his teacher had asked the students in the class to apply the tripartite structure of *History in Three Keys* to a historical event of their choosing as a term paper assignment. The popularity of the book led the publishers to put out a second edition in 2005. But the problems in the translation were not dealt with, prompting the Social Sciences Academic Press (Shehui Kexue Wenxian Chubanshe) of the Chinese Academy of Social Sciences (Beijing) to reissue the book in corrected form in 2014 with a new introduction by me and a substantial foreword by Lei Yi, one of China's leading intellectual historians.[38]

The Prepublication Backstory of History in Three Keys

The backstory of *History in Three Keys*—its prepublication history—was very different from that of *Discovering History in China* (see chapter 4). The striking success of *Discovering History in China*, first published in

1984, meant that instead of being a young historian with two specialized monographs to his credit, I was now a more known quantity. More specifically, it had been demonstrated that I could write a book with wider appeal than a standard scholarly monograph and thereby hopefully reach a larger readership. Columbia University Press, the publisher of *Discovering History in China*, was interested in *History in Three Keys* from the start. But so was the University of California Press, partly because it had published Joseph W. Esherick's award-winning *The Origins of the Boxer Uprising* (1987), which received high praise in my book, and partly because of my friendship with Sheila Levine, who was the editorial director of the press. As a result of this situation, for some months prior to my completion of the manuscript, I was in regular consultation with both Sheila and Kate Wittenberg of Columbia's editorial department, and it was understood that I would be submitting it to both presses simultaneously. Inevitably, although the book still had to go through the customary process of evaluation, this put me much less in the position of a supplicant than had been the case with *Discovering History in China*.

I sent the manuscript of *History in Three Keys* to Columbia and California in late August 1995. I was a trifle nervous at the time. I had been working on the book for almost ten years, no one had read the manuscript through in its entirety, and because of its atypical form I was uncertain how it would be received. Two weeks later I got a letter from Kate, whose comments frankly blew me away: "I find it to be one of the most extraordinary works of scholarship that I have ever read. Both in content and structure, its originality and importance is stunning. The writing is absolutely wonderful, and your research and argument are as strong and powerful as anything I have read in years. In short, it would be an honor and a pleasure to work with you on the publication of what, in my opinion, is going to be one of the major works ever published in this field."

I immediately dropped Kate a note (dated September 17) thanking her for her enthusiastic response. As she knew, I had envisioned the book as one that, "even though expressing itself in the language of Chinese history, would also be of interest to a wider readership of intelligent, educated, intellectually curious persons," people who would be willing to "brave Chinese," as it were, to deepen their knowledge of history. I told Kate that her response was especially meaningful to me since I envisioned her as the perfect exemplar of this wider reading public.

There were three reader reports for Columbia, one from my fellow graduate student at Harvard forty years earlier, John Israel, a second from an unidentified writer, and a third from Madeleine Zelin. In his report, Israel had this to say:

> His primary purpose is to expand our horizons on the nature and legitimacy of three approaches to the writing of history. The Boxers are a vehicle for this enterprise. At the same time, his work broadens our understanding of the Boxer uprising as such. Cohen's genius is that he is able to accomplish both tasks at the same time, interweaving expository prose with philosophical musings. The result is a work of art. . . . Since this is a many-dimensional work . . . its readers will not be confined to Sinologists. It will be used as one of a series of topical monographs in upper division or graduate level courses on modern China. It could equally as well be assigned for historiography or philosophy of history courses.

The other two Columbia reader reports were also favorable. Since the manuscript sent to the outside readers weighed in at 798 pages, all were encouraged to suggest ways the book could be trimmed, and all three obliged with helpful suggestions, as did Kate Wittenberg. I knew the manuscript was too long and happily accepted the challenge of trimming it.

At the end of October I received a phone call from Sheila Levine, followed by a letter of acceptance from California (dated November 1), with two conditions: first, that the mythologization of the Boxers in the West (as opposed to China) be amplified, and that the manuscript be substantially cut. Sheila made it clear in the letter how much she wanted to publish my book. She was then in possession of both readers' reports, the first of which (by Jeff Wasserstrom) strongly recommended publication. Jim Clark (the director) and others at the press had (according to her) "spoken positively on [the book's] behalf." The second reader's report, however, was sharply negative, judging the tripartite structure of the book to be "fundamentally unsound, arbitrary, and unsatisfying" and the remarks on history and history writing in the conclusion "obvious and uninspiring." He or she also found that my ideas about the Boxers "rarely penetrate below the surface of what is already well known." A member of the press's editorial committee was asked (presumably because of the conflicting assessments of the two outside readers) to look the manuscript over. This person's comments essentially reinforced the negative position of the second outside reader, finding the meditations on history in the book to be "superficial and outdated, rendered even more so by the chatty tone," and the references to literature, for the most part, "boastful rather than enlightening."[39]

I wrote a detailed response to the criticisms of the second reader and the editorial committee member and sent it to Sheila. But in the end, the overall reaction of California to my manuscript was frankly discouraging and, assuming that California really wanted to publish the book, self-defeating. Once a manuscript has been accepted by a press, there remains a huge amount of work that still needs to be done to turn it into a successful book. On the strength of the outside reader reports and the great enthusiasm of Kate Wittenberg, Columbia presented a welcoming environment that would be a pleasure to work in. Despite having early on accepted the book, California did not offer the same. The clincher in Columbia's case came when I went down to visit the people there and spent two hours with Kate and two of their marketing personnel, which gave me a concrete sense of how Columbia intended to handle the book if I went with them. They committed themselves to treating the book as a trade, rather than a text, book, which meant that they would be marketing it aggressively not only within academia but also beyond the ivy-covered walls. They agreed to identify the book not primarily as a "China" book but as a "general" book, which is what I wanted. Columbia also gave me a meaningful advance (which frankly had never even crossed my mind), a commitment to bring out the paperback version in one year, full control over the jacket design (which meant I would be free to use a smashing, full-color patriotic woodcut of 1900 in the possession of the British Library), and written assurance that the hardcover edition would be priced no higher than $35.

I signed a contract with Columbia in December and in early February 1996 received a letter from Kate saying that she had gone through the revised manuscript and thought it was "just wonderful": "the entire manuscript now has a tighter, crisper, and clearer quality as a result of the revisions you have made, and I think you have done a wonderful job."

There are a thousand and one reasons (some of which can never be known to an author) a press—or, to be more precise, the individuals who work at a press—will react to a manuscript in a certain way. Therefore, it is important to note that in 2009, a little over a decade after California's puzzling response to *History in Three Keys*, my next book, *Speaking to History: The Story of King Goujian in Twentieth-Century China*,[40] was brought out by none other than the University of California Press, and they did a marvelous job with it. There's a story leading up to this, of course, and it is told (along with a few other stories) in the next chapter.

Before moving on to chapter 8, I want to pause briefly and say an additional word about the difficulties I personally experienced in getting *Discovering History in China* published (see chapter 4), and then in winning over the University of California Press to unequivocal support of *History in Three Keys*. What was most troubling to me about both of these cases was that they related to perhaps my two most influential books. Yet each was met in the evaluative process with strong support and equally strong disparagement (as distinguished from constructive criticism). This says something to me about the inadequacy of the standard procedures for assessing academic book manuscripts—an inadequacy that I find frankly disturbing. There's a lesson here for the young scholar about to submit a first manuscript to a publisher. When encountering such individuals, I sometimes share my experience, particularly in regard to *Discovering History in China*, lest they assume (not unreasonably) that a rejection or a lack of enthusiasm on the part of a publisher inevitably means that their work is of poor or weak quality. That may be the case. But it may not be. This is a tough moment in a young scholar's life and it is essential, I tell them, that they ask themselves, as honestly as possible, whether they feel they've written something that is truly of value, something they believe in strongly. If the answer is in the affirmative, they have no choice but to stay with it and not lose hope, bearing in mind that the decisions made by publishers are human decisions subject to the quirkiness and vagary that so often guide such decisions.

CHAPTER 8

From the Boxers to King Goujian

Surprise Developments

After the publication of *History in Three Keys* in 1997, I became seriously interested in pursuing a topic that had an intimate tie-in with the Boxer phenomenon in China: the theme of national humiliation (*guochi*). An initial expression of my interest in this subject was a paper I presented at a conference held in Essen, Germany, in June 1998. The main theme of the conference was "Collective Identity, Experiences of Crisis, and Traumata." It was to be the first in a series of three conferences devoted to the larger question of "Chinese Historiography and Historical Culture from a New Comparative Perspective."

National Humiliation Days

The title of my paper was "Hostage to a Shameful Past: National Humiliation Days in Twentieth-Century China." (The main title was later changed slightly to read "Commemorating a Shameful Past," but the conference papers were never published so it made little difference.)[1] I had first encountered this specific theme years earlier on reading something by the influential MIT political scientist Lucian Pye in which he observed that to arouse patriotic feeling, the Guomindang government adopted the curious practice of establishing National Humiliation Days. Pye found it especially noteworthy that Chinese political leaders in the twentieth century—and he included the later Communists—"have not turned spontaneously to charismatic appeals and the themes of heroic glory that characterize the nationalism of most transitional societies. Instead, to a large degree they have sought to detail the real and imagined ways in which China has been humiliated by others."[2]

I don't recall paying particular attention to Pye's point when I read his book. In fact, it wasn't until many years later, when I began looking into how the Boxer uprising had been remembered in twentieth-century China, that I first became familiar with the huge amount of material on *guochi* or "national humiliation"; the main connection was with the draconian settlement the foreign powers had imposed on China after their victory in the Boxer War of 1900. In 1924 the newly reconstituted Guomindang, then closely allied with the Chinese Communist Party (CCP) and in its militantly anti-imperialist phase, designated September 7, the date of the signing of the Boxer Protocol in 1901, a "National Humiliation Day," and during the next few years the CCP-sponsored *Xiangdao zhoubao* (Guide weekly) annually ran a special issue in early September to mark the date. The Guomindang continued to recognize the anniversary of the Boxer Protocol signing as a National Humiliation Commemoration Day (an alternative designation) in the 1930s, long after the purge of Communists from the party's ranks.[3]

There were many other National Humiliation Days (*guochi ri*) as well (fig. 8.1). The Guomindang promoted them assiduously and issued detailed instructions on how they were to be observed in schools, factories, offices, army units, party branches, and other organizations.[4] A book that came out in 1931 reproduced a chart issued by the government, containing no fewer than twenty-six National Humiliation Commemoration Days (*guochi jinian ri*), indicating for each the date, the event's causes, the adverse consequences for China, and the foreign country involved.[5] As China experienced new humiliations in the 1930s and 1940s, mainly at the hands of Japan, the number of *guochi ri* grew exponentially. Different people counted *guochi ri* differently, depending partly on the political affiliation and ideological stance of the counter. Thus, included among the hundred (!) National Humiliation Commemoration Days listed in a Communist publication of 1995 were events relating to the labor movement in the 1920s and the civil war in the late 1940s that a Guomindang writer would not have identified as *guochi ri*.[6]

8.1. Yang Jiachang, "The busy men of May." By the late 1920s there were more national humiliation days in May than in any other month. On such days the Guomindang routinely put heightened security measures into effect. *Source: Shenbao,* May 9, 1922.

National Humiliation Days were by no means the only national days commemorated in twentieth-century China. There were also holidays of a more celebratory nature, such as the anniversary of the 1911 revolution; days of national mourning, such as the anniversary of the death of Sun Yat-sen; and so on.[7] Still, National Humiliation Days constituted a major form of national remembering and, through much of the Republican period, were the implicit or explicit focus of a vast *guochi* literature.[8] Moreover, there was a revived emphasis on *guochi* writing in the 1990s, reflecting the intensification of Chinese nationalism during that decade, focused on the patriotic education campaign in the wake of the Tiananmen Square crackdown (June 4, 1989) and the collapse of the Soviet Union (1989–91), and, on the more positive side, the resumption of Chinese sovereignty over Hong Kong (1997), widely described in the Chinese press as *xuechi* or "the wiping away of a humiliation."

The impact of *guochi* writing in the twentieth century (especially in the pre-1949 years) may be measured in several ways. First, there was its sheer abundance, as suggested already. Second, many *guochi* publications went through repeated printings, indicating a considerable reading public.[9] Third, these publications were often accompanied by some form of official seal of approval: prefatory remarks by a provincial education official,[10] the words *Jiaoyubu shending* ("examined and approved by the Ministry of Education") on the outside cover,[11] and so on. Fourth, the *guochi* theme was incorporated in school textbooks,[12] and a major effort was made to include it in popular and mass education materials. Lü Simian's *A Short History of National Humiliation* (*Guochi xiaoshi*, 1917) was published in Zhonghua shuju's Popular Education (*tongsu jiaoyu*) series and went through many printings. The *Thousand-Character Primer for Townspeople* (*Shimin qianzi ke*), issued (in 1927) by the Chinese National Association of the Mass Education Movement and approved by the Guomindang Ministry of Education, contained a lesson headed "*Guochi.*"[13] And a lesson titled "National Humiliation Day" (*Guochi ri*) was included in the *Thousand-Character Primer for the Common People* (*Pingmin qianzi ke*), published in 1922 by the National Committee of the Chinese YMCA.[14]

The foci of *guochi* writing varied. Some books dealing with this theme were general in nature and were in effect surveys of China's suffering at the hands of imperialism from the Opium War (generally) until the book's date of publication (or, in the case of Communist overviews, from the Opium War until the late 1940s). Other *guochi* publications were more specific. Among those I have personally examined, one focuses on the evolution of the unequal treaty system,[15] another on the causes and consequences of the Opium War,[16] and another on Japanese incursions of the late Qing and early Republican periods.[17] I have also seen two books that concentrate on the Twenty-One Demands of 1915 (the occasion for the first—and for a while the only—National Humiliation Days: May 7 and/or May 9), another on the Manchurian (or Mukden) Incident of September 18, 1931.[18]

In the *guochi* literature, the assignment of responsibility for China's plight appears to have shifted to some extent over time, reflecting changes in China's external circumstances, the ideological orientation of its rulers, and the mood of the public. During the Republican period, extending at least into the early 1930s—a time when foreign imperialism was a pervasive (and in important respects growing) presence in Chinese life—there was a conspicuous tendency to turn the spotlight on the deficiencies of the Chinese as a people. Liang Xin, for example, in his frequently reissued *A Concise History of National Humiliation* (*Guochi shiyao*), unambiguously attributes China's repeated humiliations since the Opium War to the absence of patriotic feeling in the national character. In the preface to his work (which originally appeared in 1931), Liang writes:

> Try accosting someone on the road and asking him: Do you have any concept of the state? Do you have any sense of the nation? Nine people out of ten, I fear, will stare at you speechless, not knowing how to respond. Alas, this is how the people of a subjugated nation behave! . . . Over the past eighty years, our nation has almost ceased to exist as a nation. When people discuss this they say the blame should be borne by our weak government. They don't realize that the government is a product of the people and that if the government is no good it is because the people are no good. . . . If we are to wipe away the humiliations of the past and avert national destruction, we must first fundamentally transform the loathsome character of the Chinese people.[19]

This spirit of self-reproach is sometimes reinforced by the pictorial images that appeared during the 1920s and 1930s. Frequently encountered in these images (as in *guochi* writing generally) is the late Spring and Autumn period (Eastern Zhou) story of Goujian, king of Yue (r. 496–465 BCE), who after being defeated in battle by his rival, the king of Wu, hung a gallbladder above his bed and tasted gall in everything he ate and drank, so that the memory of his humiliation—and his resolve to avenge it—would never fade.[20] (The story of King Goujian and its impact in twentieth-century China is the focus of chapter 9.) The lesson on national humiliation in the *Thousand-Character Primer for Townspeople* is accompanied by two illustrations: one, of a despondent Goujian reclining on a bed of brushwood and gazing at the gallbladder suspended before him, the other of a Chinese man sitting on a map of China, stripped to the waist, with his ankles bound and his arms secured to a post behind him.[21] *The Painful History of National Humiliation* (*Guochi tongshi*), dealing with Sino-Japanese relations in the late Qing and early Republic, has on its cover an image of a Chinese gentleman with tears streaming down his cheeks; his head is being split in two by an ax, on the blade face of which is inscribed the date of China's acceptance of the Twenty-One Demands (May 9) (fig. 8.2).[22]

What is significant about this illustrative material, as well as the writing of the 1920s and 1930s as it pertains to *guochi*, is that it typically depicts Chinese in positions of submission, impotence, and helplessness, rather than in postures of struggle and heroic resistance. In this respect as well as others, the *guochi* literature of the Communist period is very different. For one thing, it refers not to a problem that is ongoing in the present but to one that existed in the past and then ended abruptly with the Communist triumph in the civil war in 1949. Accordingly, the emphasis is not on figuring out how China got into its existing situation and what was required to get out of it; rather, it is on the importance of "not forgetting" the suffering and humiliation of the imperialist interval in China's history.[23]

Another feature of post-1949 *guochi* literature that differentiates it from the *guochi* writing of the Republican period is the master narrative it incorporates. To be sure, as in the earlier period, a good deal of attention is paid to the details of imperialist incursion. The emphasis, however, is much less on the defects of the Chinese body politic that facilitated this incursion and much more on the Chinese people's defiant struggle against it. "Modern Chinese history," Liang Yiqun tells us, "is not just a history of humiliation, it is also a history of resistance, of the wiping out of humiliation." Prior to 1949,

the modern anti-imperialist struggle of the Chinese people was unable to achieve real victory, it was unable to alter China's semifeudal, semicolonial status, and as a consequence was unable to reach the goal of eradicating national humiliation. Only after the overthrow of the three big mountains [imperialism, feudalism, and bureaucratic capitalism] by the entire people under the leadership of the Chinese Communist Party, and the founding of the People's Republic of China, did the great Chinese nation acquire new life and, bringing a permanent end to the history of our allowing ourselves to be trampled upon and subjected to endless bullying and insult, thoroughly wipe away China's century of national humiliation.[24]

8.2. The pain of national humiliation. This image appears on the cover of an anonymous work titled *Guochi tongshi* (The painful history of national humiliation). The ax blade bears the characters for May 9, the date of China's acceptance of the Twenty-One Demands. *Source: Guochi tongshi* (1920?).

These differences in the *guochi* literature of the Republican and Communist periods are important. But the fact remains that even in the latter era (in particular in the 1990s, it seems), efforts to stir up nationalistic passion among the populace focused less on the greatness and glory of the Chinese past or the rich folk culture of China or even the substantial economic achievements of China in the 1980s and 1990s than on the shameful interlude of China's victimization at the hands of imperialism in the century following the Opium War.[25] In my Essen conference paper, I explored this issue in a very preliminary way, but didn't really have a satisfactory explanation of the puzzle. I concluded the paper by pointing to a number of aspects of the national humiliation phenomenon that I hoped to look into in greater depth in the future. One of these—the fear of forgetting that lies at the heart of the Goujian narrative and crops up again and again in China's twentieth-century history—became the central theme of an article I published in 2002.[26]

Remembering and Forgetting National Humiliation in Twentieth-Century China

The Chinese sensitivity to national humiliation in the twentieth century is well known and constituted a major form of national remembering. Much less familiar is a persistent sense of anxiety over what appeared to many intellectuals as China's obliviousness to such humiliation. This anxiety took different forms in different periods. In the late Qing, the complaint most often heard was that Chinese, unlike other peoples, were somehow impervious to feelings of national shame (fig. 8.3). The fear that the memory of humiliating experiences, instead of serving as a constant goad to action, would fade over time lay at the very heart of the Spring and Autumn period saga of King Goujian of Yue, who went to extreme lengths to keep the humiliations he had experienced alive in his heart. Then, early in the Republican period, the problem shifted, in the view of many commentators, from imperviousness to forgetfulness. It was now argued that after being subjected to acts of national humiliation, Chinese erupted in anger for a short time but then promptly forgot the source

8.3. After the foreign forces took Tianjin in July 1900, "shameless" Chinese "who cared for nothing except saving their own skins" carried flags proclaiming that they were "people who submitted" (*shunmin*) to the foreign occupiers. The foreigners detested such persons and killed them anyway. *Source: Anhui suhuabao, jiachen* 10/1 (November 7, 1904), no. 15.

of their anger and retreated to their original condition of indifference. Anniversaries were regularly observed and formulaic memory markers widely circulated in society, but patriotic Republican-era intellectuals frequently expressed concern over what they perceived as a propensity of the Chinese people to forget the painful history to which the anniversaries alluded. "Nationalism," Prasenjit Duara maintains, "is inculcated and can be intense, but its appearance is relational and contextual." To dramatize his point, Duara presents a schematic depiction of the Chinese reaction to the U.S. bombing of the Chinese embassy in Belgrade in May 1999: "Day 1: Eat at McDonalds; Day 2: Throw rocks at McDonalds; Day 3: Eat at McDonalds."[27]

In the final decade of the twentieth century, the problem with respect to remembering national humiliation assumed yet another guise.
For the great majority of Chinese, the humiliations of the past were no
longer a matter of immediate, personal experience. Since an important
source of legitimation for China's ruling Communist Party was its part in
vanquishing imperialism in the 1940s—and the closure this brought to
the country's "century of humiliation"—the challenge facing patriotic
educators in the climate of revived nationalistic feeling and weakened
faith in Communism that characterized the 1990s was to fill the minds of
the young with narratives of the suffering and humiliation of the imperialist interval in China's history and entreat them to "not forget." Indeed,
"do not forget"—*wuwang*—became the mantra of the *guochi* writing of
this decade.

What are we to make of the seeming contradiction between an obsession with national humiliation, on one hand, and the recurrent apprehension over it not being treated with adequate seriousness or its threatened disappearance from the national consciousness, on the other? If the
sense of national shame was so powerful, how is it that it was so readily
muted or forgotten?

There is no simple, generic answer to this question. The three points
in time with which I've dealt—the late Qing and the eras of Guomindang and Communist rule—were fundamentally different from one another, and within each time period, in a complex society, there were sizable differences from group to group and individual to individual. These
differences clearly have to be taken into account in any effort to address
the issue. For this purpose, it may be helpful to distinguish between the
parts taken by state and society for each period. During the late Qing,
when the issue of national humiliation first began to emerge in public
discussion, the state tended to be a silent bystander. To be sure, the foreign policy of the central government after 1900 was, as a number of
scholars have shown, increasingly shaped by a nationalist agenda focused
explicitly on the preservation and recovery of Chinese sovereignty.[28] But
with a revolutionary movement in progress that defined nationalism in
terms of the overthrow of the Manchus and the explosive growth in the
first decade of the twentieth century of other forms of nationalism that
often were linked with demands for popular rights and political power

sharing,[29] the Qing had no great interest in the nurturing of Chinese Nationalist sentiment. In other words, there was an important distinction
to be drawn between a nationalism-driven foreign policy, over which the
state could exercise a modicum of control, and popular nationalism, which
could easily spin out of control and turn against the dynasty. In the late
nineteenth and early twentieth centuries, the issue of national humiliation, with its potential to feed directly into popular nationalism, was
raised almost exclusively at the society level, by a small (albeit rapidly
growing) minority of Chinese intellectuals.

During the two decades or so that followed China's acceptance of
the Twenty-One Demands, the situation was in some ways more complicated. Initially, the anger and outrage triggered by this event seem to
have been widespread geographically (at least in urban centers) and to
have cut across social class lines. But by the summer of 1915, only a few
short months after the original issuance of the demands, there was a conspicuous decline in political activism at all social levels, and observers
began to worry out loud about the Chinese people's "precious 'ability to
forget'" (to cite the memorable words of the great writer Lu Xun).[30] In
the ensuing years, the memory of the Twenty-One Demands was undermined, paradoxically, by the numbing profusion of the very means—
mainly anniversary observances and slogans—that were deployed for
the purpose of keeping this memory intact. It was further undermined
by the economic and political uses it was made to serve. Business firms,
partly out of patriotic sentiment but clearly also with a view to expanding sales and increasing profitability, linked the public's purchase of their
products to wiping away national humiliation. On anniversaries of the
demands, students transferred the anger associated with the original event
to whatever political grievances happened to be uppermost in their minds
at the time. After coming to national power in the late 1920s, the Guomindang sought to exercise greater control over the entire commemorative
process, partly to establish and reinforce its own reading of postimperial
Chinese history and partly to keep anniversary observances, especially
of the Twenty-One Demands (but of other national humiliation days as
well), from generating political instability and jeopardizing the government's position vis-à-vis the Communists and an increasingly aggressive
Japan. The idea wasn't to make all memory of China's past humiliation
disappear but to assert the state's prerogative to serve as arbiter of what

was to be remembered—and how. Popular nationalism was to be transformed into official nationalism, a form of nationalism "the one persistent feature" of which (to cite Benedict Anderson) "was, and is, that it is *official*—i.e. something emanating from the state, and serving the interests of the state first and foremost."[31]

This ambiguous relationship between popular and official nationalism was also a factor in the 1990s. To a degree, the two worked in tandem. But much as in the Guomindang period, in spite of significant contextual differences, there was also considerable tension between them.[32] Chinese leaders welcomed popular nationalism to the extent that it served as a substitute form of political validation and had a genuine interest in reminding the Chinese people of past humiliations at the hands of the West and Japan and in celebrating all instances (such as the Hong Kong reversion and the victory over Japanese aggression in 1945) in which these humiliations were "wiped clean." But they feared a completely unfettered popular nationalism that might imperil the stability of the regime, undermine China's modernization efforts, and interfere with the government's foreign policy, especially in regard to the always sensitive relationships with the United States and Japan.[33] The government therefore prohibited mass gatherings (or other expressions of popular sentiment) relating directly or indirectly to national humiliation or, when the costs of complete prohibition were too steep, made every effort to keep such outpourings of popular feeling under tight state supervision.[34]

Where, then, does this leave us? In light of the widely variant ways national humiliation was experienced, remembered, manipulated, and forgotten in the course of the twentieth century, does it make sense, as I suggested earlier, to posit a simple contradiction between a national obsession with *guochi*, on one hand, and the tendency to disregard or forget it, on the other? I think not. On both ends, the actual situation was more complicated than this. First, although Chinese sensitivity to national humiliation was unquestionably a prominent theme throughout the century, it did not have the same significance or salience in every period. Nor, at any given juncture, was it uniformly prevalent among all segments of the population or equally energized even within a given segment at all times. "Obsession" may be too crude and imprecise a term to describe it.

Second (and this is closely related to the first point), the Chinese who at each historical moment were most vocal in leading the charge against their compatriots' propensity to ignore or forget were intellectuals who happened to feel very strongly about the repeated humiliations China had sustained. Although Chinese intellectuals in the last century operated within a venerable tradition of viewing themselves as the rightful custodians of China's national memory—at times tacitly competing with the state, in this respect—there is no need to assume that the rest of the population (or, for that matter, all intellectuals) saw the world in the same way. Many Chinese in the 1990s, including quite a few intellectuals, were happy to forget all about national humiliation and go out and get rich, and many others (farmers in the interior provinces and factory workers, in particular), left out of the country's growing material well-being, felt victimized less by foreign imperialism than by their own government's policies.

Third, there was the matter of differential generational experience. I've pointed this out with respect to the 1990s. But it was true of the early Republic as well. When it came to remembering and forgetting, it made a great deal of difference whether one had experienced the Twenty-One Demands directly, as a conscious person, or only indirectly, as later transmitted via older members of society or the school system or the press. One couldn't really expect someone who was only a child in May 1915 or not yet born to look back on the events of that time with the same kinds of feelings as someone who had experienced them directly. There was likely to be an attrition of memory in either case, but a critical difference existed between the firsthand and secondhand remembering of the same experience.[35]

Fourth, although there was clearly a tension between remembering and forgetting in each of the periods I have discussed, as students of memory have pointed out (and historians have long known), all remembering takes place in the present and incorporates a sizable component of the present.[36] It is a myth that memory has to do only with the past. It stands to reason, therefore, that as the political, social, intellectual, and international environments of China changed in the course of the twentieth century, the meanings of "remembering" and "forgetting"—and the nature of the tension between them—also underwent significant change. Being indifferent to the repeated humiliations of one's own day, forgetting the initial outrage over a humiliation that occurred some time before (or linking the memory of this outrage to unrelated, or at best remotely related, purposes), and having to be taught in books about humiliations one had never personally experienced were quite different phenomena, reflective of the very different "presents" of the three time periods I have dealt with.

Finally, I want to underscore the vast difference that existed between the late Qing/early Republican tendency to view imperviousness or forgetfulness as a Chinese problem, something peculiar to the Chinese people, deeply ingrained in their culture, and the late twentieth-century perception of forgetting as contingent in nature, a problem that for historical reasons had belatedly turned up in China but was not in any inherent sense Chinese. Culture and history were alternative sources of forgetting, and they operated in different ways and with varying degrees of strength at different points in time.

An Unanticipated Interruption in My Work

In early November 2001, as I was putting the finishing touches on the article just summarized, I received a letter from the British publisher Routledge inviting me to contribute to its new book series, Critical Asian Scholarship, a series intended "to showcase the most important individual contributions to scholarship in Asian studies."[37] I was both flattered and hesitant in my reactions—flattered because the initial group of invitees was very small and included, aside from myself, Patricia Ebrey and George Kahin, two highly esteemed scholars,[38] hesitant because preparing such a volume would mean an interruption of the work I was fully engaged in on the problem of national humiliation in twentieth-century China. As I began to think about what to include in such a book and how, in an introductory essay, I might address and work through certain unresolved issues in my past scholarly work, my unease abated and I became increasingly enthusiastic about the multiple challenges the project offered.

Two people who were particularly important in moving me forward in this process were Mark Selden and Elizabeth Sinn. Having had as a mentor in graduate school John Fairbank, whose gifts as a nurturer of successful manuscripts were legendary (see chapter 1), I held Mark Selden, the editor of the Critical Asian Scholarship series, to an impossibly high standard. Mark, doing the impossible, met this standard at every step of the way. As an unusually experienced editor, he exercised exceptionally good judgment in helping me decide what to include (and not include) in the book. By the end of December, just two months after initially hearing from Routledge, Mark and I had agreed on a basic plan. His detailed comments on the writings to be included were unfailingly constructive, all the more remarkable because his specific interests and starting point for approaching history tended (with some exceptions) to be quite different from mine. Mark's comments covered everything from style and word choice to weaknesses or illogicalities in my argument to bibliographical lacunae. He pushed me especially hard on the introductory essay, which he rightly judged to be critical to the success of the volume as a whole. The finished piece (from which portions of chapter 5 of this memoir are drawn) benefited greatly from his many specific suggestions, insightfulness, and tireless prodding.

My partner, Elizabeth Sinn, was a good deal more excited by the idea of the Routledge book than I was and did much to overcome my initial misgivings. Beyond this, she read through multiple versions of several chapters, pointing out ambiguities and infelicities in the writing, lapses in documentation, and places where the analysis was in clear need of sharpening. Knowing the author well, including his very considerable capacity for defensiveness, Elizabeth navigated with practiced adroitness the treacherous border area between criticism and encouragement, for which I was deeply grateful.

Putting together a volume of my writings, spanning a publishing career at the time stretching to almost a half-century, was fascinating in a number of ways. For one thing, it involved rereading things that in some cases I hadn't laid eyes on in decades, reminding myself, sometimes happily, sometimes not, of where I stood intellectually at various points in my evolution as a historian. For another, it afforded me the opportunity to play historian to myself, identifying some themes—my teacher Benjamin Schwartz referred to them as "underlying persistent preoccupations"[39]—that had endured from the beginning of my writing life, although taking different forms at different times, and others that had emerged at one point or another but weren't there at the beginning.

In other words, the exercise enabled me to gain a clearer picture of how my thinking had changed over time and, equally important, how it hadn't. This distinction was brought out in the introduction I wrote for the book.

The book was eventually titled *China Unbound: Evolving Perspectives on the Chinese Past*, and it embraced a wide spectrum of topics, including Wang Tao, American China historiography, the writing of history in general, the Boxers, nationalism, reform, popular religion, and continuities across historical divides. Although the substantive themes varied, my effort throughout was to identify and explore fresh approaches to the Chinese past, alternately interrogating Western historians, Chinese historians, and the history itself. My ultimate hope—which I was confident most other Western students of China shared—was to demystify Chinese history, to undermine parochial perspectives that continued to cordon it off in a realm by itself, so that it could be rendered intelligible, meaningful, and even important to readers in the West.

An Unexpected Shift in Intellectual Direction

As it turned out, the Routledge project took less time than I had initially anticipated, and by the last months of 2002 I was able to get back to the book on national humiliation in twentieth-century China. But before coming to that, let me say a word or two about the personal side of my life. After all, I didn't write one book or article after another sitting up in the sky someplace. As my relationship with Elizabeth Sinn grew—we had met at a conference at the University of Aberdeen in Scotland in April 1997—I began to spend two or three months a year in Hong Kong, which was her home, and she several months in Boston, where I lived, so that eventually we were able to be together for roughly half of every year. When in Hong Kong, my host institution at first was the University of Hong Kong's Centre of Asian Studies (of which Elizabeth was deputy director for a number of years), then the Hong Kong Institute for the Humanities and Social Sciences, also part of the University of Hong Kong. Both presented ideal working environments. I was appointed a visiting scholar and given a private office. I had intelligent and stimulating colleagues and a first-class research library at my disposal. So when I wasn't living in Boston and making use of the research facilities of Harvard, my needs were very well taken care of at the University of Hong Kong (fig. 8.4).

After finishing the Routledge book and returning to the topic of national humiliation full-time, something happened that was completely unforeseen. The book I had started working on after the publication of *History in Three Keys* had begun to turn into a substantially different book. In my exploration of the theme of national humiliation, I kept running into the story of King Goujian, a story that spoke to national humiliation and much else. Already at the time of the Essen conference in 1998, I had written Jeff Wasserstrom of my fascination with the Goujian story.[40] Clearly, if I stayed with my original book plan, I would have to omit vital parts of the Goujian story's engagement with recent Chinese history, something I was increasingly loath to do. During the year I was at work on the Routledge book, I was able to put this quandary aside. But as I returned to the work on national humiliation in late 2002, it had to be confronted. I talked it over with Elizabeth, and she helped me out of the predicament I was in with the eminently sensible proposal that in-

8.4. Clowning around as mobsters at a Hong Kong restaurant, with former Harvard professor Leo Lee, a friend of many years now living in that city. Photograph by Elizabeth Sinn.

stead of the book on national humiliation, I consider writing one on the impact of the Goujian story in all of its facets (including but not confined to national humiliation). A disarmingly simple suggestion, but also a radical one, as it meant a shift in the book's principal focus and in the broader issues that would ultimately form its core—above all, the relationship between story and history. Although only half realizing at the time the adventure that was in store for me, I responded eagerly to her suggestion. In time, I became aware of the degree to which the interaction between story and history that was so central to the book on Goujian was another aspect of my writing that may be said to have had its germination in *History in Three Keys* and had been lurking in the back of my mind ever since I began work on that book.

Jeff Wasserstrom, an old friend and perennial intellectual interlocutor—we had started to exchange letters, writing, and ideas as early as the mid-1980s, when he was a young graduate student at Harvard and I was just getting into my research on the Boxers—could see that I was really excited by the stuff I was into. Several years before I made the decision to do a book on Goujian rather than national humiliation, I was already writing him about my growing interest in Goujian. He "loved the story about tasting gall" (Goujian) and could see how "there might be a short book (FOR TAM AND MY California SERIES THIS TIME!)" in the new direction he sensed my work taking. This last was in an email of August 21, 1998, responding to an email I had just written him. The series he mentioned, edited by Jeff, Hue-Tam Ho Tai (the "TAM" he referred to), and Kären Wigen, was Asia: Local Studies/Global Themes, a new series the University of California Press had recently introduced.

In 1998, of course, the idea of doing a book on Goujian was not even on my mental horizon. But I was in regular contact with Jeff on how things were going in my work. In mid-August 2001 I wrote him about my travails reading the Chinese newspaper *Shenbao* for commentary on the National Humiliation Day anniversary observances associated with the Twenty-One Demands of May 1915 ("lots of good material of all sorts but the print is so tiny and often indistinct on the page that I fear premature blindness"). Not long after this I informed him of my newly hatched plan to write a book on Goujian rather than national humiliation and told him about the intriguing contrast between insider and outsider that the Goujian story addressed directly (a core theme of chapter 9).

Jeff was also intrigued by the insider/outsider contrast and invited me to give a talk on it at Indiana University, where he was then teaching.[41]

A few years later, Jeff learned that I was moving toward completion of the Goujian book and approached me again about submitting it to his series at California. He knew that I had already sent the manuscript to the Harvard University Asia Center, had served on the center's publications committee, and had a very high regard for John Ziemer, the chief editor of its publications. But he thought my book would be a particularly good fit for the new California series he coedited and hoped I would give it serious consideration. I asked Jeff what the procedure would be if I were to submit it to California. He contacted Sheila Levine, who was in Argentina on a sabbatical but was still involved at the press on a part-time basis. Sheila emailed me from Buenos Aires telling me how pleased she would be if I decided to send my book to California and assured me that if I did, she personally would shepherd it through the publication process. I decided to submit the book to California, partly because of Sheila's genuine enthusiasm and in no small measure because of the chance to work with Jeff and Tam (the latter a colleague at Harvard's Fairbank Center for Chinese Studies). California sent the manuscript to two outside readers, Tim Brook and Keith Schoppa, both of whom gave it strongly favorable reviews. On June 8, 2007, I received the following email from Randy Heyman, Sheila's assistant at the press: "On behalf of Sheila, I am pleased to report that your manuscript was enthusiastically approved by the Editorial Committee with no recommendations or conditions. The Editorial Committee reader who presented the project gave a glowing review, and the motion to approve was unanimous."[42]

The AAS Roundtable of 2007 on My Contributions to Chinese Historical Studies

On June 17, 2006, I received an unusual invitation from Jeff Wasserstrom, which came out of the blue. I quote it at some length:

> I hope that it is safe to take for granted that, especially since it will be in your home town, you are planning to attend the 2007 AAS [Association

for Asian Studies] meetings. If so, I have a rather unusual invitation to issue that I hope will please you. I'm putting together a roundtable devoted to your work . . . and am hoping you are game to come and respond to the presentations. The plan is to have individual scholars working on related issues revisit each of your books. . . .

The idea for it came in part from realizing . . . just how many people of Bill [Kirby]'s, my and Robert [Bickers]'s cohorts at least (there are people trained earlier and later for whom this is true as well, I am sure) have been influenced not just by your work but also by our interactions with you (your lectures or talks, your comments on our papers, just conversations). Not formally your graduate students, some of us owe a very large debt to you as a mentor, very much like that we owe our formal advisors. So this could be thought of as something of a festschrift gathering or belated retirement party [I had retired from teaching at Wellesley in 2000] put together by your "students" (even if most of us never encountered you in the classroom). . . .

I was reminded just how far back my own debt to you goes, by the way, while recently going through old papers in preparation for our move West in late July. I found some letters (we used to communicate via paper, if you can believe that) from twenty years ago in which you told me what you liked and disagreed with about a couple of papers I did on the Boxers while in grad school, and described in tentative but quite eloquent ways this idea you were playing with of doing a book that would approach the Boxers from three different angles. . . .

I'll pass on the final details about the session when I have them, but I did want to let you know that it was being cooked up and that most of it is sorted out well in advance. To really make it work, you will need to agree (as I hope you will) to be there to react to what we say.

My response to Jeff's invitation: "Wow, what a lovely surprise. And what a nice letter (I know, it was an e-mail, but some e-mails deserve to be categorized more elegantly). Yes, of course, I will be at the AAS and will be more than happy to respond to the panelists. And thank-you, Jeff, I'm both flabbergasted and deeply touched."

The official title of the roundtable was "Revisiting Paul Cohen's Contributions to Chinese Studies" (see fig. 8.5). Its sponsoring organization was the Chinese Historians in the United States, which later published the proceedings in its journal *Chinese Historical Review* (Fall 2007). There was an excellent turnout with a striking generational spread. (In regard

8.5. With Jeff Wasserstrom and journalist and scholar Ian Johnson (standing), at breakfast in a Hong Kong hotel (November 2017). Photograph by Elizabeth Sinn.

to the latter, Jeff wrote me afterward about a second-year UCLA graduate student who emailed him ahead of time to make sure the roundtable was about the work of Paul A. Cohen, not some other Paul Cohen, as she "was a big fan of works such as *History in Three Keys* and didn't want to be disappointed if there was another less interesting Paul Cohen in the field.") The roundtable was moderated by Bill Kirby, the only person involved who had been a true student of mine: way back in the early 1970s when he was a Dartmouth undergraduate, he spent a semester at Wellesley and took my modern Chinese history course. Bill's opening remarks were generous and hilariously funny. The other participants—Ryan

Dunch (commented on *China and Christianity*), Hanchao Lu (*Discovering History in China*), Robert Bickers (*History in Three Keys*), Rudolf Wagner (*Between Tradition and Modernity* [Wang Tao]), Dong Wang (*Speaking to History* [the still-to-be-published book on Goujian]), and Jeff (miscellaneous other writings)—were each allotted ten minutes to say what they wanted. They spoke well, and I learned something from all of them about the different perspectives from which my own work could be viewed.

When Jeff originally broached the prospect of a roundtable on my work, he took note of the fact that the date coincided with the fiftieth anniversary of the appearance of my first published work, an article in Harvard's *Papers on China* in 1957. That was a lot of years. When he wrote this, my mind traveled back to an amusing incident that took place several years earlier at the University of Hong Kong. I was waiting with Elizabeth Sinn for an elevator when we encountered a priest affiliated with the university who had earned a doctorate relating to the history of Christianity in China. Elizabeth knew him and introduced us. Not long before, she later told me, she had mentioned to him that I would soon be visiting Hong Kong, at which point a somewhat bewildered expression crossed his face: clearly he thought Paul Cohen had long since died and gone up to heaven.

I wouldn't go so far as to suggest that that's how I felt after the conclusion of the roundtable. But from my perch here on Earth, I would have to say that the proceedings marked an extraordinary moment in my life as a scholar, and for some time thereafter, every time I recalled the event, a big smile filled my heart.

CHAPTER 9

The Problem of Insideness
versus Outsideness

Speaking to History

A t the end of chapter 5, I discussed some of the problems created by an excessive emphasis on cultural contrast. I touched on this issue again in a talk I gave on the Boxers in the summer of 2001. The talk had the unlikely (and, for a largely Western audience, somewhat provocative) title "Humanizing the Boxers." The position I took was that, in addition to forming the prism through which communities express themselves in thought and action, culture also has the potential to distance one community from another, thereby facilitating processes of stereotyping, caricaturing, and mythologization. In light of the unusual degree to which the Boxers had been subjected to such processes in both China and the West in the twentieth century, I made a special effort in the talk to focus on what the Boxers shared with people of other cultures who faced comparable historical challenges. My point was not to deny the Boxers their cultural particularity (nor, certainly, to portray them as angels); rather, it was to rescue them from the grip of dehumanizing exceptionalism that had misrepresented and distorted their history almost from the beginning.[1]

Cultural difference relates very closely to the polarity between insideness and outsideness, and the many different forms both of these perspectives can assume. This is an issue that I've wrestled with throughout my career. In the preface to the second paperback edition of *Discovering History in China*, I revisited the matter of the "outsider's perspective" in historical writing. I noted that although in the final chapter I had discussed outsideness and regarded some of its forms as less detrimental than others, I had consistently portrayed it "as a *problem*, as a burden upon the historical enterprise, rather than an asset."[2] A number of scholars took issue with this stand, raising the possibility that in certain situations, the historian's outsideness could confer an advantage—a position I eventually came to accept (see the concluding section of chapter 6).

The Importance of the Goujian Story in China

The book I discuss in this chapter, *Speaking to History: The Story of King Goujian in Twentieth-Century China* (2009), deals with an ancient Chinese story that may be the ultimate demonstration of the tension between insideness and outsideness. But before getting to that, I want to say a few words about another core aspect of the book: the powerful relationship in it between story and history. American playwright Arthur Miller once observed in regard to his 1953 drama *The Crucible*: "I can almost tell what the political situation in a country is when the play is suddenly a hit there—it is either a warning of tyranny on the way or a reminder of tyranny just past."[3] Miller's play deals with the late-seventeenth-century witch hunt in Salem, Massachusetts, but it was also a thinly disguised reflection of the author's outrage at the witch hunt of his own day (McCarthyism), thus making it serviceable as a metaphor for political oppression wherever or however it might occur. This resonance between story and situation, between a narrative and a contemporary historical condition that prompts those living in it to attach special meaning to that narrative, is what *Speaking to History* is mainly about.

Although such narratives can in theory be ancient or modern, fictional or factual, indigenous or foreign, the most potent ones are often those that derive from a culture's own past. Certainly this has been true in China, where from ancient times to the present people have demonstrated a strong affinity for stories dressed in historical garb. The tale of King Goujian provides an intriguing example of just such a story, one that in a wide array of circumstances spoke to Chinese with exceptional force throughout the twentieth century. Although I first encountered the story while reading materials pertaining to national humiliation in the first half of the century, it did not take long for me to discover that the narrative related to many other concerns as well. Prior to the late Qing, the main vehicles for transmitting the story, apart from ancient texts, were opera, historical romance, and other forms of literary endeavor (oral and written). After the turn of the twentieth century, the story began to be disseminated by a wide range of other means as well, including the newspaper and periodical press, school primers, mass education materials, spoken drama, and later radio, film, and television.

Although the story's core structure has persisted with little change from its first emergence in ancient times up to the present day, like most ancient Chinese historical narratives, it evolved over time, some elements being reworked, others dropped, and still others added.[4] A favorite diversion of opera fans that was not part of the original story, for example, is the alleged romance of Fan Li, Goujian's top minister, and the beautiful Xi Shi. The text of the story, in contrast with the relatively stable texts of a Chekhov play or a Jane Austen novel, was soft or pliable. In fact, to even speak of a "text" in the case of the Goujian saga is probably misleading. Oral transmission was still strong in China when the story first emerged. And in subsequent times, much as in the trail of stories inspired by so many other historical figures about whom there is little reliable information (Joan of Arc comes to mind), the narrative was recycled almost continuously in response to the requirements of different audiences, different historical moments, and different authorial predilections.[5] The importance of recounting Goujian's life and career for Chinese during the past century and more clearly resides less in its embodiment of historical truth than in its many-faceted allure as a story (more on this shortly).

During the so-called century of humiliation, lasting from the Opium War (1839–42) to the Communist victory in the civil war in 1949, a broad spectrum of Chinese—ranging from high Qing dynasty officials (like Lin Zexu and Zeng Guofan) and major twentieth-century political leaders (Chiang Kai-shek) to lowly immigrants detained at the Angel Island Immigration Station in San Francisco Bay or struggling to make ends meet in the Philippines—found the Goujian story unusually compelling and, when faced with seemingly intractable personal or political problems, looked to it as a source of inspiration and encouragement.[6] Even in the very different environments that prevailed after the Communists came to power and the Nationalists retreated to Taiwan, the story continued to be influential. For example, it periodically emerged in Communist theatrical productions as a vehicle for the dissemination of political messages of one sort or another, and in post-1949 Taiwan it offered psychological and political support for the Nationalist goal of eventually retaking the mainland.

One thing that this last assertion points to—and it merits underscoring—is the degree to which narratives like the Goujian story functioned as a shared Chinese cultural resource that went much deeper than political divisions. This struck me with particular force while I was leafing through the 1974 editions of the Nationalist government's Chinese-language textbooks for primary and middle school students. These were published in Taiwan while the Cultural Revolution was still in progress on the mainland and the ideological conflict between the Communists and Nationalists was at its most intense. One of the lessons in each work contained a rendering of "The Foolish Old Man Who Removed the Mountains" (*Yu gong yi shan*), an ancient fable the point of which was that, with sufficient resolve, any goal could be achieved, no matter how great the difficulty. Another lesson in the elementary school primer applied the fable to the engineering challenges in the construction of the Zengwenxi Reservoir in southern Taiwan.[7] What struck home for me was that this fable was well known for having been promoted by Mao Zedong during the Cultural Revolution—it was one of "Three Essays" everyone was supposed to memorize—to encourage the Chinese people to tear down the twin "mountains" of feudalism and imperialism.[8] Different historical settings. Different meanings. But the story, part of China's cultural bedrock, was identical.

The Goujian story was as familiar to Chinese schoolchildren as the biblical stories of Adam and Eve or David and Goliath are to many American youngsters—the story is "in our bones," a scholar from China told me some years back. Despite its far-reaching impact throughout the Chinese cultural world,[9] before the publication of *Speaking to History*, even among American historians of the recent Chinese past (those not of Chinese descent) it appears to have been mostly unknown, whereas American scholars of ancient Chinese history or literature who knew the Goujian story well were unlikely to be aware of its salience for Chinese in the twentieth century. Manifestly, the story of King Goujian is one of those artifacts of cultural knowledge, found in every society, that "insiders," people who have been raised and gone to school in the society, are apt to have instilled in them as part of their cultural training, but that "outsiders," those who learn about the culture mainly from books or from having lived in the society for brief periods as adults, almost never run into (or don't notice when they do). As a result of this curious situation—which suggests the existence of two very different tracks for learning about a culture—the place of the Goujian story in the history of China over the past century has been largely, if not entirely, omitted from the work of American historians (and, as far as I know, Western historians generally).

What is odder still is that in a certain sense Chinese historians also appear to have overlooked it. Let me be absolutely plain here. Chinese students of the twentieth century, unlike many of their American counterparts, are intimately familiar with the Goujian story and keenly aware of the pervasiveness of accounts of (and references to) it, especially at certain historical junctures.[10] But I have found little indication that they see the relationship between story and situation in itself as a fit object for serious historical inquiry. A possible reason for this is that such scrutiny might, at specific moments, be too sensitive politically (to be elaborated on in the next section). But a more fundamental reason, I suspect, is that most Chinese simply accept the existence of the story–situation relationship as a given. In other words, it is not something they have a high degree of self-consciousness about. The notion that stories even from the distant past can speak in meaningful ways to what is going on in the present has been drummed into them from childhood. They pay attention to such stories for the guidance or inspirational value they may offer, but there is little likelihood of stepping back and interrogating the distinctive importance of the story–situation relationship as such, either in China or in other cultural settings.

There is another reason for the failure of historians to include the Goujian story in their accounts. This is that the story, for all its importance in other respects, contributes little to the history of twentieth-century China when this history is framed as a narrative of interconnected events. Indeed, it can be omitted from this narrative almost entirely—as it has been—without significantly altering the overall picture. (This is of course also true of many other aspects of intellectual and cultural history.) However, when we shift our attention to how the Goujian story has affected Chinese perceptions of their experience—a more interior perspective on the Chinese past—we get a very different sense of things. As psychologist Jerome Bruner has stated, we "cling to narrative models of reality and use them to shape our everyday experience. We say of people we know in real life that they are Micawbers or characters right out of a Thomas Wolfe novel." Such stories become "templates for experience." What is astonishing about these templates, he adds, "is that they are so particular, so local, so unique—yet have such reach. They are metaphors writ large" or, as he puts it in another place, "root metaphors of the human condition."[11]

When the Goujian story is understood in Bruner's sense as a root metaphor—or several such metaphors—it assumes a far more imposing historical presence than we would ever guess from the standard narrative accounts of twentieth-century Chinese history. It is this presence that I try to illuminate in *Speaking to History*. My interest, I emphasize there, is not primarily in how the story of Goujian evolved as a story. That is a job best left to students of Chinese literature. Rather, it is directed to the rich variety of ways in which Chinese, sometimes instinctively, at other times more self-consciously, adapted the contents of the story to the requirements of different historical situations—and why this mating of story to history was deemed so critically important.

The Story as Known in Antiquity

Before looking at the variety of ways the figure of Goujian assumed meaning for Chinese in the twentieth century, let me say a few words about the story itself.[12] In reconstructing the Goujian story, I have not been unduly concerned with the historicity of particular incidents or details. The impact of the story in the twentieth century derived not from its accuracy as history but from its power as narrative. What I do in my book is establish a rough baseline for what was known about the Goujian narrative in the first century CE, the time when the first full-fledged version of the story (of which we are aware) appeared. To this end, I consulted such basic early sources as *Zuozhuan* (Zuo's tradition), *Guoyu* (Legends of the states), Sima Qian's *Shiji* (Records of the historian), and *Lüshi chunqiu* (The annals of Lü Buwei).[13] I relied most heavily on the Goujian chapters (the last four *juan*) of the later (and highly fictionalized) *Wu Yue chunqiu* (The annals of Wu and Yue), originally compiled by the Eastern Han author Zhao Ye from 58 to 75 CE.[14] I did this for two reasons. First, in comparison with the earlier sources, *Wu Yue chunqiu* is (as David Johnson correctly observes) "far more detailed and coherent" and contains "major new thematic elements."[15] Second, it had a seminal influence on accounts of the Goujian story written during the remainder of the imperial period and was a principal source, directly or indirectly, for many of the versions of the narrative that circulated in the twentieth century.[16]

The setting of the Goujian story was the rivalry beginning in the latter phase of the Spring and Autumn period (722–479 BCE) of the Eastern Zhou between the neighboring states of Wu (in modern Jiangsu province) and Yue (in modern Zhejiang), two newly ascendant powers on the southeastern periphery of the contemporary Chinese world. In 494 BCE, the new Yue king Goujian, in his early twenties at the time and headstrong, went against the advice of his chief minister Fan Li and launched an attack against the state of Wu. It didn't take long for the armies of the Wu king Fuchai to surround the Yue forces. Facing certain defeat, Goujian was prevailed on by his high officials to do everything possible to bring about a peaceful resolution of the conflict, mollifying Fuchai with humble words and lavish gifts and even evincing his willingness to go to Wu with his wife as prisoners of the Wu king. Swallowing his pride, Goujian acquiesced in this strategy. It was also decided that Fuchai's grand steward, Bo Pi, well known for his greed and lust, should be secretly bribed with beautiful women and precious gifts to gain internal support for Yue at the Wu court.

Goujian's servitude in Wu, along with his wife, began in the fifth year of his reign (492 BCE). Fan Li accompanied them, and the other top official of Yue, Wen Zhong, remained at home to look after the governance of Yue during the king's absence. On Goujian's arrival in Wu, Fuchai's prime minister, Wu Zixu, a clear-sighted official with long experience, urged the Wu king to kill Goujian forthwith and obliterate Yue. Fuchai, with the encouragement of Bo Pi, allowed Goujian to live. During the next three years, Goujian served as Fuchai's carriage driver and took care of the horses. He, his wife, and Fan Li were housed in a humble stone cottage near the palace, where they led the lives of poor working people, swallowing one humiliation after another without showing the least sign of anger or resentment. In the third year, Fuchai fell ill. Fan Li, using his divination skills, reported to Goujian that the Wu king was not going to die and that on a specified date his illness would take a turn for the better. Fan Li and Goujian proceeded to devise a strategy to persuade Fuchai of Goujian's loyalty. Goujian, claiming to be able to predict an illness's course on the basis of the taste of the ill person's feces, told the Wu king, after sampling his stool, that he would get well by a certain date (fig. 9.1). When Fuchai did indeed recover, he was so grateful to Goujian that he pardoned him—over the forceful objections of Wu Zixu—and permitted him to return to Yue.

After returning to Yue, Goujian, with the help of Fan Li, Wen Zhong, and other official advisers, adopted a wide range of policies geared toward building up the population and economy of Yue and rehabilitating its military—and weakening the state of Wu, through various stratagems designed to exploit Fuchai's vulnerabilities (above all, his love of beautiful women and penchant for ostentatious display). Determined on a course of revenge, Goujian immersed himself in hard work, wearing simple clothing, eating plain food, and directly sharing the grueling lives of the people. Although the phrase *woxin changdan* (to sleep on brushwood and taste gall) that became closely associated with the Goujian story in late imperial times apparently was first used only in the Song period, in ancient times we are told that Goujian hung a gallbladder at the entrance to his room, which he licked every time he passed through, to guard against complacency and as a reminder of the bitter suffering he had undergone (fig. 9.2).

Twenty years passed in this fashion. Yue became prosperous and the population multiplied. Moreover, all were determined to avenge the earlier wrong. Therefore Goujian, after getting the go-ahead from Fan Li, led his armies in a series of attacks on Wu, which ended in Fuchai's death, the destruction of the state of Wu, and the wiping out of the original humiliation.

In the vast majority of twentieth-century renderings of the Goujian story, this is where the narrative ends. But in the ancient texts, there is a darker Goujian who emerges after Wu's destruction, which, when

9.1. Goujian suffered many indignities while a slave in Wu. This figure shows him sampling Fuchai's stool for diagnostic purposes, while Fuchai looks on from his sickbed. *Source:* Chen Enhui, *Xi Shi* (Tainan: Dafang Shuju, 1953), illustration 6.

included in twentieth-century accounts may (depending on the historical context) signal the author's intent to advance a veiled criticism of the despotic rule of his own day. Immediately after Wu's destruction, according to the ancient texts, Goujian took several steps to reinforce Yue's position as a rising power among the states of the day. Knowing his master well and sensing that the unbridled ambition and envious nature of the Yue king would make life extremely dangerous for anyone in his entourage who had accumulated great merit, Fan Li decided that it was time to leave Yue and go elsewhere. He sent a letter to Wen Zhong, advising him to do the same. But Wen Zhong, to his later regret, was not persuaded. Before long he became the target of rumors at the Yue court raising questions about his loyalty. Goujian thereupon presented him with a sword, with which the devoted official committed suicide.[17]

There are a number of key themes in the Goujian story. One is humiliation, sometimes externally inflicted but at times self-imposed,

9.2. Graphic depiction of "sleeping on brushwood and tasting gall." *Source:* Zhao Longzhi, *Goujian* (Taipei: Huaguo Chubanshe, 1953).

insofar as Goujian, to realize his objectives, willingly submitted to a range of humiliating behaviors during his stay in Wu. A second theme is the quest for revenge (which applies not only to Goujian but also, in the fuller story, to Fuchai and Wu Zixu). A third theme is forbearance. The core idea here, nicely encapsulated in the proverb *renru fuzhong* (lit., to put up with humiliation in the pursuit of an important goal), is that there is a higher order of courage according to which an exceptional in- dividual will abase him- or herself, acquiescing in the most degrading forms of humiliation or indignity, if by doing so the prospect of attain- ing some greater end will be enhanced. A fourth key theme is the sys- tematic rebuilding of Yue economically and militarily after Goujian's return and the establishment, through enlightened and compassionate policies, of a positive relationship between the king and the people of Yue. Finally, there is the complex relationship that existed between Gou- jian and his top officials, as revealed in the fates of Fan Li and Wen Zhong.

The Adaptability of the Goujian Story

REPUBLICAN PERIOD

As a humiliation/revenge story, the story of Goujian was one of China's main patriotic narratives during the period from the late Qing through the Sino-Japanese War (1937–45). Chinese in the late Qing and Republi- can periods referred endlessly to the humiliations (*guochi*) their country had experienced at the hands of foreign imperialism beginning with the Opium War. In the Republican era (as we saw in the previous chapter), they even established days of national humiliation or shame (*guochi ri*) to mark the anniversaries of these painful episodes. Such days, along with the sensitivity to national humiliation they reflected, constituted a major form of collective remembering and became the implicit or explicit focus of a vast *guochi* literature. Given the persistence of this open wound—a sense of grievance that would not go away and kept being revisited—it is not surprising that the Goujian story should loom large in the minds of Chinese throughout these years.

The widespread diffusion of the Goujian story in Republican-era educational materials and popular literature—its establishment as collective cultural knowledge—meant that shorthand allusions to it in connection with national humiliation in newspapers, magazines, posters, and even advertisements, although unlikely to make sense to outsiders, would be readily deciphered by virtually the entire Chinese reading public. A nice example is an advertisement for Golden Dragon (Jinlong) cigarettes (a brand manufactured by the Nanyang Brothers Tobacco Company) that appeared in May 1925 and May 1926 in a number of Shanghai dailies. The ad ran in several consecutive issues of each paper and was timed to appear around May 9, the anniversary of China's capitulation to the Twenty-One Demands imposed by Japan in 1915. In addition to asking people not to forget May 9, it explicitly identifies smoking Golden Dragon cigarettes as a patriotic act. An inset at the far left side of the ad shows a group of people standing under a tree on the branches of which are hung strips of paper with *guochi* written on them. At the bottom of the ad, just to the left of center, is a modern-day Goujian seated uncomfortably on a pile of brushwood, holding a gallbladder up to his mouth, his gaze directed toward the paper strips on the tree. What is interesting is that although the purpose of the ad, apart from marketing cigarettes, was to establish a clear connection between Goujian and the admonition not to forget China's humiliation, the ad's creators obviously saw no need to indicate to readers who the seated figure was or what he was holding in his hand (fig. 9.3).[18]

Another major arena in which the story took a significant part during these years was that of Guomindang ideology, in particular the mindset of Chiang Kai-shek. The front entrance of the Whampoa Military Academy (Huangpu junxiao), which was headed by Chiang, displayed on either side the flags of the Republic of China (ROC) and the Guomindang and at the top center, draped across the archway, a large light banner on which was written in bold black characters the proverb *woxin changdan* (to sleep on brushwood and taste gall). In the aftermath of the Mukden Incident of September 18, 1931, which served as a pretext for Japan's takeover of Manchuria, the Commercial Press in Shanghai came out with a volume titled *National Humiliation Illustrated* (*Guochi tu*) that, like so many other books published subsequent to the Guomindang's assumption of national power, clearly reflected the ruling party's point of view. The book contained ten large, full-color foldouts of charts, maps,

9.3. Advertisement for Golden Dragon (Jinlong) cigarettes. *Source: Shenbao,*
May 7–11, 1925; May 9, 1926. Also in *Shibao* (Eastern times), May 7–12, 1925; *Shishi
xinbao* (China times), May 8–10, 1925, and May 9, 1926.

and other pictorial matter pertaining to China's victimization at the
hands of imperialism. One of the foldouts, "A Chart of the Different
Kinds of National Humiliation," superimposes a list of the wrongs
China has suffered as a result of the unequal treaties over the proverb
woxin changdan, drawn in large block characters. On either side of the
foldout is depicted a sword passing through a crown of thorns—a symbol, interestingly, derived from Christian iconography, where it represents the mocking humiliation of Jesus by the Roman soldiers who
placed the crown on his head. From each crown of thorns is suspended a
gallbladder dripping bile into the open mouth of a Goujianesque figure
clad only in shorts and lying against a pile of brushwood. As in so many
of the other shorthand allusions to the Goujian story that newspapers
and magazines were filled with, it is taken for granted that Chinese readers (inevitably insiders) will know that *woxin changdan* refers to the story
of Goujian and the burden of suffering and shame (including the mockery) he endured and will interpret the image accordingly (fig. 9.4).[19]

   Although perhaps it cannot be demonstrated in a categorical way, it
is certainly plausible to argue that the strong identification of the Guomindang with the example of Goujian during these years reflected the profound sense of connection that Chiang Kai-shek felt with the Yue
king. Chiang had great admiration for Goujian's capacity to withstand

9.4. Illustrated chart of different kinds of national humiliation. *Source: Guochi tu* (National humiliation illustrated) (Shanghai: Shangwu Yinshuguan, 1931 or 1932), 2nd foldout.

the most horrific abuses and indignities: "During Goujian's captivity," he wrote in his diary in 1934, "not only did he lie on brushwood and taste gall, he also drank urine and tasted excrement. Compared to me today, his ability to put up with hardship and tolerate humiliation was many times greater." In informal remarks to his subordinates in Zhejiang around the same time, Chiang made explicit his identification with Goujian: "We must emulate King Goujian of Yue," he said, "everyone must become a King Goujian of Yue. . . . In all our actions, all our methods, we must follow his example. . . . With such a model as Zhejiang's King Goujian of Yue, if we are unable to save the nation, truly we will be unable to face our ancestors." In an article on Chiang's Japan strategy in the years leading up to the outbreak of war between China and its neighbor, one PRC historian concluded (based mainly on Chiang's unpublished diaries) that the rare "power of restraint" Chiang exhibited at the time "can only be related to the influence of Goujian."[20]

THE GUOMINDANG ON TAIWAN

The humiliation/revenge theme in the Goujian story continued to be widely encountered after 1949 during the rule of Chiang Kai-shek and the Guomindang on Taiwan. The story was disseminated at all levels of the educational system and in opera, film, fiction, plays, newspapers, magazines, comics, television, and radio. The messages distilled from it were now, however, somewhat different. For one thing, as befit the self-image of the Republic of China as the last bulwark of traditional Chinese culture, the figures in the story were often heavily Confucianized. For another thing, there was much emphasis on the aspect of the story that dealt with the uphill battle faced by the small, weak state of Yue (now represented by the ROC) in achieving its goal of overcoming the much larger and more powerful state of Wu (the People's Republic of China, PRC) and recovering the territory over which it had previously ruled. An example was an illustrated comic book account of the story published in 1976 with the support and authorization of the powerful National Editorial and Translation Office (Guoli bianyi guan) and targeting young readers; the comic contained a boxed message at the very end explicitly stating the author's view of the relevance of the Goujian story to Taiwan's contemporary situation. The message read: "This is an example from our country's history of the few attacking the many, of enduring humiliation and wiping out disgrace, of launching a counterattack and recovering the nation. We must bear in mind the lessons of history and obliterate the Mao bandits [*Mao fei*]."[21] The reference to "launching a counterattack and recovering the nation" (*fangong fuguo*) was important. This slogan (as noted in chapter 1) was ubiquitous in Taiwan after 1950; it expressed the foundational policy of the Nationalist government at the time. If further evidence were needed of the resonance between the Goujian story and this policy—or indeed of the identification of Goujian with Chiang Kai-shek—it is seen in the repeated use of *Goujian fuguo* (Goujian recovers his country) as the title of Taiwan renderings of the story in the domains of opera, spoken drama, and film.

THE PRC UNDER MAO ZEDONG

On the Chinese mainland also, starting in the early 1960s—a time of crisis when China was beset by severe famine (owing to the Great Leap Forward) and growing tensions in its relationship with the Soviet Union— the Goujian story was widely used (primarily in operatic and spoken drama performances but also in essays and articles) to convey timely political messages. There was nothing accidental about this. It had long been held that historical drama should have immediate relevance to present concerns. Thus, one writer observed in 1961,

> in the initial days after the country's liberation, *Li Zicheng Enters the Capital* [*Chuang wang ru jing*], by warning people not to get carried away with success, had great educational value; during the Resist-America Aid-Korea period, *The General and the Prime Minister Make Peace* [*Jiang xiang he*] showed us how to become more effectively united when confronting a formidable enemy; and in the present day, when the party has called on us to engage in arduous struggle [*jianku fendou*] and to work hard to strengthen the nation [*fafen tuqiang*], the story of King Goujian of Yue's sleeping on brushwood and tasting gall has appeal for large numbers of viewers.[22]

Mao Dun, the minister of culture in the early 1960s, said that he himself had read over fifty different opera scripts dealing with the *woxin changdan* theme and estimated that there were more than a hundred in existence. He was so impressed by the widespread attention given to the story throughout the country that he published a book on it in 1962. The central idea in the works, according to him, was the importance of "self-reliance" (*zili gengsheng*) in enabling Yue to turn weakness into strength and successfully avenge the humiliations to which it had been subjected by Wu. Clearly this was an allusion to the situation China had been thrown into as a result of the growing rift with the Soviet Union and suggested an appropriate response to it.[23]

In Mao Dun's judgment, the most successful of the *woxin changdan* dramas from the early 1960s—and the only one that wasn't an opera—was the eminent playwright Cao Yu's five-act play *The Gall and the Sword* (*Dan jian pian*), which was first performed in Beijing in 1961 at a time when Cao Yu was at the height of his prestige. Some have suggested that this play, which includes an entire act devoted to a famine in Yue and touches on tensions between Wen Zhong and Goujian, contained implied "criticism of Mao Zedong's . . . policies" during the Great Leap Forward—policies that were openly criticized by Minister of Defense Peng Dehuai at the Lushan Conference of July 1959, leading to Peng's dismissal in September.

There are several problems with this judgment. First, although in Cao Yu's play Goujian is initially irritated by the forthright criticism of Wen Zhong, unlike Mao at Lushan, he eventually accepts it. No less important, he is presented in the famine act as a ruler who is directly and intimately involved in his people's travails, as compared with Mao, who during the Great Leap Forward distanced himself from the sufferings of Chinese farmers. Second, my sense is that Cao Yu, who was genuinely and deeply distressed by the suffering in rural China at the time *Dan jian pian* was being written, deliberately assigned a prominent place to famine, not to take a dig at Mao but as a means of reinforcing the play's overall contemporary relevance. The troubled relationship Goujian had with his top officials is more complicated. In light of Cao Yu's political timidity and abiding faith in the Communist Party, it seems extremely unlikely that he would engage in even the most indirect criticism of the party's paramount leader. We must distinguish clearly, however, between an author's intent and the range of possible meanings his or her language might assume in the minds of reading and viewing audiences, who have their own concerns and preoccupations and their own distinct social biographies. In the atmosphere of the early 1960s, marked as it was by widespread sentiment sympathetic to Peng Dehuai, it seems entirely plausible that readers and viewers of *Dan jian pian*, most of whom would have also been acquainted with a broader, more inclusive set of renderings of the Goujian story, might equate Wen Zhong with the dismissed minister of defense, even though Cao Yu's play ended with Yue's destruction of Wu and didn't deal with the tragic fate that overtook Wen Zhong later. In short, they might, on the basis of their wider experience of the Goujian story, fill in imagined blanks in the drama that Cao Yu had no intention of putting there.[24]

THE POST-MAO YEARS

In the early 1980s, in the works of two major writers, Xiao Jun and Bai Hua, neither of whom shared Cao Yu's political timidity, the cruel and despotic Goujian who emerged after Yue's conquest of Wu was resurrected as political allegory to form a critique of the autocratic quality of Maoist rule. This phase of the Goujian story had generally been omitted from earlier twentieth-century renderings, partly because Yue's final triumph over Wu constituted a natural and appropriate ending (especially during the first half of the century when China was under constant threat from Japanese aggression) and also for the reason that its inclusion could too easily be interpreted as a veiled critique of Chiang Kai-shek before 1949 or Mao after 1949. Xiao Jun and Bai Hua thus crossed an important invisible line in their treatments of the story.[25]

In the period from the 1990s to the present, the Goujian story began to be handled in still other ways, again closely mirroring things that were happening in China at the time.[26] The nationalistic side of the story, which predominated in the Republican era, continued to be exploited, now, especially after 1989 (the year of the suppression of the Tiananmen protest demonstrations), mainly in connection with the new emphasis on patriotic education. Much more prevalent—and I think more interesting— were some of the other usages that became rampant in the waning years of the century. The story was used to critique the corruption among party cadres and leaders; Fuchai in particular was trotted out as a negative example of what happened when leaders forgot the concerns of the people and the state and lavished attention on their own private interests. Managers in industries that were slumping were encouraged, emulating Goujian, to work hard and not give up hope. Job hunters were told that they shouldn't insist on getting the perfect position right away: "Putting up with adversity for a short period," it was observed in one article, "isn't really such a bad thing. As a twenty-first-century 'Goujian,' you will be more self-confident and have a greater competitive edge" when you try for your next job. The use of the Goujian story as a motivational vehicle was frequently touted by educators concerned about the "little emperor" syndrome fostered by the one-child policy; these youngsters were spoiled rotten and, unless handling adversity (*cuozhe*) was incorporated into their educations, it was feared, they would be paralyzed in the face of the inevitable frustrations of real life.

The use of the Goujian story as a motivational spur, to teach people not to be discouraged by setbacks and show them how they could better their lives by hard work and persistence, was by no means a completely new development in these years. But the frequency with which the story was deployed in the 1990s and later in connection with personal motivation—and the great variety of contexts in which this occurred—signaled something new, reflecting the dramatic shift that had taken place in the post-Mao years from national and collective involvement to a newly opened space centering on individual apprehensions and goals.

This shift was vividly symbolized by a grisly event that took place in a village in Dujiangyan, Sichuan, on the first night of the lunar new year of 2004 (January 22). One of the villagers, Hu Xiaolong, after practicing martial arts for many years, went on a murderous rampage, butchering three members of a single household to avenge a private grievance dating back twenty years. Several days after the killings, reporters went to Hu's home. The wall opposite the entrance to the courtyard was covered with crude graffiti he had scrawled with a piece of charcoal, apparently the night before the murders. One stated "King Goujian of Yue slept on brushwood and tasted gall, three thousand Yue soldiers at long last destroyed Wu." Other scribblings also referred to the Goujian story, although more indirectly. What is fascinating about these allusions is that they were totally personalized, even to the point where the murderer identified with the Yue king and perceived the story as a prototype for his own behavior. In starkly horrific terms, the killings mirrored the degree to which the pendulum had swung from public to private concerns in China.[27]

In this same period, beginning in the early 1990s, the adaptability of the Goujian story was tested against yet another set of circumstances distinguishing the recent evolution of Chinese society. I refer to the story's marketing in response to the growth of the domestic tourism industry and of television, not to mention the proliferation of new print outlets accompanying the extraordinary expansion of China's tertiary educational sector in the post-Mao years—and, no less important, the emergence of new research technologies for accessing these outlets. Let me give a simple example from my own work. In preparing the final chapter of the Goujian book, I made extensive use of a Chinese database (*China Academic Journals*) that enabled full-text searches of more than 7,200 journals, magazines, newsletters, and other vehicles of periodic scholarly communication, representing a vast range of specialized interests and covering the years from 1994 to 2007 (the final year in which my research was conducted).[28] To give some idea of the power of such a database, as of January 13, 2007, a search for "Goujian" resulted in hits in 5,549 articles, and a search for "*woxin changdan*" hits in 7,292 articles. Clearly, without such a search engine, along with the process of digitization that lay at its heart, the research on which much of the chapter was based would simply not have been possible.

Like so much else in China, the Goujian story has undergone a process of commodification, becoming a significant source of revenue for Shaoxing (the site of the ancient Yue capital), for travel agencies in the lower Yangzi region, and for the television industry in general. In 2006 and 2007 alone, it was the subject of no fewer than three long-running TV historical dramas, each featuring a star actor in the role of Goujian. The money-making potential of blockbuster TV dramas like these is suggested by one of them, *Yue wang Goujian* (King Goujian of Yue). A joint production of China Central Television (CCTV), Shaoxing TV, and media companies in Hangzhou and Beijing, it had forty-one segments and aired before a nationwide audience in 2007. Apart from hefty advertising revenues, broadcasting and adaptation rights to the film were sold to Japan for a record high sum. A novel based on the script was published in 2006, and, as with other TV historical dramas, a digital video version soon followed.

Heavily promoted dramatizations of the Goujian story such as the foregoing interacted synergistically with the growth of Chinese tourism. A precedent was set in the 1990s with the explosion of interest in Fan Li's alleged paramour, Xi Shi. Operas dealing with the famous beauty enjoyed great popularity in a wide area including Zhejiang, Shanghai, Jiangsu, Anhui, Shanxi, and even Taiwan; two very long novels about Xi Shi appeared in 1995. The local government of Xi Shi's home place, Zhuji (now a city under the administrative jurisdiction of Shaoxing), after renovating the Xi Shi Temple and opening it to the public, embarked on promoting a tourist economy centered on its most famous daughter (whose historicity, as it turns out, has not gone unchallenged by modern Chinese scholarship). "Overnight, it seemed, from every side there was a sudden burst of interest in this beautiful woman who lived more than two thousand years ago."[29]

Apart from conveying the spirit of Goujian to people all over China, the TV drama *Yue wang Goujian* promised to generate considerable economic benefits for Shaoxing. The fact of the drama being partly filmed in the Houshan scenic area in Shaoxing promoted the city nationally as a prime site for domestic tourism. CCTV went to considerable expense to build a set at Houshan—it included a reproduction of Goujian's palace, his ancestral shrine, the Zhongli forge for sword making,[30] the stable, and other structures—and it was left in place after the filming was completed late in 2005, creating an additional attraction for visitors. The Houshan authorities suspended a large red banner over one of the entrances to the park that announced, "The set from *King Goujian of Yue* lends even greater enchantment to the scenery of Houshan" (fig. 9.5). In response, numerous travel agencies scrambled to sign agreements of touristic cooperation with the Houshan authorities, supplying a boost to the scenic area and of course an infusion of new revenue into Shaoxing.[31]

As a historian working on a book about the Goujian story in twentieth-century China, I was naturally determined to visit Shaoxing, especially after the developments just described. Elizabeth and I flew from Hong Kong to Hangzhou in early January 2007 and hired a car to take us to Shaoxing (an hour's ride) for the day. Among the more interesting places we visited in Shaoxing was the King of Yue Temple (Yue wang dian), which was perched on a hill in Fushan Park (Fushan Gongyuan), only a short walk from the grave of Wen Zhong. The temple had been destroyed

9.5. Banner at the entrance to the Houshan Scenic Area announcing the added attraction created by the set from the TV film *Yue wang Goujian* Shaoxing. Photograph by author, January 5, 2007.

by Japanese bombing during the war but was rebuilt in 1982 following the original design. As you enter the temple, you see on the right and left walls two huge paintings of Goujian, one of them with the king alone, seated cross-legged on a brushwood mat with a gallbladder suspended above his left shoulder and a sword on his lap, the other painting showing him flanked by Fan Li and Wen Zhong, avowing his determination to "recover his state and wipe out his humiliation." As soon as I saw the paintings, especially the one of Goujian alone, I knew these images had to grace the front and back jackets of my book when it was published. I took photos of the images and, on my return to Boston, sent them to the designer at the University of California Press. She agreed that the images would make for a terrific book jacket, but unfortunately the resolution of my photos wasn't nearly high enough to permit their use for that purpose. No problem, I told her, and immediately consulted with my daughter Lisa, who is a professional photographer. Lisa and I made a deal. She had been wanting to go to China for a long time, so I offered her a two-week trip to Hong Kong and China in return for her shooting the paintings in the King of Yue Temple properly. She was overjoyed, I was much relieved, and when I went back to Hong Kong in the fall, Lisa was with me. We returned to Shaoxing and took the pictures (using a stepladder to avoid distortion owing to

9.6. Wall painting of Goujian in King of Yue Temple (Yue wang dian), Shaoxing. This photograph, taken by Lisa Cohen, was used on the front cover of *Speaking to History: The Story of King Goujian in Twentieth-Century China* (Berkeley: University of California Press, 2009).

the unusual height of the paintings), and when I returned to the States and sent the images to the University of California Press designer, she said they would work splendidly (fig. 9.6).

Nothing could be more China-centered than a book that probes the impact on Chinese history of a story that, while deeply ingrained in Chinese culture and widely known among East Asian peoples generally, is for the most part unknown to outsiders. This is China-centeredness

with a vengeance. At the same time, for a non-Chinese like myself, someone not born to the culture, it seemed natural, once having become familiar with the Goujian story and its remarkable impact throughout
China's tumultuous twentieth century, to move to the next level and pose
the larger—and plainly non-China-centered—question of what
prompts a people to look at their current historical experience through
the lens of a story that seems to prefigure that experience.

Although perhaps unusually prevalent in China, the part taken by
such stories—the ways they speak to history—has been compellingly
demonstrated in many other societies as well. One thinks of the resonance
the Masada story, symbolizing the willingness of a people to make the ultimate sacrifice in preference to acknowledging defeat (in 73 CE), had
among perennially threatened Jews during the span of several decades surrounding the founding of the state of Israel (1948), or the inspiration late
twentieth-century Serbs drew from their ancestors' traumatic defeat in the
Battle of Kosovo more than 600 years earlier (1389), or Barack Obama's
insertion of himself into a biblically structured history of the American
civil rights movement, in which (as he put it in a talk in Selma, Alabama,
in March 2007) Martin Luther King Jr. and others represented "the Moses
generation"—"the men and women of the movement, who marched and
suffered but who, in many cases, 'didn't cross over the river to see the
Promised Land'"—and his own generation, "the Joshua generation."[32]

Clearly, the multifaceted connection developed in *Speaking to History* between the Goujian saga and China's recent history can serve as the
opening wedge into a larger intellectual discussion. To gain a fuller understanding of the issues involved, Chinese history will have to be joined
by Jewish history, Serbian history, U.S. history, and all the other histories. So, we encounter one final paradox: even as, in the course of a deeply
China-centered scrutinizing of Chinese history in the twentieth century,
an outsider's perspective may be helpful in recognizing the pervasiveness
and importance of the story–history connection in human experience
generally, once having gotten to that point there is a strong likelihood
that with cultural particularity diminished in importance, the old distinctions between insider and outsider may perhaps be less salient. This
theme will be explored further in chapters 10 and 11.

CHAPTER 10

The Power of Story

History and Popular Memory

A n important goal of my most recent book, *History and Popular Memory: The Power of Story in Moments of Crisis* (Columbia University Press, 2014), was to contribute to a broadening of the study of Chinese history, to treat China not from the perspective of the proverbial frog in the well that sees a small part of reality and thinks it is the whole world but by placing Chinese history in a larger context, to shed a different sort of light on it. This is something that in various ways other Western historians of China also have been doing in recent years. In my case it followed a pattern that has marked my work since the end of the last century when I published *History in Three Keys*. A major way that book departed from my previous writing was the new interest in stories that it embodied— rumor stories about the beliefs and activities of the Boxers, stories the Boxers themselves told about their beliefs, stories describing the magical skills of the Red Lanterns (the Boxers' female associates), and the mythic narratives that grew up among Chinese and Westerners long after the Boxers had passed into history. I became so fascinated by this storytelling aspect of history that it became the central focus of *Speaking to History*, discussed in the preceding chapter.

In *Speaking to History*, I examined in some detail the influence among Chinese over the past 100 or so years of the saga of King Goujian, who ruled the state of Yue in the fifth century BCE. Although in different historical situations in the twentieth century Chinese fastened on different aspects of the Goujian story, its impact was greatest in moments of protracted crisis. Thus, in the context of the Japanese military threat in the 1920s and 1930s, Chiang Kai-shek and the Guomindang stressed in their writings and pronouncements the core Goujianesque theme of humiliation and revenge. After fleeing to Taiwan following their defeat by the Communists in the civil war (1945–49), when the main threat to the Guomindang's survival was no longer a foreign nemesis but the People's Republic of China with its vastly greater population, territory, and resources, the part of the story that fixed the Guomindang's attention was the fact that the state of Yue, despite the great disparity in size and wealth and power between it and Wu, was able, after taking twenty years to build up its population and military strength, to completely obliterate Wu. In both situations, the story of Goujian served as a metaphor for the challenges facing Chiang Kai-shek. The right story, in such instances, by presenting a model of the world that incorporated a favorable outcome for the crisis, pointed to a more hopeful future.

This powerful interplay between story and history, far from being peculiar to China, has also been widely encountered in other societies around the world. The British-born historian Simon Schama, for example, goes so far as to argue that Shakespeare's histories were not just the making of the Bard but also the making of the English. Here is what he has to say about Laurence Olivier's film rendering of *Henry V*, which was released just months after D-Day in 1944:

> Shakespeare awakened the historian in me. He seemed to deliver a certain idea of England at a time when all that was left otherwise was tea and cricket. In 1955, just 10 years after the war, it was as though the Bard had scripted Churchill; that the original "happy few" were prototypes for the boys who flew in Spitfires. What now looks like the shamelessly chauvinistic film version made by Olivier in 1944 as a morale booster for D-Day made perfect sense to us even after the war had ended. Hadn't we all been in it together, Exeter, Harry the King, George the King, Winston, Dunkirk, the Blitz, Normandy? "We band of brothers, for he who today sheds his blood with me shall be my brother"! We needed the pennants of Agincourt and the Crispin-St. Georgery of it all, for London was still a sooty pea-soup fog-shrouded place; bombed out buildings in the city and East End sticking up like stumps of blackened teeth.[1]

There are an infinite number of possibilities, as far as precise subject matter is concerned, for the interaction between story and history. In the process of writing the Goujian book, I became sensitized to the overall pattern of how this interplay operated and thought it might be interesting to see what happened if I assembled a number of cases relating to a specific set of issues. This got me started on my new book. In talks I gave on the book, someone in the audience could always be counted on to ask how, from all the possible historical cases, I selected the ones I did. A perfectly legitimate question. I knew from the outset that one chapter would deal with the Goujian story, the new book's clear ancestor and progenitor. In the conclusion of *Speaking to History*, I had placed the Goujian story in comparative perspective and singled out the Masada and Kosovo stories, which I happened to be familiar with, as two other instances in which memory of a historical event played an important part in shaping people's consciousness many centuries later. Similarly, I knew enough about the story of Joan of Arc to see that it would also fit nicely into the larger plan of the book. At a dinner in Hong Kong, I described the new book's main themes to my friend and fellow historian Chris Munn (fig. 10.1). His eyes brightened as he urged me to include Laurence Olivier's *Henry V*; and much the same thing happened again some months later when, over lunch at Harvard's Fairbank Center for Chinese Studies, Steve Goldstein, who taught Chinese politics at Smith College, said that if I were going to include *Henry V*, I needed to consider adding Sergei Eisenstein's *Alexander Nevsky* as well. Not a very systematic way to determine a book's contents, but that's how things sometimes work in practice.

The six countries that are the book's focus—Serbia, Palestine/Israel, the Soviet Union, Great Britain, China, and France—all faced severe crises in the course of the twentieth century. The crises I singled out all involved war or the threat of war, in response to which older historical narratives embodying themes that were broadly analogous to what was happening in the historical present were drawn on by the populations and states affected. Creative works—plays, poems, films, operas, and the like—often played an important role in the recovery and revitalization of these narratives, and, as we would expect in the twentieth century, nationalism took a vital part in each case.

10.1. With Hong Kong historian Chris Munn in the University of Hong Kong Senior Common Room (November 2017). Photograph by Elizabeth Sinn.

This reverberation between (ancient) story and (present) history is a phenomenon of no little historical interest. But it is exceedingly complex, reflecting deeply on how individual leaders or entire peoples or subgroups within a society position themselves in the space of historical memory. The manner of this positioning varies significantly from case to case. Yet running through them all is a constant: the mysterious power that people in the present draw from stories that sometimes derive from remotest antiquity and often recount events that have only the thinnest basis in an actual historical past. The question psychologist Jerome Bruner poses in reference to this storytelling phenomenon, although not referring explicitly to history, is central. "Why," he asks, "do we use story as the form for telling about what happens in life and in our own lives? Why not images, or lists of dates and places and the names and qualities of our friends and enemies? Why this seemingly innate addiction to story?"[2]

The power of story, so common and yet so poorly understood, merits far more scrutiny than it has generally received from practicing historians.[3] In response to his own question, Bruner cautions, "Beware an easy answer!"[4] My hope is that the multifaceted connections developed in my book between story and history in a range of cultural settings and historical circumstances go some way toward illuminating the problem he raises.

Since the older stories involved never supplied an exact match to what was currently happening in history, they were regularly modified to some degree to make the fit closer. This is where popular memory became important. Popular memory—what people in general believe took place in the past—is often a very different animal from what serious historians, after carefully sifting through the available evidence, judge to have actually taken place. This distinction between memory and history, vitally important to historians, is often blurred in the minds of ordinary folks, who are likely to be more emotionally drawn to a past that fits their preconceptions—a past they feel comfortable and identify with—than a past that is "true" in some more objective sense. This blurring is greatly facilitated when, as a result of a dearth of historical evidence or the unreliability of such evidence as has survived, even professional historians cannot know with absolute confidence what occurred in the past. Such is the case with the examples I explore in the book. But as I point out again and again, even when there exists a minimum core of certainty about what happened in the past—that Joan of Arc was burned at the stake in 1431, that in the year 73 CE a confrontation took place at the mountaintop fortress of Masada on the eastern edge of the Judean Desert overlooking the Dead Sea between a small group of Jewish warriors and a vastly stronger Roman force, or that a young Russian prince known to history as Alexander Nevsky (1220–63) in 1242 led the citizens of Novgorod (a large trading city in northwestern Russia) in the defeat of an invading force of German knights—even when this minimum core of certainty about the past exists, the power of the historian's truth often has a difficult time competing with the power of the right story, despite (or some would say because of) the latter having been seriously distorted by myth or political manipulation. A major goal of my book is to attain a deeper understanding of why this is so.

But I also see it as having a larger import. As a lifelong historian of China, my work has centered on a single country and culture. This book is different. Although there is a chapter drawn from Chinese history, it is just one case among several, having the same weight as the chapters devoted to the other countries. The focus of the book, rather than being on a particular country or culture, is on a supracultural phenomenon—the part taken by story in popular memory—that may well be universal and, if not, is certainly encountered in a vast array of places around the world, regardless of the linguistic, religious, social, cultural, and other differences that pertain among the peoples inhabiting these places. In brief, what we have, I would maintain, is a different sort of world history, not the conventional kind based on conjunctures, comparisons, and influences, but one that is manifested in recurring patterns, clearly bearing a family resemblance yet independently arrived at and very possibly rooted in certain human propensities—above all, the universality of storytelling in the human experience—that transcend the specificities of culture and place.

Story and History: Matching and Adaptation

The phenomenon of story adaptation that I discuss in the book differs in detail from case to case, but the underlying process is reasonably consistent. We've already looked at the Goujian story (which is treated in chapter 3 of *History and Popular Memory*). Let me give a few additional examples. One is the Battle of Kosovo of 1389, widely perceived by Serbs as the central event in their history and eventually serving as the cornerstone of Serbian national consciousness.[5] The battle, which took place on the Field of Blackbirds (Kosovo Polje) several kilometers from the modern-day Kosovo capital of Pristina, was fought between the Serbs, led by Prince Lazar, and an invading army of the Ottoman Empire under the leadership of Sultan Murad I. The differences between the mythology and the actual historical circumstances surrounding the battle are substantial. In terms of its military consequences for the fate of the early Serbian state, the Battle of Kosovo was not nearly as important as an earlier Ottoman victory in the Battle of the Maritsa River Valley, which took place in 1371 in what is now Bulgaria, or the events of 1459, seventy years later, when Serbia finally succumbed to the Ottoman Turks. Although remembered by Serbs as a calamitous defeat, the military outcome of the Battle of Kosovo seems to have been fairly inconclusive, the leaders on both sides, as well as most of the combatants, being killed. The myths and legends that grew up around the battle were fashioned soon after its end in epic poems and folk ballads and were given a strongly Christian reading by the Serbian Orthodox Church (most conspicuously in the Christlike characteristics invested in Prince Lazar, who was said to have chosen a kingdom in Heaven over a kingdom on Earth, opting to die heroically rather than live in shame). A core theme in the Kosovo myth was the tension between loyalty and betrayal, as epitomized in the figures of Miloš Obilić and Vuk Branković. This tension reflected the historical reality that after the crushing defeat of 1371, numbers of Serbian warriors went over to the Ottoman side and very probably, in sharp contradiction to the legend, fought alongside the Turks in the Battle of Kosovo. No less subversive of the myth, scholars now question whether the historical Vuk Branković, the very picture of evil in Serbian popular memory, truly betrayed the Serbian side in the battle and whether Miloš Obilić, the iconic representative of Serbian loyalty, ever existed.

During the four and a half centuries of Ottoman rule (1455–1912), a number of important changes took place in Kosovo. One was a dramatic shift in the ratio of Serbian to Albanian inhabitants of the area. At the outset there was an overwhelming Serb majority in Kosovo, but by the late nineteenth century the Kosovo population consisted of a little over 70 percent Albanians. A second important change was the increasing Islamization of the populace (most of the Albanians, originally Roman Catholic, having become Muslims). Despite these developments, much as in the case of the Jewish people and Palestine, the ethnic and religious changes in Kosovo under the Ottomans had little apparent effect on the enduring belief among most Serbs that Kosovo represented "sacred soil."

By the time we get to the nineteenth century and the first stirrings of nationalism among the Serbian people, the Kosovo legend, embodying sizable departures from what is now believed to have actually taken place historically, was firmly in place. But this did not keep its mythic character from continuing to evolve, as two celebrated figures from the world of Serbian letters, Vuk Karadžić (1787–1864) and Petar Petrović Njegoš (1813–51) (see fig. 10.2), adapted the Kosovo legend to the new tide of nationalism. Karadžić published compilations of Serbian epic ballads that transformed the stories of Lazar and the Battle of Kosovo from oral lore into coherent written narratives that supplied Serbian national ideology with its mythical foundations. Njegoš, who ruled the ethnically

ПЕТАР ПЕТРОВИЋ ЊЕГОШ
(1813—1851)

10.2. Drawing of Petar Petrović Njegoš (1813–1851), artist unknown. *Source:* P. P. Njegoš, *The Mountain Wreath*, trans. and ed. Vasa D. Mihailovich (Irvine, CA: Schlacks, 1986), by permission of Vasa D. Mihailovich.

Serbian territory of Montenegro in the mid-nineteenth century, through his enormously influential poetic drama, *The Mountain Wreath* (*Gorski vijenac*), introduced into Serbian nationalism a strain of rhetoric marked by uncompromising violence, departing in flagrant fashion from the actual history of Muslims in Montenegro (which was far less bloody) and incorporating a vision of Christianity in which nothing was holier than taking revenge against one's enemies.

A leading Serbian literature scholar, Vasa Mihailovich, has contended that Serbs, whenever faced with critical junctures in their history, have invariably turned to the Kosovo story as a source of strength and inspiration. In this light, it is significant that for some time after the conclusion of World War I, which brought an end to the Ottoman Empire and the liberation of all Serbian lands (including Kosovo) from Turkish rule, there was a sharp decline of Kosovo motifs in Serbian literature. The flip side of this was that the allure of Kosovo traditions and stories might be expected to return the moment the Serbs as a people again felt humiliated, victimized, and oppressed, which is exactly what happened in the latter decades of the twentieth century, when Kosovo themes once again dominated Serbian cultural and political consciousness.

The Battle of Kosovo has been usefully viewed by psychiatrist Vamik Volkan as an example of what he calls a "chosen trauma," a concept that he applies to a number of other famous battles as well.[6] The concept of chosen trauma refers to "the shared mental representation of a large group's massive trauma experienced by its ancestors at the hands of an enemy group, and the images of heroes, victims, or both connected with it. Of course," Volkan tells us, "large groups do not intend to be victimized, but they '*choose*' to mythologize and psychologize the mental representation of the event." Thus, "the '*reality*' of what happened during . . . [the Battle of Kosovo] did not matter to the next generations of Serbian people. What mattered . . . was the evolution of the mental representation of this battle as a chosen trauma."[7]

Another example of the process of adaptation of ancient story to current historical circumstances is that of Joan of Arc in World War II France.[8] This example is in some ways more complicated than the Kosovo one owing to the fact that Charles de Gaulle and Philippe Pétain, the two main French political leaders during the war, strongly identified with Joan even though they were on opposite sides of the conflict.

The story of Joan of Arc (fig. 10.3), who was a French patriot and became a Roman Catholic saint, is known the world over. She was born in 1412 into a farming family in the town of Domremy in northeastern France, during the Hundred Years' War between England and France, when much of northern France was occupied by the English. In 1425, Joan, still a girl, first heard voices from God that instructed her to go into the heart of France. In 1429, after repeatedly hearing voices, Joan left with a retinue of six men for the western city of Chinon, where the French heir apparent Charles had his castle. Although at times in her brief career Joan described her mission broadly as being to drive the English from France, on reaching Chinon she announced that she had two specific objectives: to raise the English siege of Orléans, which had begun some months earlier, and to escort the Dauphin (the French heir apparent) to the city of Rheims to be anointed and crowned. She accomplished these goals and won other battles against the English. Eventually Joan was captured by the Burgundians (French allies of the English), subjected to a rigged trial on several charges, condemned to death, and burned at the stake. Within twenty-five years, Charles, now King Charles VII, drove the English from France, bringing an end to the Hundred Years' War.

In the hands of a leader like de Gaulle, the meaning of the Joan story was fairly straightforward: just as Joan of Arc had devoted her brief life to bringing an end to foreign occupation of France in the fifteenth century, de Gaulle led the resistance to the German occupation during World War II. Pétain also identified with this core theme in the Joan narrative, but his was a more literal identification: as an ally of France's German conquerors, the Vichy leader was free to target the English specifically as the object of Joan's enmity and to portray himself, because he had made peace with the Germans (thereby saving France from utter devastation), as a Joan-like savior of France in the 1940s. If the latter identification strikes us today as somewhat strained, it seemed far less so to many French people in the immediate aftermath of the swift German victory in spring 1940. In other respects, Vichy's reinvention of Joan of Arc as an example for French youth in an environment heavily imbued with fascist values and as a model of conventional female domesticity praised more for her sewing than for her military prowess must have struck a hollow note among many of Joan's twentieth-century compatriots. Nevertheless,

TALIS IN ARMA RVIT BELLACI SCHEMATE VIRGO.

IOHANNA DARC AVRELIANENSIS PVELLA VVLGO NVNCVPATA

L. Gaultier sculp. 1612.

Pugnate audentes Galli: si tale tenebat
Palladium titubans Troia, perennis erat.

Jeanne Darc. — Tiré de l'ouvrage de Jean Hordal de 1612.

10.3. Joan of Arc in full armor astride her horse. Engraving by Léonard Gaultier (1612). *Source:* Jean Hordal, *The History of the Most Noble Heroine Joan of Arc, Virgin of Lorrain, Maid of Orléans* (in Latin) (Ponti-Mussi, France: Apud M. Bernardum, 1612), reprinted in Joseph Édouard Choussy, *Vie de Jeanne Darc* (Moulins, France: Imprimerie Bourbonnaise, 1900).

although Vichy's efforts to align the Joan of Arc story with the Pétain government's values and goals were forced, to say the least, the fact that the Pétainists saw such alignment as important was in itself of great significance. It spoke to the desirability, shared by many in France at the time, of having Joan of Arc on (and by) their side during a time of severe national crisis, regardless of what she was said to represent.

The Function of Stories in Time of Crisis

What I call the power of story, although bearing a special relationship to history, permeates virtually all human activities. Indeed, I argue in my book that the use, creation, telling, and remembering of stories are an essential part of what it means to be human. If this is so, I argue further, a plausible answer to the question Jerome Bruner poses concerning human beings' "seemingly innate addiction" to story may well be that, like walking erect on two legs, having opposable thumbs, and thinking that babies are cute,[9] our reliance on story is a direct consequence of biological evolution, and without our ability to frame virtually all the things we think, dream, desire, do, and experience in narrative form we would not be able to function—or at least not in ways recognizable to us today. In short, there is a strong possibility that our brains' capacity to organize nearly everything that happens in our lives in narrative terms, thereby introducing intelligibility (including an understanding of cause and effect) into what would otherwise be utter chaos, at some point in the remote past gave humans an incalculable survival advantage over those species that could not do this or did it less well.[10]

The fact that story is ubiquitous and, in the words of one leading scholar, "takes the same basic form across cultures,"[11] doesn't mean that all stories are alike or that they perform the same kinds of functions in the lives of all people and societies. Although focusing in some cases on individuals, in other cases on important battles, and in yet other cases on a combination of the two, the stories dealt with in my book possess a common and quite specific set of characteristics. However much modified, mythologized, distorted, and misrepresented over the centuries, none of the stories was totally fabricated: they all had roots in actual historical occurrences and may thus be referred to as "history" stories. Although oral transmission played an important part in keeping some of the stories alive, they were all eventually set down in writing, circulated for centuries, and were known far and wide in the lands of their origin. All of the stories, with the partial exception of Masada,[12] had named human protagonists and more often than not supplied cognitive models that people, individually or collectively, could readily relate to and measure their thoughts and actions against. Finally, it is noteworthy that the stories I deal with were in every instance revived and popularized in the twentieth century in response to societal crises (mainly war or the threat of war) and sooner or later in this setting received strong support from the state.

Much of the power of the stories in my book derived from their capacity to speak metaphorically to what was happening—or had only recently happened or was threatening to happen in the near future—to people in the historical present. This symbolic parallelism between story and historical setting is a fundamental reason for the pervasive appeal of each story explored. The right story in such circumstances hammers away at a particular theme or set of themes very clearly and compellingly, thus challenging people to see through the clutter of their everyday lives and recognize what is truly important to them at a particular historical moment. Such stories are not personal stories. Rather, they are collective in nature, shared with other members of the community, almost all of whom were introduced to them from a very early age.

Israeli philosopher Avishai Margalit, in discussing his notion of a "community of memory," asserts that "human beings . . . lead collective existences based on symbols that encapsulate shared memories."[13] These shared memories—not the past itself, Ernest Renan cautioned, but the stories we tell one another about the past—are what bind national communities together in the present, becoming a part of the "rich legacy of memories" such communities hold in common.[14] In other words, the power of the stories I discuss, although deriving in substantial measure from their metaphoric embodiment of what was happening in the historical present, also fed on the fact that the stories constituted a vital part of a shared (or popular) store of memories (sometimes referred to as a form of folk knowledge) that fostered group coalescence and made it possible for the members of the group to think of themselves and behave as a community. Bruner has similar things to say about the relationship between "common stories" and the human groups or communities in which they circulate. Sharing such stories, he states, "creates an interpretive community" that is critically important "for promoting cultural cohesion."[15] Or, as Jonathan Gottschall has pithily put it: "Story is the glue of human social life—defining groups and holding them together."[16] What all these people are apparently suggesting is that some form of symbolic sharing (in the form of stories or memories) is absolutely key both to a culture's objective existence and to an individual's subjective sense of belonging to that culture.

Objectively, as China historian Mark Elvin puts it, "shared stories . . . define the space" in which a particular human group operates—"its conceptualized physical landscape."[17] Subjectively, common stories and memories are the very stuff out of which the imagined communities Benedict Anderson describes are formed. Although Anderson's notion of imagined communities is applicable to a variety of communal realms—religious, cultural, and so on—he uses it primarily to refer to nations (a particular kind of political community). According to him, a nation is "imagined" "because the members of even the smallest nation will never know most of their fellow-members, meet them, or even hear of them, yet in the minds of each lives the image of their communion." A nation is imagined as a "community" because, despite the differences prevailing within it, it "is always conceived as a deep, horizontal comradeship."[18] The stories that circulate among the members of such a community, I would add, constitute at all times a special cultural language for discussing matters of immediate concern; and in time of peril, they supply a floor of reassurance that individual fears and worries about what is happening—or what may happen—are shared in common by other members of the community.

In addition to the horizontal comradeship Anderson refers to, there is a vertical dimension to the stories that circulate in and to some extent define a national community. This dimension ties the community's members to a shared—or at least a partially shared—past. It fleshes out the sense of identity of the community members by telling them where they have come from and where they might be headed.

It should be clear at this point why the members of a national community instinctively turn to certain kinds of stories when the community's survival is at stake. Personal stories—the primary concern of many writers on narrative, based on the premise that stories are a fundamental part of how individuals process experience and understand the world—won't do in such situations. Instead, collective stories—stories that are widely known within a community, that are part of its heritage—are needed. But not just any old collective stories. The ones needed must be closely aligned in content and structure with the crisis in which the community is embroiled. This is what Margalit is getting at when he asks:

> "Why did Stalin, an arch-manipulator, when locked in a war of life and death with the invading Nazis, invoke the national memories of great patriots from czarist Russia rather than working-class memories that he was ideologically supposed to represent? Stalin invoked the memory of Alexander Nevsky, who defeated the Teutonic knights (in the thirteenth century), rather than the memory of Karl Marx, and of Ivan the Terrible, who defeated the Tartars at Kazan [the capital and largest city in the republic of Tatarstan, Russia] in the sixteenth century, rather than Friedrich Engels."[19]

Beyond being attracted to collective narratives that bear a metaphoric likeness to the crisis a community is undergoing, the members of the community, as I suggested earlier, are also commonly drawn to tales that show a way out of the crisis and are therefore a source of sorely needed hope and encouragement. Clear examples of this are the two films discussed in the final chapter of my book—Eisenstein's *Alexander Nevsky* and Olivier's *Henry V*—which conclude with the triumph against all odds of the central character over his archenemy.

Popular Memory and Critical History: Concluding Thoughts

At the end of my book, I turn to the key issue of the tension between critical history and popular memory.[20] History, according to French historian Roger Chartier, while "one among many forms of narration, . . . is nevertheless singular in that it maintains a special relationship to truth.

More precisely, its narrative constructions aim at reconstructing a past that really was."[21] No one ever said this was easy. But as another well-known historian, Georg Iggers, has put it, "[there remains a fundamental difference between postmodern theories that deny] any claim to reality in historical accounts and a historiography that is fully conscious of the complexity of historical knowledge but still assumes that real people had real thoughts and feelings that led to real actions that, within limits, can be known and reconstructed."[22] As I make amply clear in my book (the mythology surrounding the Battle of Kosovo and Joan of Arc serving as cases in point), this view of the aim of history is sometimes accompanied, compromised, or even completely displaced by other aims, the common element of which is their structuring of the past in such a way that it lends support to present purposes and aspirations. A concern for truth may be part of the process—or it may not. But either way a truthful picture of the past is not the thing that is of paramount concern. What is of the utmost importance is framing the past interpretively in such a way that it makes the present—the desired present—seem to evolve directly, or at least plausibly, from it—the construction (to put it somewhat differently) of a narrative that, while professing to square the present with the past, in fact does the very reverse of this, redefining the past so as to accommodate a preferred present.

Although the rewriting of the Masada and Kosovo stories (not to mention the Joan of Arc story under Vichy) was particularly blatant, the fact is, all of the stories dealt with in my book, and a great many other "history" stories not included in it, have undergone a comparable rewriting process. It doesn't seem to matter to most people, even if they suspect (as some surely must) that the stories have been modified over time. As British historian David Lowenthal writes,

If Oliver Goldsmith was appalled by the "ecclesiastical beggars" who rattled off lies and legends as facts at Westminster Abbey's Poets' Corner, most viewers neither seek objective veracity nor mind if it is absent. Echoing Washington Irving's indulgence of spurious Shakespeare relics at Stratford in 1815, they are "ever willing to be deceived, where the deceit is pleasant, and costs nothing. What is it to us, whether these stories be true or false, so long as we can persuade ourselves into the belief of them?"[23]

What is the basis for this apparent indifference to truth? I've already hinted at an answer. Let me enlarge on it.[24] Another British historian, J. H. Plumb, in *The Death of the Past* (1969), maintained that "the past," by which he meant what I call popular or folk or collective memory, should never be confused with critical history. "True history," he wrote, is at bottom "destructive," its role being "to cleanse the story of mankind from those deceiving visions of a purposeful past." French historian Pierre Nora, in his celebrated seven-volume work *Les lieux de mémoire* (Realms of memory) (1984–1992), made much the same point when he wrote that "Memory is always suspect in the eyes of history, whose true mission is to demolish it, to repress it." However, he did not think this was a good thing at all and so, along with his collaborators, he set about reconstructing as many sites as possible that were evocative of French collective memory. Lowenthal, although using the term "heritage" for collective memory in his book *Possessed by the Past* (1996), fully agrees with Nora, contending that "heritage, no less than history, is essential to knowing and acting" and arguing that "by means of it, we tell ourselves who we are, where we came from, and to what we belong." (The connection Lowenthal draws between heritage and identity is beautifully captured in an exchange between American novelist Jonathan Safran Foer and his six-year-old son, to whom he often read children's versions of Old Testament stories. After hearing about the death of Moses for the umpteenth time—"how he took his last breaths overlooking a promised land that he would never enter"—the son asked if Moses was a real person. "I don't know," Foer told him, "but we're related to him."[25])

American historian Bernard Bailyn also addressed the uneasy relationship between history and memory with great eloquence at a 1998 conference on the Atlantic slave trade that almost broke up when many black scholars in attendance and others reacted heatedly to the cold, statistically grounded scholarly presentations on the trade. Bailyn drew a sharp contrast between critical, scientific historical writing, which was all head and no heart and kept its distance from the past it was bent on recovering, and memory, the relationship of which to the past was more an embrace. Memory, he contended, "is not a critical, skeptical reconstruction of what happened. It is the spontaneous, unquestioned experience of the past. It is absolute, not tentative or distant, and it is expressed in signs and signals, symbols, images, and mnemonic clues of all sorts. It shapes our awareness whether we know it or not, and it is ultimately emotional, not intellectual."

Although these writers all accentuate the contrast between critical history and popular memory—a contrast I repeatedly emphasize in my book—this distinction is not the whole story. The truth is that there is a great deal of overlap between academic history and the "history" stories I deal with, which is a prime reason for the confusion between the two in many people's minds. Popular memory, I point out repeatedly, often has a genuine historical component. There really was a battle between the Serbs and Turks at Kosovo in 1389, a Roman siege of Jerusalem and destruction of the Second Temple of the Jews in 70 CE, a plucky French maid named Joan who fought the English occupiers of northern France and was burned at the stake in 1431, a King Goujian who ruled a state called Yue in the latter part of the Zhou dynasty and eventually triumphed over his rival, and so on. How is a person untrained as a historian—or even a historian if he or she happens to be unfamiliar with the aspect of the past that the story relates to—to know which parts of the stories dealing with such people and events are authentic and which are the product of inventive minds? People confront this problem today constantly when we see historical dramatizations in film, TV, or the stage or read historical fiction based on a core of actual historical persons and events.

I recently read two remarkable works of historical fiction by Stanford University psychoanalyst/author Irvin D. Yalom: *The Spinoza Problem: A Novel* (2012) and *When Nietzsche Wept: A Novel of Obsession* (1992). Unlike many authors of historical novels, Yalom includes a note at the end of each work telling the reader what parts and which characters are fabricated. These notes are helpful but also deceptive because by fictionalizing the environment within which the nonfiction aspects of the works operate, he unavoidably ends up fictionalizing those nonfiction aspects as well.[26]

This is one side of the problem: the frequent difficulty of distinguishing clearly between fact and fiction. Another is that serious historians, although striving to reconstruct the past as it really was, can never fully succeed in this venture. Where full and reliable data are lacking (which is almost always the case), we habitually make inferences, some of which are later shown to be wrong. Beyond this, historians are never entirely impervious to the collective memory of the society in which they live, which means that even as we strive to identify and undermine the mythic aspects of our knowledge of the past, we inevitably introduce into our accounts new myths (although we may not think of them as such) that are reflective of the values and thought patterns that happen to be important to people in our own day. This is what we mean—part of it, at any rate—when we say that each generation makes its own history. It is what sociologist Barry Schwartz means when he says that the remembering of Abraham Lincoln (and presumably other important historical figures) must be regarded "as a constructive process as opposed to a retrieval process," that, within limits, each generation of Americans has had its own Lincoln who differed in major or minor ways from the Lincoln of earlier generations.[27] Shifting from heroic individuals to complex, large-scale events, it is what acclaimed documentary filmmaker Ken Burns means when he writes of the American propensity to periodically rethink the meaning of the Civil War.[28]

What this complicated relationship between critical history and popular memory suggests is that Bailyn's comment at the Atlantic slave trade conference would perhaps benefit from a slight shift of emphasis. At the moment he made his remarks—to say nothing of the sensitivity of the issue to which they were addressed—it must have seemed necessary and desirable to draw the line between critical history and popular memory hard and fast. Although it is true that good history writing is always attentive to the distance of the real past from the present—David Lowenthal, as noted in the introduction to this memoir, famously referred, in another of his works, to the past as a foreign country—it is not true that it is always all head and no heart. Bailyn himself seems to acknowledge as much when he asserts that "perhaps history and memory . . . may act usefully upon each other."[29] I would reframe this in stronger language and ask whether it is not inevitable that they interact in this way. In J. H. Plumb's view, distinguished French historian Marc Bloch "possessed the power to abstract himself from any preconceived notions about the past and to investigate an historical problem with detachment. And yet, detached as he was, his imagination, his creative invention, his sense of humanity infused all that he did."[30] This infusion, in my judgment, is what good historical scholarship should aspire to. But it would be a mistake to believe that it can ever give us the past as it really was. Despite the most painstaking efforts to reconstruct such a past (efforts I wholeheartedly applaud), the questions we ask—and that guide our research and writing—will unavoidably be informed in substantial measure by the present in which we live, with all its values, assumptions, anxieties, foibles, and mythic preferences. This circumstance more or less ensures that the product of our efforts as historians will embody a tension between the past as it really was and the past we seek to clarify and understand.

CHAPTER II

Then and Now

The Two Histories

At various points in this memoir I've alluded to the double meaning of the word *history*. History refers to what happened *then*—what took place in the past. But it is also used to refer to how historians view the past *now*, how we understand and write about it. In this case I happen to be the principal figure in both phases—the "then" and the "now"—so the title *A Path Twice Traveled: My Journey as a Historian of China* seemed fitting.

The basic objective of this memoir has been to trace the development of my career over a sixty-year period of time. When my most recent book, *History and Popular Memory: The Power of Story in Moments of Crisis*, was published (in 2014) I was about to turn eighty. At the time of this writing, it is eighteen years since my retirement from Wellesley College (2000), where I taught for thirty-five years. Obviously, during the course of a long career as a student of China, important changes have taken place in my life: I'm older and I no longer teach.

In recent years, one thing has become plain to me: aging and retirement mean different things to different people. Many years ago a colleague told me that when he retired he planned to go sailing every day, while another said that he looked forward to a joyous retired life of playing golf from morning to night. In my case, after retiring from Wellesley, I have occasionally been asked by younger colleagues approaching the age of possible retirement what I would advise them to do. (In the United States, I hasten to note, there is no set retirement age for academics.) I've always responded that there were a number of factors they needed to consider: whether they would have enough money to live on, how their health was holding up, and what they planned to do with themselves once retired. The answers to these questions came easily to me. I was financially comfortable, I was in excellent health, and I loved doing research and writing, so retirement meant more time for these activities.

I can't resist quoting something I wrote Ezra Vogel, my longtime friend and colleague at the Fairbank Center, at the time of his retirement from teaching at Harvard in 2000, the same year as mine. In the months leading up to my own retirement, I wrote him, nonacademic friends and relatives asked me with growing frequency, "So what are you going to do after you're finished?" Although a perfectly reasonable question, I was nonplussed when I first heard it since I had never assumed that after my teaching career was over I would be "finished." I added that I was sure this applied to him also.[1] As for me, since the end of my teaching career, I've published three books and more than two dozen articles (including a few that have represented significant departures from the usual tenor of my work[2]). I've also remained actively involved at Harvard's Fairbank Center for Chinese Studies, with which I have been affiliated since 1965, and at the University of Hong Kong's Hong Kong Institute for the Humanities and Social Sciences, where I continue to spend three months of every year. Furthermore, as I have throughout my career, I still respond to requests from colleagues and younger scholars around the country to read and comment on their work in progress. So, yes, the pattern of my career has changed, but there's been a good deal of continuity as well.

As I stated at the beginning of chapter 1—and this gets to the heart of my motive for undertaking to write a memoir in the first place—what I hoped to do was "take stock of the path I've followed: where I started, how and why my views changed at certain points, and where I find myself now." My interest was not, in good Aristotelian fashion, to create an airtight narrative with a beginning, a middle, and an end, but to reconstruct, as closely as possible, the process I went through in the course of my career as a historian of China. My part in this process obviously has to end at a certain point, either because I die or because I abandon my interest in Chinese history and switch to farming or running marathons. But the larger process—the effort to understand and explain the history of China—existed before me and will continue to exist after me. It is my *engagement* in this process that has been the subject of this memoir.

There's another reason for writing a memoir. It's not just something you do because it's the right time in your life to do it. It can also be a fascinating learning experience. Although this is something I had no inkling about when I started, in the course of putting the memoir together and coming to grips with the two distinct forms of consciousness referred to earlier (see the introduction), I began to think about things I had never really thought about previously.

The most obvious example of this pertains to the narrative account of my career in general. A lot of what I now know concerning what happened in the course of my life as a historian is not stuff that I knew at the outset. I didn't know, for example, while working on my first book, *China and Christianity*, that the next book would be an intellectual biography of Wang Tao. The same holds true for subsequent books I wrote. Indeed, as the reader will recall, in one instance I started out with every intention of writing one book (on national humiliation) and ended up doing another one instead (on the impact of the story of King Goujian in twentieth-century China), which entailed a major change in the work's specific content and in the larger issues that would eventually lay at its heart—above all the relationship between story and history.

Another example of history's capriciousness relates to *Discovering History in China*. When I finished writing that book, I naively anticipated, given my previous experience with Harvard University Press, that it would be accepted by Harvard more or less as a matter of course. Not only did this prove not to be the case, the book was also rejected or treated with minimal enthusiasm by three other publishers before finally being accepted by Columbia. The tribulations I experienced in my efforts to get the book published, which are detailed in chapter 4, never before constituted part of the public story of my career.

As a form of history, a memoir often addresses perspectives that were originally either well hidden or not present at all. An example of this is the shift that took place between the societal realities that prevailed during my early career and the discoveries I subsequently made about these realities from my new vantage point as a memoir writer. What is interesting here is the fresh insight I gained when I looked back over my life and applied my present consciousness to situations that existed many years before when social conventions were very different. There are two examples of this in my memoir, each of which deals with a different form of social constraint. The first, which is treated in the introduction, relates to the theme of patriarchy, as played out initially in the relationship between my father and his father, and subsequently in a radically different way in my relationship with my father, the direction of generational change moving toward less control and greater freedom in making key life decisions.

This freer pattern, happily, continued in the case of my relationship with my own children, Joanna, Nathaniel, Lisa, and Emily (fig. 11.1), each of whom, when it came to important life choices, has enjoyed freedom from efforts at parental control. Joanna has taught English at a number of Massachusetts high schools and more recently ESL (English as a second language) at Johnson & Wales University in Providence, Rhode Island, where her classes not infrequently are filled with students from China. Within the immediate family, Nathaniel is still called Didi ("Little Brother" in Chinese), the name he acquired from spending the first six months of his life in Taipei. He is an artist and craftsman, trained in sculpture, woodcarving, drawing, and design and has taught studio art at several institutions, including Hampshire College in Amherst, Massachusetts. Lisa, as noted in chapter 9, is a professional photographer, dividing her time between the commercial and art photography arenas. Emily (the only child from my second marriage), after creating and running an organic herbal products business (Revival Herbs) for five years, returned to school for training in acupuncture and Chinese herbal medicine, which she has practiced in Northampton, Massachusetts, since 2005, alongside a growing interest in homesteading. Also to be noted, Emily's child and her two stepdaughters all attend a Chinese-immersion charter school in western Massachusetts.

The other example has to do with male entitlement in gender relations, which, as pointed out in chapter 1, was still strong at the beginning of the 1960s but underwent dramatic change in the course of that decade in the direction of greater gender equality—not in all respects, to be sure, but certainly in regard to career choice. Shortly after getting divorced in 1968, I married Jane Maslow, who was eleven years younger than me. On graduating from college, she headed straight for law school and a career in law. What is eminently clear to me now is that my own

11.1. With my four children at the ninetieth birthday party of my sister Barbara in New York City (September 2017). From left: Nathaniel, me, Lisa, Joanna, and Emily. Photograph by Peter Black.

perspective on gender issues had undergone an important change during the 1960s: it seemed perfectly normal to me, by the end of that decade, to have a wife who was a working lawyer, just as it has seemed perfectly normal to me, over the past twenty years, to be partnered with a woman who makes her home in Hong Kong (not Boston), though, like me, she is also a professional historian of China.

Insideness and Outsideness

Let me turn to my career as such, focusing on the main topics that have preoccupied me as a historian of China. As I noted in my discussion of the assembling of a selection of my writings for the Routledge volume *China Unbound* (see chapter 8), there are certain themes in my work that have been there from the beginning and have never really gone away (although they have taken different forms at different times), while other themes have emerged at certain points but really weren't there at the beginning of my career. A prime example of the former kind of theme is the contrast between insideness and outsideness. An abiding concern through much of my career, as I wrote in the introduction to *China Unbound*, "has been my determination to get inside China, to reconstruct Chinese history as far as possible as the Chinese themselves experienced it rather than in terms of what people in the West thought was important, natural, or normal." There was a context for this resolve. The idea was to move beyond approaches to the Chinese past that suffered overmuch from Eurocentric or Western-centric preconceptions. Such preconceptions represented the "outsideness" in this situation; the "insideness," which I strongly endorsed, was what I eventually called the "China-centered approach."

The China-centered approach—and I want to reiterate that although I gave it a name, I didn't invent it—began to take hold among historians in the United States around 1970 (or just before). One of its most important expressions was its repudiation, explicitly or implicitly, of the conventional paradigms of the past, which began Chinese history in the West and incorporated a Western measure of significance, and its replacement of these with a Chinese story line that, far from grinding to a halt in 1800 or 1840 and being preempted or displaced by the West, continued to be of central, paramount importance right through the nineteenth century and into the twentieth.

The resulting restructuring of our picture of nineteenth-century Chinese history could be seen in a number of areas. A conspicuous example was reform, which came to be viewed by many Western scholars as part of a long-standing indigenous reformist tradition that in its origins, its style, and much of its actual content, owed little or nothing to the West. Few would argue that the West was unimportant or that it did not have a significant shaping effect on Chinese reform thought and activity over time. But there was a strong reaction against the facile representation of reform as Western-oriented and Western-inspired and an equally strong sense of the need to redefine the entire phenomenon of reform in Chinese perspective.[3]

In more general terms, the understanding of Chinese history in the nineteenth century now began to look quite different. Where there had been widespread agreement among earlier historians that the decisive break between the modern period of Chinese history and the traditional period was the Opium War (1839–42), there was significant gravitation after 1970 to the view that the more critical breakpoint event of nineteenth-century Chinese history was the Taiping Rebellion (1850–64), which, along with the other rebellions that arose in its wake, rained unprecedented devastation on the population of the Qing empire.[4]

Focusing on the Taiping Rebellion not only calls attention to blind spots in the earlier perspective of U.S. historians, it also highlights a problem of periodization.[5] To be sure, we can identify proximate causes of the Taiping upheaval in the nineteenth century. But when we inquire more deeply into the factors that culminated in the rebellion, we are inevitably drawn back to the eighteenth century and the truly mammoth changes (largely endogenous) that took place at that time. The problems identified by Philip Kuhn (above all, population explosion and intensified competition for land) generated growing strains in Chinese society that were already beginning to show in the latter decades of the eighteenth century. This socioeconomic crisis was aggravated toward the end of the century by the external impact of the expanding West (above all, the trade in opium) and the familiar marks of dynastic decline (bureaucratic corruption, popular rebellion), with the result that by the early years of the nineteenth century, long before the outbreak of the Opium War, the Qing bore little resemblance to the vigorous condition characterizing the Kangxi (r. 1662–1722), Yongzheng (r. 1723–1735), and early Qianlong (r. 1736–1796) eras.[6]

Another example of the contrast between insideness and outsideness is dealt with, at least by implication, toward the end of chapter 6, where I discuss the "outsideness of the historian." Viewed from one perspective, the outsideness of the historian—for example, a male historian reconstructing the experience of women or a white historian probing black history—has the potential to misconstrue and distort, to introduce meanings alien to the material under examination. In such cases, the historian's outsideness clearly poses a problem, and that was the position I emphasized in my early writing. But a number of colleagues (including the late Lin Tongqi,[7] the translator of *Discovering History in China* into Chinese) took exception to this stand, arguing that in certain respects, outsiders (say, U.S. historians of China) might have an advantage over insiders (Chinese students of their own past). In the course of writing *History in Three Keys* and thinking long and hard about the differences especially between the direct experiencing of the past (a quintessentially insider perspective) and its later reconstruction by historians (inevitably outsiders), I came to accept this criticism, recognizing that while the historian's outsideness can be a problem, it is a crucial aspect of what differentiates us from the original experiencers of the past and enables us, in our role as historians, to render the past fathomable and meaningful in ways simply unavailable to those directly involved.

A very different example of the contrast between insideness and outsideness is presented by the story of King Goujian in twentieth-century China. "The Goujian story," I wrote in chapter 9, "was as familiar to Chinese schoolchildren as the biblical stories of Adam and Eve or David and Goliath are to many American youngsters." Yet the story was almost completely unknown to inhabitants of the American cultural world, even including (at least before publication of *Speaking to History*) serious students of the recent Chinese past.

In *Speaking to History* I refer to stories like that of King Goujian as "insider cultural knowledge": "It is not a form of knowledge that Chinese [insiders] deliberately conceal from non-Chinese [outsiders]. It tends to be hidden, rather, mainly because the ways in which it is acquired—transmission within the family setting, early school lessons that are heavily story-centered, popular operatic arias heard on the radio, and the like—are not generally available to people who have not had the experience of growing up in a Chinese cultural milieu."[8]

Insider cultural knowledge is by no means exclusive to China. It is found in all cultures and in the different phases of a given culture's evolution through time. As an instance of the latter, Marina Warner observes that when Joan of Arc "reached for metaphors that . . . came . . . close to rendering what she felt about her voices," the three images she chose—Michael the Archangel, St. Catherine of Alexandria, and St. Margaret of Antioch—"were as well known to her contemporaries, both French and English, as a football player's or a tennis star's or a singer's are today." Such saintly images were learned in fifteenth-century France and England in the settings of home and church. The access to them among twenty-first-century French and English people is far less prevalent.[9]

The circumstances of the functioning of insider cultural knowledge and the degree of its hiddenness are likely to differ from case to case. In China, the mere mention of the proverb *woxin changdan* (sleeping on brushwood and tasting gall) immediately calls to mind the main outlines of the Goujian story. Something comparable to this is often true in the West as well. In March 2005, while driving back to Boston after visiting my son, Nathaniel, and his family, I was listening to "On the Media," a national weekly radio program devoted to media criticism and analysis. The guest on the program was Charles Lewis, the founder (and from 1989 until 2004, the director) of the Center for Public Integrity, a nonprofit, nonpartisan organization in Washington, DC, that does investigative reporting and research on public policy issues. The program host, Bob Garfield, was discussing with Lewis the effectiveness of his center's work in bringing about constructive change. "Let me ask you something, Don Quixote," he quipped, not very encouragingly, "what are your top three windmills that you've tilted at that you thought deserved far more public attention and media attention but somehow amounted to nothing?" Instantly comprehending the allusions to the Cervantes character Don Quixote (an impractical dreamer whose repeated efforts to right the world's wrongs came to naught) and "tilting at windmills" (a metaphoric reference to the idealistic, impractical nature of Quixote's labors), Lewis proceeded to discuss a few of his least successful endeavors. A few minutes later, Garfield asked Lewis how often his efforts resulted in real change taking place. Lewis conceded that it probably wasn't more than 10 percent of the time. "All right," Garfield interjected, "let me change mythic archetypes here. Never mind Don Quixote. [AUDIENCE LAUGHTER] Let's talk about Sisyphus"—"Yeah," Lewis broke in, "that [LAUGHS] might be more accurate [LAUGHS]." Garfield finished his interrupted sentence, describing Sisyphus "pushing the boulder perpetually up the hill." But Lewis, it is clear, had understood the metaphor from the start and didn't need to have it decoded.[10]

In this radio exchange, words like "Don Quixote" and "Sisyphus" and phrases like "tilting at windmills" served as metaphors that, even though not as widely prevalent as *woxin changdan* in China, for many Westerners required little further elucidation. If, on the other hand, the conversation had taken place before a listening audience of Chinese, most of whom would have been totally unacquainted with the Don Quixote or Sisyphus stories, such decoding would have been a necessity.

Cultural Patterning and Universal Human Patterning

Another theme that has cropped up periodically in my writing, from the beginning to the present, is the distinction between thinking and behavior that are culturally conditioned and thinking and behavior that are reflective of universal human attributes. Very early in my study of Wang Tao, I published an article in which I cautioned against overlooking "those less visible aspects" of modern Western civilization and the traditional civilization of China that, "without in any sense being identical," did nonetheless "converge or overlap." Such points of convergence between cultures that in other respects were so far apart, I suggested, could be significant in a number of ways, one of which was that "in them we have a reflection of basic human responses to inherently human—and hence to a degree supracultural—predicaments."[11]

Wang Tao, in very different language, regularly made a distinction that was akin to the one I made. During his visit to Europe in the late

1860s, after a speech before the graduating class at Oxford (in 1868), he was asked by some of the graduates to compare the *dao* (the right path or "way") of Confucius and the *dao* of Christianity. In both cases, he responded, *dao* had its basis in humanity. From one of China's classical texts, he quoted the words of a famous wise man: "The East has its sages, and in mind and principle they are one; the West has its sages, and in mind and principle they are one." In sum, he said, "The *dao* of the East and the *dao* of the West form a great unity [*datong*]." Twenty years later, Wang reiterated this stance in his critique of the view of a growing number of Chinese Westernizers that Western learning had its origins in ancient China. He forcefully rejected the parochial notion that China's culture was the only culture, historically, to have seriously concerned itself with *dao*. *Dao* belonged to humanity. Sageness was a universal quality that *all* peoples, Western and Eastern, had the capacity to generate and cherish. In fact, it was precisely this quality, natural to human beings everywhere, that gave to the human enterprise its underlying unity.[12]

In grappling with Wang Tao's understanding of the common humanity underpinning the cultures of China and the West, I became sensitized to the general issue, and it became an increasingly important aspect of my historical perspective in general. A notable example is my understanding of the Boxer uprising. Conventionally, the Boxers and the foreigners saw themselves as contrasting in just about every respect. Westerners at the turn of the twentieth century portrayed the Boxer uprising as a struggle between the forces of progress, civilization, and enlightenment, on one hand, and barbarism, savagery, superstition, and xenophobia, on the other. In China, over the past century, the uprising has been quite differently viewed, above all by those in the Marxist camp, who have shown a strong inclination to define the conflict as one between foreign imperialism and the Chinese people's patriotic resistance to this force.

I found both of these viewpoints, focusing entirely on the contrast between the Boxers and the foreigners, inadequate. Inadequate because of their failure in each instance to take into account what the two sides shared in common. In my research into the Boxer episode, I was struck by the degree to which, at the time, this struggle—as well as the circumstances surrounding it—was understood by both sides in profoundly religious terms. As a corollary to this, I noted the general tendency of each party to the conflict to view itself as acting in behalf of a supernatural force that was authentic and good—God or the gods—and the other side as representing false gods that were, at bottom, either powerless or the very embodiment of evil.[13]

For Christians at the close of the nineteenth century, God's hand was everywhere. If He wanted his flock to survive, He would deliver them from danger. If He wanted the missionaries to continue in their work, He would see to it that their material needs were satisfied. And if, as one missionary wrote in reference to the protracted drought conditions of 1900, "He thot best," God "could send relief thru rain."[14] Conversely, if the Christians faced a deadly threat like that of the Boxers, it was not because God was asleep on the job. The Boxer uprising took place because He had permitted it to happen.

What is remarkable is the degree to which contemporary Chinese—non-Boxers as well as Boxers—also viewed everything that happened in the world, including whether it rained, as being in the control of Heaven or "the gods." In fact, although the Chinese construction of reality differed greatly in specifics from that of the missionaries, in a number of broad respects it formed almost a mirror image of the missionaries' construction. The missionaries saw themselves as representatives of the Lord, sometimes describing themselves as "God's soldiers,"[15] and often believing quite literally that they had been called by Jesus Christ to go to China to labor for that country's salvation. In jingles repeated and notices circulated throughout north China in 1900 the Boxers were often portrayed in comparably salvific (and martial) terms, as "spirit soldiers" (*shenbing*) sent from Heaven to carry out a divine mission or as mortals whose bodies had been possessed by spirits (thereby rendering them divine) for the same purpose.

Again, where the missionaries constructed the Boxer movement as a satanic force, whose capacity for evil knew no bounds, the Boxers (and, one presumes, millions of Chinese sympathizers who were not active participants in the movement) saw the missionaries, and by extension all other foreigners (as well as Chinese Christians), as the root source of evil in their world, the immediate occasion for the anger of the gods. The explanation of the drought found in Boxer notices was embedded in a full-blown religious structuring of reality; the notices also provided participants in the movement with a clear program of action designed to mollify the gods and restore the cosmic balance.[16] There is every reason to believe, moreover, that this judgment held true for the population at large as well. "There come the foreign devils, that[']s why we don't have any rain," a missionary reported hearing a street boy call out in Tianjin in May 1900.[17]

The gods who withheld rain were often seen as angry, jealous, vengeful gods—gods who were prepared to punish an entire community of believers if representatives of this community either turned to other gods or violated established rules of behavior. When, on the other hand, believers perceived themselves not as harborers of miscreants but as innocents at risk in situations marked by danger, they expected their gods to perform a protective function. This function was plainly evidenced in both Boxer and Christian understandings of the role of supernatural agency in the context of war.[18]

Story and History

The main new development in my evolution as a historian (not just of China but also in general) was a fresh appreciation—I seem to have arrived at it at some point in the mid-1980s—of the importance of story and storytelling in history. If you had looked at me in the 1970s and asked, "But what about story? Where does that fit in?" I honestly wouldn't have known what you were talking about. In retrospect I would say that, although my interest in story didn't become explicit and central to my work until I began to explore the part the Goujian saga took in twentieth-century China, I was unconsciously starting to appreciate the importance of story—or "narrative," to use a somewhat more formal term—at some point in the mid-1980s in connection with the tripartite approach I had adopted in my research on the Boxers.

In the course of exploring the different ways the past may be viewed, I tried to be as clear as possible concerning what separated event, experience, and myth. As noted earlier (see chapter 7), I wrote the different parts of the book in reverse order, so that by the time I sat down to write the prologue to part 1 (The Historically Reconstructed Past), I had already drafted parts 2 (The Experienced Past) and 3 (The Mythologized Past).

With this behind me, I was in a position to distinguish with greater confidence between experience, which is messy, complicated, and opaque, and history, which brings order and clarity into the chaos. As I wrote at the time, the problem basically had to do with how we went about defining the relationship between "history" (in the sense of the history that historians write) and "reality" (in the sense of the history that people make and directly experience). This has been a very controversial issue among historians as well as philosophers and literary theorists who concern themselves with historical matters. Some individuals (like Hayden White) have taken the position that there is a fundamental discontinuity between history and reality. History, they believe, is basically narrative in form, while reality is not. Therefore, when historians write history, they impose on the past a design or structure that is alien to it. Other individuals (among whom I have found David Carr to be one of the clearest and most persuasive) argue that "narrative structure pervades our very experience of time and social existence, independently of our contemplating the past as historians." Since narrative is, for Carr, an essential component of the past reality historians seek to elucidate, the relationship between history and reality, or as he puts it, "narrative and everyday life," is one marked not by discontinuity but by continuity.[19]

My stance lies somewhere between these polar alternatives, although it is closer by far to Carr's. I agree with Carr that narrative is a basic component of everyday existence, not only for individuals but also for communities, and therefore the narrativization of the historian does not, in itself, create a disjuncture between the historically reconstructed past and the experienced past. However, there are other characteristics of the process of historical reconstruction, as practiced, that do create, if not a complete disjuncture, at least a very different set of parameters from those demarcating immediate experience.[20] At the bare minimum, all historical writing, even the best of it, entails radical simplification and compression of the past. An event, such as the Boxer episode, that took several years to unfold and spread over much of north China, is transformed into a book of a few hundred pages that can be held in the hands and read from start to finish in several hours.[21]

Although the objective of the historian is, first and foremost, to understand what happened in the past and then explain it to his or her readership, I would also caution that there is an oversimplification buried in the neat contrast between the experienced past and the historically reconstructed past that needs to be addressed. The experienced past may well be messy and chaotic to the historian, but it is not to the immediate experiencer. It is not that there isn't mess and chaos in people's lives, but our lives, to ourselves, are not messy and chaotic (or at least not generally so). And it is precisely here that the narrative function, at the level of personal experience, is so important. As we live our lives, we instinctively place them in a narrative framework. In the language of psychology, Daniel L. Schacter writes: "Memory is a central part of the brain's attempt to make sense of experience and tell coherent stories about it. These tales are all we have of our pasts, and so they are potent determinants of how we view ourselves and what we do."[22] In other words, we "tell stories" to ourselves that make sense of our experiences: biographical, not historical, sense. So it isn't entirely correct to say, paraphrasing Geoffrey Braithwaite, the narrator in *Flaubert's Parrot*, that books explain while in life things simply happen. In life, also, there is a powerful need for understanding and explanation, which all of us experience, subjectively, every moment of every day.[23]

After a good deal of ruminating, it eventually occurred to me that by the very act of disaggregating what the Boxers were all about and suggesting in some detail the different ways we might go about understanding them, I had gained greater access to the part that story played in their history. Predictably, this came to me initially in my exploration of the mythologization of the Boxer phenomenon, the final part of the book but the part that I wrote first. The contents of the mythologization chapters in *History in Three Keys*, it gradually dawned on me, were awash with stories of all sorts. As I became more sensitized to the operation of story and storytelling, it became increasingly clear that the topics dealt with in the experience section of the book—drought, magic, female pollution, spirit possession, rumor, death—were also bursting at the seams with stories. Finally, the fresh understandings of the historically reconstructed past that I gained in the course of writing *History in Three Keys* strengthened in my thinking the ways historians engage in telling stories.[24] Story had by now become an important part of the conceptual apparatus with which I approached history writing in general.

This points to an interesting enigma relating to *History in Three Keys*. Although the book didn't come out until 1997, the core ideas embodied in it were very much on my mind a dozen years earlier, precisely at the time when *Discovering History in China*, with its strong endorsement of a China-centered approach to Chinese history, was published (1984). Yet as will be recalled from my discussion of the limits of the China-centered approach (chapter 5), although there are facets of *History in Three Keys* that are China-centered, the main object of the book was to say something not about Chinese history but about the writing of history more broadly construed. As I wrote at the time, "there's nothing especially China-centered about that." In other words, at the very moment that I was introducing and endorsing the China-centered approach, I was preparing to move away from it in my own work. The resolution to this paradox, as pointed out in chapter 5, is actually fairly straightforward. My support of the China-centered approach, after all, was in reference specifically to the history of China (indeed, the title of the chapter in *Discovering History in China* in which I described the approach was "Toward a China-Centered History of China"). But in *History in Three Keys*, although the principal material I use to illustrate my analysis is drawn from the Boxer uprising in China, from the very beginning of the book I make it plain that my main purpose in it is to shed light on what historians *in general* do when they write history, China's Boxers serving as an enabler of this larger undertaking.

My next book, *Speaking to History*, was related to *History in Three Keys* in a number of ways. Most conspicuously, its focus on a well-known humiliation–revenge motif centering on the story of King Goujian demonstrated the potential of this story as a patriotic narrative, especially during the 1920s and 1930s when China was under Japanese threat. But more important, the ways the story was adapted and readapted to successive crises called to mind the changing myths (stories) about the Boxers that were created at different points in the twentieth century. Much as myths represented different ways of extracting from the Boxer past the messages mythologizers wanted to instill in people's minds in the present, fresh versions of the Goujian story were designed, consciously or unconsciously, to speak to the shifting concerns of Chinese in the twentieth century.

Earlier I referred to stories like the Goujian story as "insider cultural knowledge," in the sense that one really had to grow up in the culture to be familiar with it. Even if American historians had visited China and could converse in the language, the likelihood that the story (or even the name) of Goujian would have any meaning for them was extremely low. When I was doing research on the Goujian story, I did an informal survey of U.S. colleagues in the modern China field, all of whom spoke Chinese and had spent time in China, and not one had ever heard of Goujian (which was precisely the situation I myself was in prior to repeatedly encountering the story in the course of my work on national humiliation).

But there was a curious thing about the Goujian story. Although unknown in most of the rest of the world, it was far from being *completely* unknown. It had been influential in other parts of East Asia, including countries that at one point or another had engaged in wars against China. The use of the Chinese writing system was key. Thus, Vietnam, with a long tradition of resistance against its much larger northern neighbor, identified itself historically with Yue; and when Ming China's occupation of Vietnam was brought to an end in 1428, the great Vietnamese scholar-patriot Nguyen Trai marked the occasion in his *Binh Ngo Dai Cao* (*A Great Proclamation on the Pacification of Wu*) by equating China with Wu. It was much the same in other parts of East Asia. The story was alluded to in late Meiji Japan at times of national crisis, such as the Tripartite Intervention (1895) following the Sino-Japanese War of 1894 and again during the Russo-Japanese War (1904–5), both instances in which Japan (like Yue) faced much larger adversaries.[25] Literary references to the Goujian story also made regular appearances in the writings of East Asians with classical Chinese training and required no special explanation. In short, the point is that although the Goujian story was part of the Chinese cultural tradition, this tradition did not belong solely to China; intellectuals from elsewhere in East Asia were until quite recently also steeped in it, nurtured on the Chinese classics, much as European elites were schooled in the classical learning of Greece and Rome.[26] Not only for Chinese, but for Vietnamese, Koreans, and Japanese as well, the Goujian story was a form of insider cultural knowledge.

Speaking to History, as noted in chapter 10, also served as a point of departure for the multiple story–history interactions described in my most recent work, *History and Popular Memory*. Although one of that book's chapters focuses on the Goujian story, others deal with Serbia, France, Britain, Israel/Palestine, and the Soviet Union. This was my first book that was not primarily about China. Indeed, as previously indicated, a major part of my motivation for writing it was to place China in a wider world setting, subverting parochial perspectives that continued to cordon China off in a realm by itself.

I made the distinction earlier between aspects of my understanding as a historian that were there from the start of my career and aspects that only emerged later in my thinking. Ironically, *History and Popular Memory* in a very real sense embodied both of these aspects. A major theme in the book is a supracultural phenomenon that I describe in chapter 10 as "a different sort of world history, not the conventional kind based on conjunctures, comparisons, and influences, but one that is manifested in recurring patterns, clearly bearing a family resemblance yet independently arrived at and very possibly rooted in certain human propensities—above all, the universality of storytelling in the human experience—that transcend the specificities of culture and place." What is interesting is that this supracultural, universally human dimension, which was part of my intellectual armory from the outset (see the discussion of Wang Tao in chapter 2), is now firmly joined to storytelling, an aspect of my historical thinking that only began to come to the fore in the 1980s when I started to think about the ingredients in what became *History in Three Keys*.

Once I became convinced of the importance of stories and storytelling, it became a central feature of my thinking as a historian. I had encountered it initially in the shifting myths created about the Boxers over time. It later assumed prime importance for my understanding of the protean character of the Goujian story, which took on different guises in response to different circumstances. It lay at the heart of the "popular memory" described in my latest book. There, as we saw in the preceding chapter, I make a clear distinction between popular memory and critical history. Although for historians this distinction is of paramount importance, I note that it is routinely blurred in the minds of nonhistorians, and the historian's truth is often unable to compete with the power of a compelling story from the past that, while professing to be an account of what really happened, in fact has been seriously distorted by myth or political manipulation.

From the historian's point of view, critical history is to be preferred to popular memory. But the relationship between the two is far more difficult and complicated than is commonly acknowledged. One reason for this is that, as we have seen, popular memory often embodies a real historical component, and it is not always easy for nonhistorians—or even in many cases historians themselves—to distinguish clearly between what is fact and what is fiction. Another reason is that historians, in our efforts to reconstruct the real past, are generally (if not inevitably) faced with an insufficiency of evidence—the more complex the past under scrutiny, the greater the insufficiency—which forces us to fill in the blank spots by inferring what we think took place. The trouble is, it is hard to keep these inferences from reflecting the values and assumptions that happen to be dominant in the society in which we currently live and work, which means that even as we endeavor to challenge the old myths that encumber people's understanding of the past, we end up, however involuntarily, introducing new myths into our accounts.

So we return, at least in a sense, to the note of historical ambiguity on which this chapter opened. But only in a sense. The points made in the chapter's opening refer specifically to this memoir. But memoirs are only one form of history and a highly singular one at that. There are many other forms, and these other forms often raise issues that memoir writers tend to ignore because they're not of immediate concern. For example, the past that memoir writers seek to know—what happened *then*—encompasses a recent and well-defined period of time (generally the subject's adult life) and tends to be focused mainly on a single individual. Therefore, memoirists (at least if they are writers) only have to tell their readers what books and articles they have written, the main themes in their work, the accolades and awards they have won, the criticisms encountered, and so forth. Of course, this is a deliberately oversimplified depiction of what one is actually likely to find in a memoir, given that the writer faces countless choices and is free to decide what to include and what not to include. But in the final analysis, it remains a relatively simple operation, especially compared to what a historian of, say, the French Revolution has to contend with, where things were a lot more complicated. The past that a historian of the French Revolution seeks to know is about a huge number of diverse people, not a single person. Its spatial embrace, moreover, is vast, and it can never come close to being grasped in full, partly because many of the things that took place were never recorded and partly because much that was recorded has been forgotten. In addition, our French Revolution historian, in shaping the picture he or she wants to convey, will also consciously or unconsciously include certain items of information in his or her account and exclude other items. As pointed out in chapter 7, all historians—French Revolution historians as well as memoir writers—have personal agendas.

Which brings us to the related matter of how historians, including memoir writers, view the past now, how we understand and write about it. There will always be gaps that need closing, blank spots that need to be filled. But as historians endeavor to do this closing and filling, we have no choice but to do so in the language of our own day, to tell a story that comes as close as possible to reconstructing what actually took place *then* but in a way that speaks meaningfully to people living *now*.

In other words, historians, memoirists as well as French Revolution scholars, must be polyglot, conversant in the language of the present but also, to the extent humanly possible, in the language of the past. And it is our need to move back and forth between these two utterly different realms, each posing its own special problems of understanding, that is perhaps the greatest difficulty we face in our work. It is not a difficulty that can ever be entirely overcome—and certainly the difficulty is greater in direct proportion to the distance between then and now. But as any seasoned historian will affirm, grappling with the challenge, even embracing it, is one of our greatest sources of fulfillment as historians, taking us to the heart of the mysteries we seek to clarify and make less opaque.

Appendix

Author's Publications

This listing is arranged chronologically, based on original date of publication.

Books (English-language)

China and Christianity: The Missionary Movement and the Growth of Chinese Antiforeignism, 1860–1870 (Cambridge, MA: Harvard University Press, 1963).

Between Tradition and Modernity: Wang T'ao and Reform in Late Ch'ing China (Cambridge, MA: Harvard University Press, 1974); paperback reprint with new preface (Cambridge, MA: Council on East Asian Studies, Harvard University, 1987).

Reform in Nineteenth-Century China, coedited with John E. Schrecker (Cambridge, MA: East Asian Research Center, Harvard University, 1976).

Report on the Visit of the Young Political Leaders Delegation to the People's Republic of China (New York: National Committee on United States–China Relations, 1977).

Discovering History in China: American Historical Writing on the Recent Chinese Past (New York: Columbia University Press, 1984); second paperback ed. with new preface, 1996; reissue with new introduction by author, 2010.

Ideas Across Cultures: Essays on Chinese Thought in Honor of Benjamin I. Schwartz, coedited with Merle Goldman (Cambridge, MA: Council on East Asian Studies, Harvard University, 1990).

Fairbank Remembered, compiled with Merle Goldman (Cambridge, MA: John K. Fairbank Center for East Asian Research, Harvard University, 1992).

History in Three Keys: The Boxers as Event, Experience, and Myth (New York: Columbia University Press, 1997).

China Unbound: Evolving Perspectives on the Chinese Past (London: Routledge Curzon, 2003).

Speaking to History: The Story of King Goujian in Twentieth-Century China (Berkeley: University of California Press, 2009).
History and Popular Memory: The Power of Story in Moments of Crisis (New York: Columbia University Press, 2014).

Articles, Chapters, and Shorter Writings (English-language)

"Missionary Approaches: Hudson Taylor and Timothy Richard," *Papers on China* 11 (1957): 29–62.
"The Hunan-Kiangsi Antimissionary Incidents of 1962," *Papers on China* 12 (1958): 1–27.
"The Anti-Christian Tradition in China," *Journal of Asian Studies* 20.2 (February 1961): 169–80; reprinted in *Christian Missions in China: Evangelists of What?*, ed. Jessie Lutz (Boston: Heath, 1965).
"Some Sources of Antimissionary Sentiment during the Late Ch'ing," *Journal of the China Society* 2 (1962): 1–19.
"Wang T'ao and Incipient Chinese Nationalism," *Journal of Asian Studies* 26.4 (1967): 559–74.
"Wang T'ao's Perspective on a Changing World," in *Approaches to Modern Chinese History*, ed. Albert Feuerwerker et al. (Berkeley: University of California Press, 1967).
"Ch'ing China: Confrontation with the West, 1850–1900," in *Modern East Asia: Essays in Interpretation*, ed. James Crowley (New York: Harcourt Brace and World, 1970).
Foreword to Sidney A. Forsythe, *An American Missionary Community in China, 1895–1905* (Cambridge, MA: East Asian Research Center, Harvard University, 1971).
"Europe Goes East," in *Half the World: The History and Culture of China and Japan*, ed. Arnold Toynbee (London: Thames and Hudson, 1973).
"Littoral and Hinterland in Nineteenth-Century China: The 'Christian' Reformers," in *The Missionary Enterprise in China and America*, ed. John K. Fairbank (Cambridge, MA: Harvard University Press, 1974).
"Discussion," in *Medicine and Society in China*, ed. John Z. Bowers and Elizabeth F. Purcell (New York: Josiah Macy, Jr. Foundation, 1974), 75–81.
"The New Coastal Reformers," in *Reform in Nineteenth-Century China*, ed. Paul A. Cohen and John E. Schrecker (Cambridge, MA: East Asian Research Center, 1976).
"China Reaches a Milestone—and Relaxes: Some Signs Hint a Letup," *Boston Globe*, July 31, 1977, A3.
"Christian Missions and Their Impact to 1900," in *The Cambridge History of China*, vol. 10, ed. John K. Fairbank (Cambridge: Cambridge University Press, 1978).
"Sino-American Relations, 1850–1900," in *The Historical Precedents for Our New Relations with China* (Washington, DC: Wilson Center, Occasional Paper No. 7, 1980).
"Modern History," coauthored with Merle Goldman, in *Humanistic and Social Science Research in China*, ed. Anne F. Thurston and Jason Parker (New York: Social Science Research Council, 1980), 38–60.

"Sinological Shadowboxing: Myers and Metzger on the State of Modern China Studies in America," *Republican China* 9.1 (October 1983): 5–10.

"The Quest for Liberalism in the Chinese Past: Stepping Stone to a Cosmopolitan World or the Last Stand of Western Parochialism?—A Review of *The Liberal Tradition in China* by Wm. Theodore de Bary," *Philosophy East and West* 35.3 (July 1985): 305–10.

"'State' Domination of the China Field: Reality or Fantasy? A Reply to Robert Marks," *Modern China* 11.4 (October 1985): 510–18.

"A Reply to Professor Wm. Theodore de Bary," *Philosophy East and West* 35.4 (October 1985): 413–17.

Review essay on Jacques Gernet, *China and the Christian Impact: A Conflict of Cultures* (Cambridge: Cambridge University Press, 1985), *Harvard Journal of Asiatic Studies* 47.2 (December 1987): 674–83.

"Self-Strengthening in 'China-Centered' Perspective: The Evolution of American Historiography," in *Qingji ziqiang yundong yantaohui lunwen ji* 清季自强运动研讨会论文集 (Collected papers from the Conference on the Self-Strengthening Movement in the Late Qing) (Taipei: Institute of Modern History, Academia Sinica, 1988), 1:3–35.

"Our Proper Concerns as Historians of China: A Reply to Michael Gasster," *American Asian Review* 6.1 (Spring 1988): 1–24.

"The Post-Mao Reforms in Historical Perspective," *Journal of Asian Studies* 47.3 (August 1988): 518–40.

"Introduction," coauthored with Merle Goldman, in *Ideas Across Cultures: Essays on Chinese Thought in Honor of Benjamin I. Schwartz*, ed. Paul A. Cohen and Merle Goldman (Cambridge, MA: Council on East Asian Studies, Harvard University, 1990), 1–13.

"Response to Introduction: Situational versus Systemic Factors in Societal Evolution," in *Two Societies in Opposition: The Republic of China and the People's Republic of China after Forty Years*, ed. Ramon Myers (Stanford, CA: Hoover Institution Press, 1990), xlvii–liv.

"The Contested Past: The Boxers as History and Myth," *Journal of Asian Studies* 51.1 (February 1992): 82–113.

"John King Fairbank (24 May 1907–14 September 1991)" [biographical memoir], *Proceedings of the American Philosophical Society* 137.2 (June 1993): 279–84.

"Cultural China: Some Definitional Issues," *Philosophy East and West* 43.3 (July 1993): 557–63.

"Obituary for Lloyd Eastman," coauthored with Parks M. Coble and Patricia Ebrey, *Journal of Asian Studies* 52.4 (November 1993): 1110–12.

Foreword to Edward V. Gulick, *Teaching in Wartime China: A Photo-Memoir, 1937–1939* (Amherst: University of Massachusetts Press, 1995).

"Imagining the Red Lanterns," *Berliner China-Hefte* 12 (May 1997): 83–97.

Review essay: Daniel H. Bays, ed., *Christianity in China: From the Eighteenth Century to the Present* (Stanford: Stanford University Press, 1996), *China Review International* 5.1 (Spring 1998): 1–16.

"Time, Culture, and Christian Eschatology: The Year 2000 in the West and the World," *American Historical Review* 104.5 (December 1999): 1615–28.

"Memorial to Benjamin I. Schwartz," coauthored with Merle Goldman and Roderick MacFarquhar, *China Quarterly* 161 (March 2000): 299–301. ˙

"Introduction: Politics, Myth, and the Real Past," *Twentieth-Century China* 26.2 (April 2001): 1–15.

"The Asymmetry in Intellectual Relations between China and the West in the Twentieth Century," in *Ershi shiji de Zhongguo yu shijie: lunwen xuanji* 二十世纪的中国与世界: 论文选集 (China and the world in the twentieth century: selected essays), ed. Zhang Qixiong 张啓雄 (Taipei: Institute of Modern History, Academia Sinica, 2001), 1:61–93.

"Remembering and Forgetting the Twenty-One Demands: A Case Study in Manipulation of National Memory," in *Measuring Historical Heat: Event, Performance, and Impact in China and the West* (conference volume) (November 2001).

"Reflections on a Watershed Date: The 1949 Divide in Chinese History," in *Twentieth-Century China: New Approaches*, ed. Jeffrey N. Wasserstrom (London: Routledge, 2002). A substantially enlarged version of this essay, with the title "Ambiguities of a Watershed Date: The 1949 Divide in Chinese History," appears in Paul A. Cohen, *China Unbound: Evolving Perspectives on the Chinese Past* (London: Routledge Curzon, 2003), 131–47.

"Remembering and Forgetting National Humiliation in Twentieth-Century China," *Twentieth-Century China* 27.2 (April 2002): 1–39.

"Between China and America: The Career of Madame Chiang Kai-shek," *Wellesley* 88.2 (Winter 2004): 34–38.

Foreword to Ye Weili (with Ma Xiaodong), *Growing Up in the People's Republic: Conversations between Two Daughters of China's Revolution* (New York: Palgrave Macmillan, 2005).

"Humanizing the Boxers," in *The Boxers, China, and the World*, ed. Robert Bickers and R. T. Tiedemann (Lanham, MD: Rowman and Littlefield, 2007), 179–97.

"Epilogue: Thoughts in Response," 204–8, in "Forum: Reflections on Paul A. Cohen's Contributions to Chinese Historical Studies," *Chinese Historical Review* 14.2 (Fall 2007): 179–211.

"Coming Distractions: Speaking to History" (interview), *The China Beat*, September 26, 2008, http://thechinabeat.blogspot.com/2008/09/coming-distractions-speaking-to -history.html.

"Boxer Uprising," in *Encyclopedia of Modern China*, ed. David Pong (Farmington Hills, MI: Charles Scribner's Sons/Gale Cengage Learning, 2009), 146–48.

"The Tenacity of Culture: Old Stories in the New China," in *The People's Republic of China at 60: An International Assessment*, ed. William C. Kirby (Cambridge, MA: Harvard University Asia Center for the Fairbank Center for Chinese Studies, 2011), 388–400.

"Boxers, Christians, and the Gods: The Boxer Conflict of 1900 as a Religious War," in *Critical Readings on Religions of China*, ed. Vincent Goossaert, 4 vols. (Leiden: Brill, 2012), 4:1451–80.

Biography of Wang Tao (coauthored with Elizabeth Sinn), in *Dictionary of Hong Kong Biography*, ed. May Holdsworth and Christopher Munn (Hong Kong: Hong Kong University Press, 2012).

Biography of Hong Ren'gan, in *Dictionary of Hong Kong Biography*, ed. May Holdsworth and Christopher Munn (Hong Kong: Hong Kong University Press, 2012).

"Peter Hessler: Teacher, Archaeologist, Anthropologist, Travel Writer, Master Storyteller," *Journal of Asian Studies* 72.2 (May 2013): 251–72.

"Between History and Memory: A Conversation with Paul A. Cohen," *Chinese Historical Review* 23.1 (May 2016): 70–78 (interviewer: Hanchao Lu).

"Change over Time in Qing History: The Importance of Context," *Late Imperial China* 37.1 (June 2016): 10–13.

"Nineteenth-Century China: The Evolution of American Historical Approaches," in *A Companion to Chinese History*, ed. Michael Szonyi (Hoboken, NJ: Wiley Blackwell, 2017), 154–67.

"How Has the Way We Study China Changed in the Last Sixty Years?," in *The China Questions: Critical Insights into a Rising Power*, ed. Jennifer Rudolph and Michael Szonyi (Cambridge, MA: Harvard University Press, 2018).

"My Taipei Days: A Reminiscence," in *The Field of Chinese Language Education in the U.S.: A Retrospective of the 20th Century*, ed. Vivian Ling (London: Routledge, 2018), 337–42.

Books, Articles, and Shorter Writings (East Asian Languages)

"Meiguo de Zhongguo jindaishi yanjiu" 美国的中国近代史研究 (Research on modern Chinese history in America), *Lishi yanjiu* 历史研究 no. 2 (1980): 85–88.

"Meiguo yanjiu Qingmo-Minchu Zhongguo lishi de xin dongxiang" 美国研究清末民初中国历史的新动向 (New directions in American historical scholarship on late Qing and early Republican China), *Fudan xuebao* 复旦学报 no. 6 (1981): 73–84.

"Meiguo yanjiu Qingmo-Minchu Zhongguo lishi de xin dongxiang" 美国研究清末民初中国历史的新动向 (New directions in American historical scholarship on late Qing and early Republican China), in *Lun Qingmo Minchu Zhongguo shehui* 论清末民初中国社会 (Essays in late Qing and early Republican Chinese society), ed. Cai Shangsi 蔡尚思 et al. (Shanghai: Fudan daxue chubanshe, 1983), 317–57 (fuller treatment of previous piece bearing same title).

知の帝国主義— オリエンタリズムと中国像 (テオリア叢書)(Discovering history in China: American historical writing on the recent Chinese past), trans. Sato Shinichi 佐藤 慎一 (Tokyo: Heibonsha, 1988).

Zai Zhongguo faxian lishi: Zhongguo zhongxin guan zai Meiguo de xingqi 在中国发现历史：中国中心观在美国的兴起 (Discovering history in China: American historical writing on the recent Chinese past), trans. Lin Tongqi 林同奇 (Beijing: Zhonghua shuju, 1989); expanded edition, Zhonghua shuju, 2005; reprinted 2017 (Beijing: Zhongguo shehui kexue wenxian chubanshe [Social Sciences Academic Press]).

Zai Zhongguo faxian lishi: Zhongguo zhongxin guan zai Meiguo de xingqi 在中国发现历史：中国中心观在美国的兴起 (Discovering history in China: American historical writing on the recent Chinese past), trans. Lin Tongqi 林同奇 (Taipei: Daoxiang chubanshe, 1991).

Meiguo de Zhongguo jindaishi yanjiu: Huigu yu qianzhan 美国的中国近代史研究： 回顾与前瞻 (Discovering history in China: American historical writing on the recent Chinese past), author: 柯保安（Chinese name used in Taiwan), trans. Li Rongtai 李荣泰, proofreader: Gu Weiying 古伟瀛 (Taipei: Lianjing Publishing, 1991).

"You zhengyi de wangshi: zuo wei lishi yu shenhua de Yihetuan" 有争议的往事： 作为历史与神话的义和团 (The contested past: The Boxers as history and myth), in *Yihetuan yundong yu jindai Zhongguo shehui guoji xueshu taolunhui lunwen ji* 义和团运动与近代中国社会国际学术讨论会论文集 (Collected articles from the international conference on the Boxer movement and modern Chinese society) (Jinan: Qi-Lu shushe, 1992).

"Wo de xueshu shengya" (My scholarly career), *Wenshizhe* 文史哲 (Literature, history, and philosophy) 2 (March 1994): 61–63.

"We de laoshi Fei Zhengqing" 我的老师费正清 (My teacher John King Fairbank), *Wenshizhe* 3 (May 1994): 72–75, 71.

Zai Zhongguo faxian lishi, xin xu 在中国发现历史，新序 (New preface to *Discovering History in China*), *Lishi yanjiu* 6 (December 1996): 95–105.

"Yi renleixue guandian kan Yihetuan" 以 人类学观点看义和团 (Anthropological perspectives on the Boxers), *Ershiyi shiji* 二十一世纪 (Twenty-first century) 45 (February 1998): 93–102.

Zai chuantong yu xiandaixing zhi jian: Wang Tao yu wan Qing geming 在传统与现代性之间：王韬与晚清革命 (Between tradition and modernity: Wang T'ao and reform in late Ch'ing China), trans. Lei Yi 雷颐 and Luo Jianqiu 罗检秋 (Nanjing: Jiangsu renmin chubanshe, 1998).

"Lijie guoqu de san tiao tujing: Zuowei shijian, jingyan he shenhua de Yihetuan"理解过去的三条途径： 作为事件，经验 和神话 的 义和团 (Three pathways toward understanding the past: The Boxers as event, experience, and myth), *Shijie hanxue* 世界汉学 (World Sinology) 1 (May 1998): 122–32.

"Ershi shiji wanqi Zhong-Xi zhi jian de zhishi jiaoliu" 二十世纪晚期中-西之间 的 知识交流 (Knowledge flows between China and the West in the late twentieth century), *Wenshizhe* 4 (June 1998): 21–29.

Fei Zhengqing de Zhongguo shijie: tong shidai ren de huiyi 费正清的中国世界：同时代人的回忆 (Fairbank remembered), compiled with Merle Goldman, trans. Zhu Zhenghui 朱政惠 et al. (Shanghai: Dongfang chuban zhongxin: Xin hua shudian Shanghai faxingsuo jingxiao, 2000).

Lishi san diao: zuowei shijian, jingli he shenhua de Yihetuan 历史三调：作为事件，经历和神话的义和团 (History in three keys: The Boxers as event, experience, and myth), trans. Du Jidong 杜继东 (Nanjing: Jiangsu renmin chubanshe, 2000).

"Yihetuan, Jidutu, he shen: Cong zongjiao zhanzheng jiaodu kan 1900 nian de Yihetuan douzheng" 义和团，基督徒，和神：从宗教战争角度看 1900 年的义和团斗争 (Boxers, Christians, and the gods: The Boxer conflict of 1900 seen as a religious war), *Lishi yanjiu* 1 (February 2001): 17–28. Also in *Yihetuan yanjiu 100 zhounian guoji xueshu taolunhui lunwen ji* 义和团研究 100 周年国际学术讨论会论文集 (Collected essays from the international conference on the 100th anniversary of Boxer studies), ed. Su Weizhi 苏位智and Liu Tianlu 刘天路 (Jinan: Shandong daxue chubanshe, 2002), 1:59–80.

"Zhongguo zhongxinguan de youlai ji qi fazhan: Kewen jiaoshou fangtan lu" 中国中心观的由来及其发展： 柯文教授访谈录 (The origins and development of the China-centered approach: Transcript of interview with Professor Paul A. Cohen), *Shilin* 史林 4 (November 2002): 32–42.

"Biandongzhong de zhongguo lishi yanjiu shijiao" 变动中的中国历史研究视角 (Evolving perspectives on the Chinese past), *Ershiyi shiji* 78 (August 2003): 34–49; reprinted in 2005 edition of Zhonghua shuju translation of *Discovering History in China*, 246–76.

Hak Moon ei: Jae Gook Ju ei (Discovering history in China: American historical writing on the recent Chinese past), trans. Lee Nam Lee (Seoul: Sanhae Publishing, 2003); new edition 2013 (Seoul: SCH Press).

"Shixue yanjiu de biaoqian baozheng" 史学研究的标签暴政 (The tyranny of labels in historical studies), *Ershiyi shiji* 87 (February 2005): 118–19.

"Goujian gushi zai 20 shiji Zhongguo: Kua wenhua shijiao" 勾践故事在 20 世纪中国：跨文化视角 (The Goujian story in 20th-century China: Cross-cultural perspectives), in *Shihuaci yu Zhongguo* 史华慈与中国 (Schwartz and China), ed. Xu Jilin 许纪霖 and Zhu Zhenghui 朱政惠 (Changchun: Jilin chuban jituan youxian zeren gongsi, 2008), 427–50.

"Lishi shuxie de wusheng zhi chu: yiwei lishixuezhe de zibai—yi *Lishi san diao: zuowei shijian, jingli he shenhua de Yihetuan* de zhuanxie wei li" 历史书写的无声之处：一位历史学者的自白—以《历史三调：作为事件，经历和神话的义和团》的撰写为例 (Silences in historical writing: A historian's confessions—using the writing of *History in Three Keys: The Boxers as Event, Experience, and Myth* as an example), *Wenshizhe* 3 (May 2012): 5–12.

Lishi san diao: zuowei shijian, jingli he shenhua de Yihetuan; reissued with corrections and new author's introduction (*Lishi sandiao* 《历史三调》中文再版序), trans. Du Jidong 杜继东 (Beijing: Zhongguo shehui kexue wenxian chubanshe [Social Sciences Academic Press], 2014); new author's introduction was also published in *Lanzhou xuekan* 兰州学刊 (November 2014), with the additional title "Lishi shishi yu lishi xuxie" 历史事实与历史叙写 (Historical facts and historical narrative).

Zai chuantong yu xiandaixing zhi jian: Wang Tao yu wan Qing gaige 在传统与现代性之间：王韬与晚清改革, trans. 雷颐 and 罗检秋 (Beijing: Citic Publishing Group, 2016).

Notes

Introduction

1. Benedict Anderson, *A Life Beyond Boundaries* (London and Brooklyn: Verso, 2016), 101; see also 189–90. Compare Anderson's emphasis on the importance of cultural difference to that of the historian H. Stuart Hughes, one of my graduate school teachers at Harvard. Hughes's parents took him on a tour of Europe at age eight, which resulted in a discovery not entirely different from mine after my first trip abroad. He was "traumatized," Jeremy D. Popkin writes, "by some of the things he saw, such as wax models of prisoners in the medieval dungeons of Mont-Saint-Michel," but he was also "attracted by the differentness of life in another country" (*History, Historians, and Autobiography* [Chicago: University of Chicago Press, 2005], 132). Unlike me, Hughes claims in his autobiography to have immediately sensed the connection between his travel experiences and his later decision to become a historian: "And so this early I had discovered my vocation: I was to be a historian of Europe. To pursue the study of history . . . was the only way to sort out the confused and contradictory residue of my travels" (*Gentleman Rebel: The Memoirs of H. Stuart Hughes* [New York: Ticknor & Fields, 1990], 24).

2. David Lowenthal, *The Past Is a Foreign Country* (Cambridge: Cambridge University Press, 1985). The opening line of Hartley's novel *The Go-Between* (London: Hamish Hamilton, 1953): "The past is a foreign country; they do things differently there."

Chapter 1. Beginnings

1. Paul A. Cohen, *China and Christianity: The Missionary Movement and the Growth of Chinese Antiforeignism, 1860–1870* (Cambridge, MA: Harvard University Press, 1963), vii.

2. Ryan Dunch, "On *China and Christianity*," in "Paul A. Cohen's Contributions to Chinese Historical Studies," special issue of *Chinese Historical Review* 14.2 (Fall 2007): 183. The Zongli Yamen was a special office established by the Qing government in 1861 to handle China's relations with foreigners.

3. Paul A. Cohen and Hanchao Lu, "Between History and Memory: A Conversation with Paul A. Cohen," *Chinese Historical Review* 23.1 (May 2016): 72. A copy of the standing invitation to the Thursday afternoon teas is found in Ronald Suleski, *The Fairbank Center for East Asian Research at Harvard University: A Fifty Year History, 1955–2005* (Cambridge, MA: John K. Fairbank Center for East Asian Research, Harvard University, 2005); it is among the images following page 144.

4. "Missionary Approaches: Hudson Taylor and Timothy Richard," *Papers on China* 11 (1957): 29–62.

5. Fairbank's article was "Patterns behind the Tientsin Massacre," *Harvard Journal of Asiatic Studies* 20 (1957): 480–511.

6. "The Hunan-Kiangsi Anti-Missionary Incidents of 1862," *Papers on China* 12 (1958): 1–27.

7. Cohen, *China and Christianity*, chapter 3, esp. 86–109.

8. Ma Jingheng, one of my teachers in Taipei, asked me to write a short essay on my experience studying Chinese in Taiwan, to be included in a larger study she and Vivian Ling were working on dealing with Chinese language training among Americans in the twentieth century. This section is partly drawn from Paul A. Cohen, "My Taipei Days: A Reminiscence" in *The Field of Chinese Language Education in the U.S.: A Retrospective of the 20th Century*, ed. Vivian Ling (London: Routledge, 2018), 337–42.

9. An exception to this pattern was found in those women who pursued doctorates in Chinese studies and went on to productive academic careers. Examples that come to mind from my Harvard experience were Merle Goldman, who taught at Boston University, while her husband, a specialist on the Soviet economy, taught at Wellesley College, and Mary Rankin, who worked as an independent scholar in Washington, DC, where her husband was based as a geologist.

10. Jeremy D. Popkin, *History, Historians, and Autobiography* (Chicago: University of Chicago Press, 2005), 146–47. See also the interview with Davis in Henry Abelove et al., eds., *Visions of History* (New York: Pantheon, 1984), 99–122. The Australian historian Jill Ker Conway, one of Davis's close colleagues in the History Department of the University of Toronto in the late 1960s and later a president of Smith College, wrote of the near impossibility, after doing graduate work at Harvard, of a woman landing a teaching position there in the early 1960s. *True North: A Memoir* (New York: Vintage Books, 1995), 31, 58–59; see also Popkin, *History, Historians, and Autobiography*, 147–48.

11. Jane Kramer, "Eat, Memory," *New Yorker*, September 19, 2016, 84. Janet Yellen, former chair of the Federal Reserve, noted in a speech on May 5, 2017, that only with the passage of a new law in 1974 were women allowed to apply for loans without a male cosigner. Binyamin Appelbaum, "To Lift Growth, Help Women Go to Work, Fed Chief Says," *New York Times*, May 6, 2017, B3.

12. Interview with Philip Galanes, "The Road to Activism," *New York Times* (Style Section), September 18, 2016, 17.

13. Fairbank, letter to author, November 15, 1960.

14. Fairbank, letter to author, March 20, 1961.

15. Feuerwerker, letter to author, December 6, 1961.

16. The Harvard-Yenching Library had the longer work *Pi-hsieh chi-shih* (*Bixie ji-shi*) (which I dealt with at length in *China and Christianity*), but not the *Pi-hsieh shih-lu*, which was a condensed version of the *Pi-hsieh chi-shih* and appears to have been much better known within the missionary community. The translation was produced by missionaries in Tengchow (Dengzhou), Shandong, and published in Shanghai in 1870.

17. Letter to Fairbank, June 28, 1961; Fairbank, letter to author, July 27, 1961.

18. Fairbank, letter to author, June 20, 1961.

19. Letter to Fairbank, August 12, 1961.

20. The book that resulted from Irv's efforts was *Christian Converts and Social Protest in Meiji Japan* (Berkeley: University of California Press, 1970).

21. Letter to Fairbank, October 8, 1962. I should note that during the latter half of the 1950s, when I was still doing coursework, the practice of graduate students serving as teaching assistants hadn't yet begun, at least in the introductory Chinese history offerings. As a result, prior to reaching Michigan, I had had no experience whatever standing up in front of a class.

22. In early December, I wrote a long memo to Alex on what I thought the University of Michigan's priorities should be in regard to the expansion of Chinese studies. Many of the points made in the memo were drawn from a letter I had previously written to Feuerwerker.

23. Letter from Thomas J. Wilson (Harvard University Press director) to Fairbank, June 12, 1962, enclosed in Fairbank, June 18, 1962.

24. Letter to Fairbank, October 8, 1962.

25. Letter to Chen Zenghui, June 3, 1985. The title of the bibliography was *Jiao'an shiliao bianmu* (*A bibliography of Chinese source materials dealing with local and international cases involving Christian missions*) (Beiping: Yanjing University Department of Religious Studies, 1941).

26. Shortly before accepting the Wellesley job, I received a letter (dated January 20, 1965) from Fairbank formally inviting me to become an associate of the East Asian Research Center.

Chapter 2. Wang Tao

1. Paul A. Cohen, *Between Tradition and Modernity: Wang T'ao and Reform in Late Ch'ing China* (Cambridge, MA: Harvard University Press, 1974).

2. This abbreviated account of Wang Tao's life is closely based on Paul A. Cohen and Elizabeth Sinn, "Wang Tao," in *Dictionary of Hong Kong Biography*, ed. May Holdsworth and Christopher Munn (Hong Kong: Hong Kong University Press, 2012), 449–52.

3. The issue of Western influence as the main source of change in the late Qing is taken up in the preface I wrote to the paperback edition of *Between Tradition and*

Modernity (Cambridge, MA: Council on East Asian Studies, Harvard University, 1987), viii–x. See also the last section of this chapter.

4. John K. Fairbank, *China: The People's Middle Kingdom and the U.S.A.* (Cambridge, MA: Harvard University Press, 1967), 104. This section is drawn with minor modifications from Cohen, *Between Tradition and Modernity*, 143–53.

5. Wang Tao, *Taoyuan wenlu waibian* (Additional essays of Wang Tao) (Hong Kong, 1883), 7:19a–b.

6. Wang's rebuttal appears in *Taoyuan wenlu waibian*, 7:15b–19.

7. A similar theme is pursued in *Taoyuan wenlu waibian*, 5:16b.

8. The *Yijing* formula was widely quoted by nineteenth-century protagonists of reform. Its meaning, according to Yang Lien-sheng, was similar to Kroeber's "exhaustion of possibilities." See Yang's "Chaodai jian de bisai" (Dynastic comparison and dynastic competition), in *Qingzhu Li Ji xiansheng qishi sui lunwen ji* (Symposium in honor of Dr. Li Chi on his seventieth birthday), vol. 1 (Taibei: Qinghua xuebao she, 1965), 146.

9. Michael Gasster, "Reform and Revolution in China's Political Modernization," in *China in Revolution: The First Phase, 1900–1913*, ed. Mary C. Wright (New Haven, CT: Yale University Press, 1968), 83 (emphasis in original).

10. The role of story and storytelling is dealt with extensively later in this memoir.

11. Referring to Japanese political modernization, Robert E. Ward says: "While the complete modern political synthesis may date only from the 1860s and 1870s, basic elements of that synthesis . . . have histories that go back from one and a half to five or six centuries beyond that. This substantially alters the traditional time perspective on the political modernization of Japan. It is seen in these terms not as a process that has taken place in the single century that has intervened since the Restoration but as a cumulative product of two and a half to six or seven centuries of gradual preparation, the last century of which was characterized by a greatly increased pace and scope of political change." See Ward's epilogue in Robert E. Ward, ed., *Political Development in Modern Japan* (Princeton, NJ: Princeton University Press, 1968), 580; see also Gasster, "Reform and Revolution," 84.

12. Paul A. Cohen, "Ch'ing China: Confrontation with the West, 1850–1900," in *Modern East Asia: Essays in Interpretation*, ed. James B. Crowley (New York: Harcourt, Brace, & World, 1970), 48–49. In his stimulating work, Cyril E. Black, *The Dynamics of Modernization: A Study in Comparative History* (New York: Harper and Row, 1966), adopts a worldwide perspective and argues for the existence of seven distinct patterns of political modernization. Significantly, he views China and Japan as belonging to the same pattern (along with Russia, Iran, Turkey, Afghanistan, Ethiopia, and Thailand).

13. Patriotic twentieth-century Chinese, in an effort to emancipate modern Chinese history from the grip of the Western impact, have argued that the seeds of capitalism and modern science were planted in China from the late Ming onward—prior to the full onslaught of the West. Even if this is granted, it pales in significance compared with developments in Tokugawa Japan. For a critique of the view that modern scientific thought emerged independently in the early Qing, see Joseph R. Levenson, *Confucian China and Its Modern Fate: The Problem of Intellectual Continuity* (Berkeley: University of California Press, 1958), 3–14.

14. Mary C. Wright, *The Last Stand of Chinese Conservatism: The T'ung-chih Restoration, 1862–1874* (Stanford, CA: Stanford University Press, 1957), 274.

15. See Cohen, *Between Tradition and Modernity*, 67–73.

16. The evolution of Wang's justifications for change is discussed in Leong Sow-theng, "Wang T'ao and the Movement for Self-strengthening and Reform in the Late Ch'ing Period," *Papers on China* 17 (1963): 118ff.

17. Wang, *Taoyuan wenlu waibian*, 1:10; see also 1:12b, 5:17.

18. Wang, *Taoyuan wenlu waibian*, 1:10, 13, 11:13b.

19. Cohen, *Between Tradition and Modernity*, 69, 138–39, 152–53, 181, 235.

20. So many, in fact, that one frustrated reviewer charged me with "stretching the foot to fit the sock." See C. A. Curwen, *Bulletin of the School of Oriental and African Studies* 39.3 (1976): 683–84. Another reviewer who found fault with the last part was W. S. Atwell, *China Quarterly* 67 (September 1976): 640–43. The reactions of most people, on the other hand, were generally quite favorable. See, for example, Jerome B. Grieder, *Intellectuals and the State in Modern China: A Narrative History* (New York: Free Press, 1981), 130–31, 379.

21. Two important books that make a persuasive case for much higher levels of hinterland commercialization during the late Qing than had previously been acknowledged are William T. Rowe, *Hankow: Commerce and Society in a Chinese City, 1796–1889* (Stanford, CA: Stanford University Press, 1984), and Susan Mann, *Local Merchants and the Chinese Bureaucracy, 1750–1950* (Stanford, CA: Stanford University Press, 1987). On the basis of her findings, Mann explicitly questions (*Local Merchants*, 27) the validity of my suggested division of late imperial China into two distinct cultural environments. I find this part of her argument less persuasive for two reasons. First, no matter how commercialized one judges the economy of the hinterland to have become by late Qing times, it still rested on an economic base that was massively agrarian; these emphases are exactly reversed in the case of the littoral culture, which, I remain convinced, "was more commercial than agricultural in its economic foundations" (*Between Tradition and Modernity*, 241). Second, even if it should be proved that the economic contrast between littoral and hinterland was much less pronounced than I had once supposed, this still leaves the noneconomic terms of the contrast—degree of exposure to Western influence, elite value orientations, administrative and legal arrangements, and the like—basically intact.

22. Feng's best-known work on reform, *Jiaobinlu kangyi* (Straightforward words from the Jiaobin studio), was composed in Shanghai around 1860 (the preface is dated 1861). The edition I saw was published in Shanghai by the Guangren tang in 1897.

23. Liu was visiting Boston at the time in connection with the filming of *The Gate of Heavenly Peace*, a documentary about the Tiananmen events produced by Carma Hinton and Richard Gordon of the Long Bow Group (Brookline, MA). Liu spoke to my students in Chinese, with Carma interpreting for him. He also gave an evening lecture at Wellesley on "Popular Culture in Post-Tiananmen China."

24. Liu Xiaobo's lawyers and the Chinese prison authorities announced on June 26, 2017, that Liu had recently been given medical parole to be treated for liver cancer, which was likely to be terminal. Chris Buckley and Austin Ramzy, "China Paroles Imprisoned Peace Laureate for Treatment of Late-Stage Liver Cancer," *New York Times*, June 27, 2017, A7. Liu Xiaobo died in hospital on July 13, 2017.

25. Xin Ping, *Wang Tao pingzhuan* (Shanghai: Huadong Shifan Daxue chubanshe, 1990).

Chapter 3. The Next Step

1. For Fairbank's account of McCarthyism and its effects on Lattimore and himself, see his *Chinabound: A Fifty-Year Memoir* (New York: Harper & Row, 1982), 331–51.

2. The paper was titled "United States Temporary Visa Policy: Its Effects on the Foreign Scientist and on American National Interest." The prize was awarded in spring 1955. As an example of the effect of the government's policy, the brilliant English physicist P. A. M. Dirac, who shared the 1933 Nobel Prize in Physics with Erwin Schrödinger, was refused an entry visa to the United States in 1954 (probably because of his friendship with several Soviet scientists and his sympathy for Stalin's government in the 1930s). Eric Hobsbawm, *Interesting Times: A Twentieth-Century Life* (New York: New Press, 2002), 183; Graham Farmelo, "Paul Dirac: The Mozart of Science," available at http://www.ias.edu/ideas/2008/farmelo-on-dirac (accessed November 4, 2016). The sensitivities of the U.S. government in this area lasted long after the demise of McCarthyism and affected nonscientists as well as scientists. By the 1970s, Hobsbawm had become, as he put it, "an academically, if not politically, respectable and recognized figure," his membership in the Communist Party of Great Britain "seen as little more than the personal peculiarity of a well-known historian, one of that new species[,] the jet-plane academic. Only America refused to forget about Hobsbawm the subversive, for, until the abrogation of the Smith Act in the late 1980s, I remained ineligible for a visa to enter the USA and required a 'waiver' of this ineligibility every time I went there, which was more or less every year." Hobsbawm, *Interesting Times*, 304; see also 389–91.

3. In connection with the struggle to acquire the skills of a historian, Jeremy Popkin refers to "the need to prove oneself worthy in the eyes of established members of the group one seeks to enter." *History, Historians, and Autobiography* (Chicago: University of Chicago Press, 2005), 140.

4. The full text of the speech is available at http://www.historians.org/about-aha-and-membership/aha-history-and-archives/presidential-addresses/john-k-fairbank#25 (accessed August 17, 2016).

5. The introduction to this chapter is drawn in part from the preface to the original edition of Paul A. Cohen, *Discovering History in China: American Historical Writing on the Recent Chinese Past* (New York: Columbia University Press, 1984), ix–xiii; also in the expanded reissue of 2010, xxix–xxxiii.

6. Paul A. Cohen, *China and Christianity: The Missionary Movement and the Growth of Chinese Antiforeignism, 1860–1870* (Cambridge, MA: Harvard University Press, 1963), 264–65.

7. It was a very different matter in the eighteenth century (and in some respects earlier), when China's impact on the thought world, decorative arts, and economy of Europe was substantial, as has been generally recognized.

8. Paul A. Cohen, "Ch'ing China: Confrontation with the West, 1850–1900," in *Modern East Asia: Essays in Interpretation*, ed. James B. Crowley (New York: Harcourt, Brace, & World, 1970), 29–30; the Schwartz quotation is from Benjamin Schwartz, *In*

Search of Wealth and Power: Yen Fu and the West (Cambridge, MA: Harvard University Press, 1964), 1–2.

9. This is very clearly seen in some of Fairbank's more influential writings. See especially Ssu-yü Teng and John K. Fairbank, *China's Response to the West: A Documentary Survey, 1839–1923* (Cambridge, MA: Harvard University Press, 1954), and the portions of John K. Fairbank, *The United States and China*, 4th ed. (Cambridge, MA: Harvard University Press, 1979) dealing with the nineteenth century.

10. Cohen, "Ch'ing China," 29–61; and, as revised, in Paul A. Cohen, *Discovering History in China: American Historical Writing on the Recent Chinese Past* (New York: Columbia University Press, 2010 [1984]), 9–55.

11. Teng and Fairbank, *China's Response to the West*, 1.

12. Wilbert E. Moore and Neil J. Smeltzer, foreword, in S. N. Eisenstadt, *Modernization: Protest and Change* (Englewood Cliffs, NJ: Prentice Hall, 1966), iii.

13. Condorcet and Hegel are quoted in Raymond Dawson, "Western Conceptions of Chinese Civilization," in *The Legacy of China*, ed. Raymond Dawson (Oxford: Clarendon Press, 1964), 14–15. Something akin to the stance of Condorcet and Hegel was also expressed in the early 1960s by the historian Hugh Trevor-Roper, who opened a televised lecture on "The Rise of Christian Europe" with the following: "Perhaps in the future there will be some African history to teach. But at present there is none: there is only the history of the Europeans in Africa. The rest is darkness." Quoted in Roland Oliver, *In the Realms of Gold: Pioneering in African History* (London: Frank Cass, 1997), 284; see also Popkin, *History, Historians, and Autobiography*, 175.

14. Levenson's views are discussed in greater detail in Cohen, *Discovering History in China*, 61–79.

15. Mary C. Wright, *The Last Stand of Chinese Conservatism: The T'ung-chih Restoration, 1862–1874*, rev. ed. (New York: Atheneum, 1965), 9–10, 300; Albert Feuerwerker, *China's Early Industrialization: Sheng Hsuan-huai (1844–1916) and Mandarin Enterprise* (Cambridge, MA: Harvard University Press, 1958).

16. Benjamin Schwartz, "History and Culture in the Thought of Joseph Levenson," in *The Mozartian Historian: Essays on the Work of Joseph R. Levenson*, ed. Maurice Meisner and Rhoads Murphey (Berkeley: University of California Press, 1976), 108–9.

17. Lloyd I. Rudolph and Susanne Hoeber Rudolph, *The Modernity of Tradition: Political Development in India* (Chicago: University of Chicago Press, 1972 [1967]), 4–6.

18. James Peck, "Revolution versus Modernization and Revisionism: A Two-Front Struggle," in *China's Uninterrupted Revolution: From 1840 to the Present*, ed. Victor Nee and James Peck (New York: Pantheon, 1975), 88, 90; see also Victor Nee and James Peck, "Introduction: Why Uninterrupted Revolution?" in the same volume (6).

19. Nee and Peck, "Introduction," 3.

20. Philip Kuhn, *Rebellion and Its Enemies in Late Imperial China: Militarization and Social Structure, 1796–1864* (Cambridge, MA: Harvard University Press, 1970), 1–2, 5–6. Although the monetization of the Chinese economy was to some extent due to the inflow of foreign silver and was thus of partly exogenous origin, Kuhn (51) suggests that population explosion alone might have spelled "disaster of a new sort for traditional Chinese society." Although here, too, exogenous factors were at work, a number of studies

appear to place more weight on internal causation (Cohen, *Discovering History in China*, 210, n. 59).

21. "Introduction: The Evolution of Local Control in Late Imperial China," in *Conflict and Control in Late Imperial China*, ed. Frederic Wakeman Jr. and Carolyn Grant (Berkeley: University of California Press, 1975), 2.

22. Pioneering province- and county-level studies are discussed in Cohen, *Discovering History in China*, 166–69; see also the illuminating work by Stephen R. Platt, *Provincial Patriots: The Hunanese and Modern China* (Cambridge, MA: Harvard University Press, 2007).

23. For a summation of Skinner's ideas, which exercised great influence over both Western and Chinese scholarship, see Cohen, *Discovering History in China*, 164–66.

24. The areas of education, literacy, and religion and rebellion at the popular level are discussed in Cohen, *Discovering History in China*, 173–79.

25. For an interesting, theoretically oriented discussion of the "new social history," see James A. Henretta, "Social History as Lived and Written," *American Historical Review* 84.5 (December 1979): 1293–1322; the interaction between history and the social sciences is viewed in broader historical perspective in Lawrence Stone, "History and the Social Sciences in the Twentieth Century," in his *The Past and the Present* (Boston: Routledge & Kegan Paul, 1981), 3–44.

26. See Cohen, *Discovering History in China*, 180–83, for the influence of anthropology on the work of Philip Kuhn and Elizabeth Perry.

27. Philip Kuhn, "The Taiping Rebellion," in *The Cambridge History of China*, vol. 10, *Late Ch'ing, 1800–1911*, Part 1, ed. John K. Fairbank (Cambridge: Cambridge University Press, 1978), 264; William Rowe, *China's Last Empire: The Great Qing* (Cambridge, MA: Harvard University Press, 2009), 198–200.

28. See Philip D. Curtin, "African History," in *The Past Before Us: Contemporary Historical Writing in the United States*, ed. Michael Kammen (Ithaca, NY: Cornell University Press, 1980), 113–30, esp. 119–30; Nicki Keddie, "The History of the Muslim Middle East," in *The Past Before Us: Contemporary Historical Writing in the United States*, ed. Michael Kammen (Ithaca, NY: Cornell University Press, 1980), 131–56, esp. 141, 148, 151, 154–55; Charles Gibson, "Latin America and the Americas," in *The Past Before Us: Contemporary Historical Writing in the United States*, ed. Michael Kammen (Ithaca, NY: Cornell University Press, 1980), 187–202, esp. 194–95.

29. This section is adapted from the introduction to *Discovering History in China*, 6–7.

Chapter 4. Discovering History in China

1. Cochran, letter to author, April 20, 1987. For another comment on the book's value for teaching purposes, see Hanchao Lu, "A Double-sided Mirror: On Paul Cohen's *Discovering History in China*," part of a special forum titled "Paul A. Cohen's Contribution to Chinese Historical Studies," *Chinese Historical Review* 14.2 (Fall 2007): 189–91.

2. The proposal for the roundtable came from Tobie Meyer-Fong and Janet Theiss, the editor and associate editor, respectively, of *Late Imperial China*. The panelists were R. Bin Wong, Robert Bickers, Li Huaiyin, Joan Judge, and Michael Chang.

3. Li Huaiyin, *Reinventing Modern China: Imagination and Authenticity in Chinese Historical Writing* (Honolulu: University of Hawai'i Press, 2013).

4. See Hanchao Lu, "A Double-sided Mirror," 189–91; also Paul A. Cohen, "Epilogue: Thoughts in Response," in the special forum "Reflections on Paul A. Cohen's Contributions to Chinese Historical Studies," *Chinese Historical Review* 14.2 (Fall 2007): 205–6.

5. In this summation of my response to the readers' reports (dated June 3, 1981), I have changed the spelling of Chinese names and terms to pinyin and have, for the sake of convenience, referred to the two external reviewers (whose identities are unknown to me) as male.

6. Cohen, "Ch'ing China: Confrontation with the West, 1850–1900," in *Modern East Asia: Essays in Interpretation*, ed. James B. Crowley (New York: Harcourt, Brace, & World, 1970), 29–61.

7. The reference is to the well-known historian of Chinese science Joseph Needham.

8. Letter to editor, *Bulletin of Concerned Asian Scholars* 2.4 (Fall 1970): 118.

9. Paul Cohen and John Schrecker, eds., *Reform in Nineteenth-Century China* (Cambridge, MA: East Asian Research Center, Harvard University, 1976).

10. The letter, which was dated November 30, 1990, nicely conveys John's characteristic editorial thoroughness as well as a new sense of urgency:

Dear Paul:
You will see that this MS tries to give an up-to-date introductory overview, introducing the reader to major topics and issues in Chinese history to 1991, stressing work recently published and interpretations currently under discussion.
Because the text neglects art and literature, the illustrations will deal largely with objects d'art.
Of course I do not expect you to take the time to go through the whole MS. I hope you will look only at what interests you but give me guidance on these questions:
What is omitted that even at this introductory level *should not be omitted*?
What is included that on the whole *need not be included*?
Most important, what *concepts* and *books* seem inadequately represented? What *authors*?
Still to come to you:
The *last two* chapters on the Cultural Revolution and Deng's reforms of the 1980s.
The *map* program plus the *Suggested Readings* arranged by topics.
If you can give me comments by February it will be a great help.

11. The preceding several paragraphs are adapted from the tribute I wrote after Fairbank's death, as found in Paul A. Cohen and Merle Goldman, comps., *Fairbank Remembered* (Cambridge, MA: John K. Fairbank Center for East Asian Research, Harvard University, 1992), 282–84.

12. See the two letters I wrote to Aida Donald, both dated May 5, 1991, one containing general thoughts about the work, the other specific suggestions for changes.

13. The full title of Borg's book was *The United States and the Far Eastern Crisis, 1933–1938: From the Manchurian Incident through the Initial Stage of the Undeclared Sino-Japanese War.*

14. See the obituary for Borg in the *New York Times*, October 28, 1993; for more detail on her life, see Warren I. Cohen, ed., *New Frontiers in American–East Asian Relations: Essays Presented to Dorothy Borg* (New York: Columbia University Press, 1983), xvii–xxiv.

15. *Discovering History in China: American Historical Writing on the Recent Chinese Past* (New York: Columbia University Press, 1984), xiii–xiv; in expanded 2010 edition, xxxiii–xxxiv.

16. Cohen, ed., *New Frontiers in American–East Asian Relations.*

Chapter 5. Limits of the China-Centered Approach

1. Portions of this chapter are based on my "Introduction to the 2010 Reissue: Further Reflections on the China-Centered Approach to Chinese History," in Paul A. Cohen, *Discovering History in China: American Historical Writing on the Recent Chinese Past* (New York: Columbia University Press, 2010); the "Introduction to the 2010 Reissue," in turn, was adapted from Paul A. Cohen, "Introduction: China Unbound" in my *China Unbound: Evolving Perspectives on the Chinese Past* (London: Routledge Curzon, 2003), 1–22.

2. Madeleine Zelin, *The Magistrate's Tael: Rationalizing Fiscal Reform in Eighteenth-Century Ch'ing China* (Berkeley: University of California Press, 1984); William T. Rowe, *Hankow: Commerce and Society in a Chinese City, 1796–1889* (Stanford, CA: Stanford University Press, 1984); Benjamin A. Elman, *From Philosophy to Philology: Intellectual and Social Aspects of Change in Late Imperial China* (Cambridge, MA: Council on East Asian Studies, Harvard University, 1984); Philip C. C. Huang, *The Peasant Economy and Social Change in North China* (Stanford, CA: Stanford University Press, 1985); Mary Backus Rankin, *Elite Activism and Political Transformation in China: Zhejiang Province, 1865–1911* (Stanford, CA: Stanford University Press, 1986); Prasenjit Duara, *Culture, Power, and the State: Rural North China, 1900–1942* (Stanford, CA: Stanford University Press, 1988); James M. Polachek, *The Inner Opium War* (Cambridge, MA: Council on East Asian Studies, Harvard University, 1992); Kathryn Bernhardt, *Rents, Taxes, and Peasant Resistance: The Lower Yangzi Region, 1840–1950* (Stanford, CA: Stanford University Press, 1992).

3. R. Bin Wong, *China Transformed: Historical Change and the Limits of European Experience* (Ithaca, NY: Cornell University Press, 1997); Kenneth Pomeranz, *The Great Divergence: China, Europe, and the Making of the Modern World Economy* (Princeton, NJ: Princeton University Press, 2000). The work of Wong and Pomeranz was the focus of a forum in the *American Historical Review* in 2002. See Kenneth Pomeranz, "Politi-

cal Economy and Ecology on the Eve of Industrialization: Europe, China, and the Global Conjuncture," *American Historical Review* 107.2 (April 2002): 425–46; R. Bin Wong, "The Search for European Differences and Domination in the Early Modern World: A View from Asia," *American Historical Review* 107.2 (April 2002): 447–69. For lengthy critiques of Pomeranz's book, see Philip C. C. Huang, "Development or Involution in Eighteenth-Century Britain and China? A Review of Kenneth Pomeranz's *The Great Divergence: China, Europe, and the Making of the Modern World Economy*," *Journal of Asian Studies* 61.2 (May 2002): 501–38; and Robert Brenner and Christopher Isett, "England's Divergence from China's Yangzi Delta: Property Relations, Microeconomics, and Patterns of Development," *Journal of Asian Studies* 61.2 (May 2002): 609–62. Pomeranz responds to Huang in "Beyond the East-West Binary: Resituating Development Paths in the Eighteenth-Century World," *Journal of Asian Studies* 61.2 (May 2002): 539–90.

4. Although I gloss over these issues here, they constitute by far the larger portion of Wong's book and form an important part of the context for his analysis of economic developments in China and Europe over the centuries.

5. Pomeranz, *The Great Divergence*, 8, n. 13.

6. Wong, *China Transformed*, 282; Pomeranz, *The Great Divergence*, 8–10.

7. Wong, *China Transformed*, 17; Pomeranz, *The Great Divergence*, 7–8 (see also 70, 107, 112–13, 165). Pomeranz and Wong both discuss the resemblances between the economies of Asia and Europe on the eve of the Industrial Revolution, mainly in the first two chapters of their studies.

8. This is a radically simplified characterization of the carefully developed positions of the two scholars. Although both, for example, emphasize the importance of coal, Pomeranz makes much of the accident of geography that in Europe, in contrast to China, located some of the largest coal deposits (in Britain) in close proximity to excellent water transport, a commercially vibrant economy, and a high concentration of skilled craftspeople. Pomeranz, *The Great Divergence*, 59–68. For an insightful review essay comparing Wong and Pomeranz and placing them in the context of earlier efforts to address similar "macrohistorical" issues—most famously, perhaps, Andre Gunder Frank's *ReOrient: Global Economy in the Asian Age* (Berkeley: University of California Press, 1998)— see Gale Stokes, "The Fates of Human Societies: A Review of Recent Macrohistories," *American Historical Review* 106.2 (April 2001): 508–25, and Gale Stokes, "Why the West? The Unsettled Question of Europe's Ascendancy," *Lingua Franca* 11.8 (November 2001): 30–38.

9. Wong, *China Transformed*, 8.

10. Pomeranz, *The Great Divergence*, 25–26.

11. Although I focus here on Hamashita, partly because of his wide-ranging and deeply grounded historical perspective, a number of other scholars have also done work on the Asian region as a system, among them Mark Selden and Giovanni Arrighi.

12. Takeshi Hamashita, "The Intra-regional System in East Asia in Modern Times," in *Network Power: Japan and Asia*, ed. Peter J. Katzenstein and Takashi Shiraishi (Ithaca, NY: Cornell University Press, 1997), 113.

13. Takeshi Hamashita, "The Tribute Trade System and Modern Asia," in *Japanese Industrialization and the Asian Economy*, ed. A. J. H. Latham and Heita Kawakatsu (London: Routledge, 1994), 92–97 (the quotations are from 96–97).

14. Fairbank's understanding of the tribute, or tributary, system was developed in many of his writings. See, for example, the early article (jointly authored with S. Y. Teng), "On the Ch'ing Tributary System," *Harvard Journal of Asiatic Studies* 6 (1941): 135–246, and the later edited volume, *The Chinese World Order: Traditional China's Foreign Relations* (Cambridge, MA: Harvard University Press, 1968). For an insightful critique of earlier understandings of the system, see James L. Hevia, *Cherishing Men from Afar: Qing Guest Ritual and the Macartney Embassy of 1793* (Durham, NC: Duke University Press, 1995), 9–15. For more recent critical discussion of the tributary system as a concept, see Peter C. Perdue, "The Tenacious Tributary System," *Journal of Contemporary China* 24.96 (2015): 1002–14; also the summation in David L. Howell's "Editorial Preface" to a special issue of the *Harvard Journal of Asiatic Studies* devoted to scrutiny of the tributary system and its recent career in the field of international relations (77.1 [June 2017]: vii–viii).

15. As I make explicit in *Discovering History in China* (196), the China-centered approach is to be clearly distinguished from the concept of Sinocentrism, with its connotations of a world (or a region, in Hamashita's case) centering on China.

16. Hamashita, "The Intra-regional System in East Asia in Modern Times," 115. Hamashita develops other aspects of his sea-centered understanding of the Asian regional system in "Overseas Chinese Networks in the Asian Historical Regional System, 1700–1900," in *Ershi shiji de Zhongguo yu shijie: Lunwen xuanji* (China and the world in the twentieth century: Selected essays), ed. Chang Chi-hsiung [Zhang Qixiong], 2 vols. (Taipei: Institute of Modern History, Academia Sinica, 2001), 1:143–64.

17. This is not the place to get into an involved discussion of the problems posed by the term *Han* as an ethnonym. Although *Han*, according to one recent effort at clarification, is "the label that was used during the Qing to distinguish the Chinese culturally and ethnically from the non-Han Other," "'Han Chinese' is the modern ethnic label used to describe the majority of people in China, as distinct from the approximately three-score 'minority nationalities' as defined by the present Chinese state." Mark C. Elliott, *The Manchu Way: The Eight Banners and Ethnic Identity in Late Imperial China* (Stanford, CA: Stanford University Press, 2001), 383–84, n. 75.

18. Jonathan Spence, Joseph Fletcher, and Beatrice Bartlett were among the first scholars to show the way to a new understanding of the Manchu experience in China during the Qing. For a sampling of the more important studies in English that have been published over the past quarter-century, see Cohen, "Introduction to the 2010 Reissue," lxii, n. 25.

19. Elliott, *The Manchu Way*, 34.

20. Evelyn S. Rawski, "Reenvisioning the Qing: The Significance of the Qing Period in Chinese History," *Journal of Asian Studies* 55.4 (November 1996): 832–33; Elliott, *The Manchu Way*, 28, 34; James A. Millward, *Beyond the Pass: Economy, Ethnicity, and Empire in Qing Central Asia, 1759–1864* (Stanford, CA: Stanford University Press, 1998), 13–15.

21. This is the subject of Peter C. Perdue's monumental *China Marches West: The Qing Conquest of Central Eurasia* (Cambridge, MA: Harvard University Press, 2005).

22. Dru C. Gladney, *Muslim Chinese: Ethnic Nationalism in the People's Republic*, 2nd ed. (Cambridge, MA: Council on East Asian Studies, Harvard University, 1996); Jonathan N. Lipman, *Familiar Strangers: A History of Muslims in Northwest China* (Seattle: University of Washington Press, 1997).

23. Jonathan N. Lipman, "Hyphenated Chinese: Sino-Muslim Identity in Modern China," in *Remapping China: Fissures in Historical Terrain*, ed. Gail Hershatter et al. (Stanford, CA: Stanford University Press, 1996), 109, also 100. Lipman uses the term *Sino-Muslim* in his book as well as in this article.

24. The Uighurs were the second largest Muslim minority in China as of the 2000 census, at that time numbering over 8 million. Unlike the largest Muslim minority, the Hui, who are found throughout the country, more than 90 percent of Uighurs live in the Uighur Autonomous Region of Xinjiang. Dru C. Gladney, *Dislocating China: Reflections on Muslims, Minorities, and Other Subaltern Subjects* (Chicago: University of Chicago Press, 2004), 206, 220.

25. Cohen, *Discovering History in China*, 161–72.

26. Lipman, "Hyphenated Chinese," 100–102 (the quotation is from 101). The difference that serious attention to ethnic difference makes in core–periphery mapping is also suggested in Millward, *Beyond the Pass*, 10–12. With respect to violence among Muslim communities, Gladney observes that it "continues to be intra-factional and intra-ethnic, rather than along Muslim/non-Muslim religious lines." Gladney, *Muslim Chinese*, viii.

27. Examples of this burgeoning literature are cited in Cohen, "Introduction to the 2010 Reissue," lxiii, n. 34.

28. There is a very large body of literature on this subject, which I make no pretense to having mastered. For this discussion, I have drawn much stimulation from Adam McKeown, "Conceptualizing Chinese Diasporas, 1842–1949," *Journal of Asian Studies* 58.2 (May 1999): 306–37; Philip Kuhn, "Toward an Historical Ecology of Chinese Migration," in *The Chinese Overseas*, ed. Hong Liu (London: Routledge, 2006), 1:67–97; and the work of and ongoing conversation with Elizabeth Sinn, especially in regard to the key role of Hong Kong in the Chinese diaspora.

29. Elizabeth Sinn, "In-Between Places: The Key Role of Localities of Transit in Chinese Migration," paper presented at the Association for Asian Studies annual meeting, Washington, DC, April 6, 2002; also her recent publication *Pacific Crossing: California Gold, Chinese Migration, and the Making of Hong Kong* (Hong Kong: Hong Kong University Press, 2013), 304–7 and *passim*; see also McKeown, "Conceptualizing Chinese Diasporas," 314–15, 319–21; Philip A. Kuhn, *Chinese Among Others: Emigration in Modern Times* (Lanham, MD: Rowman and Littlefield, 2008), 14–15, 51–52.

30. Kuhn, "Toward an Historical Ecology of Chinese Migration." For an interesting discussion of the variety of pasts available to people of Chinese descent in Southeast Asia for fashioning new identities, see Wang Gungwu, "Ethnic Chinese: The Past in Their Future," paper presented at the conference on "International Relations and Cultural Transformation of Ethnic Chinese," Manila, November 26–28, 1998.

31. McKeown, "Conceptualizing Chinese Diasporas," 307, see also 331.

32. The Chinese diaspora is only one of several such large-scale migratory movements of recent centuries; others include the Indian, African, and Armenian diasporas.

33. Paul A. Cohen, *History in Three Keys: The Boxers as Event, Experience, and Myth* (New York: Columbia University Press, 1997), xiv.

34. As an example, Paul R. Katz explicitly applies the tripartite focus of *History in Three Keys* (history as event, experience, and myth) in his book, *When Valleys Turned Blood Red: The Ta-pa-ni Incident in Colonial Taiwan* (Honolulu: University of Hawai'i Press, 2005).

35. The Chinese diaspora involves various forms of deterritorialization. A specific instance is the notion of "cultural China," as advanced by Wei-ming Tu. Substantively, "cultural China" refers to a cluster of values, behavior patterns, ideas, and traditions that people agree to define as in some objective sense "Chinese," and to which, speaking more subjectively, those who identify themselves as "Chinese" feel themselves to belong. Strategically, the idea of cultural China affords Chinese living in the diaspora a way of talking about, shaping the meaning of, and even defining China and Chineseness without inhabiting the geographical or political space known as Zhongguo. See Wei-ming Tu, "Cultural China: The Periphery as the Center," *Daedalus: Journal of the American Academy of Arts and Sciences* 120.2 (Spring 1991): 1–32; Paul A. Cohen, "Cultural China: Some Definitional Issues," *Philosophy East and West* 43.3 (July 1993): 557–63.

36. A Uighur in Xinjiang or a Tibetan in Qinghai, while incontestably (although not necessarily without contesting it) part of political China, might well object to being considered culturally Chinese. Conversely, a recent Chinese migrant to California, while no longer inhabiting a political space called China, would more than likely continue to view him- or herself as culturally part of China.

37. For example, see my essay "The Tenacity of Culture: Old Stories in the New China," in *The People's Republic of China at 60: An International Assessment*, ed. William C. Kirby (Cambridge, MA: Harvard University Asia Center, 2011), 388–400.

38. Although not using the phrase "cultural essentialization," Sen contests the claims of cultural boundary, cultural disharmony, and cultural specificity in his "East and West: The Reach of Reason," *New York Review of Books* 47 (July 20, 2000): 33–38 (quotation from 36).

39. Fairbank begins his book by placing China's response to the West in the context of prior Chinese experience with and attitudes toward barbarians. John K. Fairbank, *Trade and Diplomacy on the China Coast: The Opening of the Treaty Ports, 1842–1854* (Cambridge, MA: Harvard University Press, 1953), chap. 1. In my book I explicitly characterize the political problem created for Chinese officials by missionaries as "derivative in nature. Underlying it was the much larger issue of Sino-Western cultural conflict." Paul A. Cohen, *China and Christianity: The Missionary Movement and the Growth of Chinese Antiforeignism, 1860–1870* (Cambridge, MA: Harvard University Press, 1963), 264.

40. Albert Feuerwerker, *China's Early Industrialization: Sheng Hsuan-huai (1844–1916) and Mandarin Enterprise* (Cambridge, MA: Harvard University Press, 1958); John K. Fairbank, Edwin O. Reischauer, and Albert Craig, *East Asia: The Modern Transformation* (Boston: Houghton Mifflin, 1965); Mary C. Wright, *The Last Stand of Chinese Conservatism: The T'ung-chih Restoration, 1862–1874*, rev. ed. (New York: Atheneum, 1965); Joseph R. Levenson, *Confucian China and Its Modern Fate: The Problem of Intellectual Continuity* (Berkeley: University of California Press, 1958), 3.

41. Cohen, *Discovering History in China*, 189–90.

42. For a fuller probing of key themes in the thinking of Schwartz, see Paul A. Cohen and Merle Goldman, "Introduction," in *Ideas Across Cultures: Essays on Chinese Thought in Honor of Benjamin I. Schwartz*, ed. Paul A. Cohen and Merle Goldman (Cambridge, MA: Council on East Asian Studies, Harvard University, 1990), 1–13.

43. I should note that not all historians accept the view of a common human condition. In his otherwise excellent book on Sino-Western cultural conflict during the late Ming and early Qing, Jacques Gernet argues that in China Western missionaries "found themselves in the presence of a different kind of humanity." *China and the Christian Impact: A Conflict of Cultures*, trans. Janet Lloyd (Cambridge: Cambridge University Press, 1985), 247. Implicitly throughout his book and explicitly in its concluding pages, Gernet advances a linguistic determinism so powerful in potential as to jeopardize any sort of meaningful cross-cultural inquiry or understanding. See my review in *Harvard Journal of Asiatic Studies* 47.2 (December 1987): 674–83.

Chapter 6. A Multiplicity of Pasts

1. Parts of this chapter are adapted from the preface and conclusion of *History in Three Keys: The Boxers as Event, Experience, and Myth* (New York: Columbia University Press, 1997); originally a talk given at the University of Charleston and Columbia University, it is substantially revised here. In a somewhat different form, the chapter was previously published in my *China Unbound: Evolving Perspectives on the Chinese Past* (London: Routledge Curzon, 2003), 200–220.

2. Paul A. Cohen, *China and Christianity: The Missionary Movement and the Growth of Chinese Antiforeignism, 1860–1870* (Cambridge, MA: Harvard University Press, 1963), 263.

3. The earliest accounts of this approach that I've been able to lay my hands on are in my grant applications made in 1985 to the John Simon Guggenheim Memorial Foundation and the National Endowment for the Humanities. Both applications were successful, which gave me the luxury of two full years of relief from teaching and committee work in the latter part of the 1980s. The substance of my proposed project, then titled "An Exploration in Historical Epistemology: The Boxers as Experience, Event, and Symbol," is summarized in a letter of August 27, 1985 that I wrote to Jeff Wasserstrom (who was also deeply interested in the Boxers):

> What I basically have in mind is an exploration in historical epistemology, using the Boxers as a case study. I don't know for certain how I shall structure the final product. But one possibility that suggests itself, given the goals I have in mind, is to construct a series of historical "cross-sections," cinematically juxtaposing different layers of historical consciousness. One layer would comprise the thought, feelings, and behavior of the immediate participants in different phases of the Boxer experience—Chinese peasant youths in straitened circumstances who, for reasons of survival, joined up with Boxer bands passing through their villages, foreigners

sequestered in the legation quarters in the steamy summer months of 1900 who didn't know, at least at the outset, whether they would emerge dead or alive—individuals, in short, who did not have the entire "event" pre-encoded in their heads and whose thought and behavior were therefore framed by a much more limited set of contextual coordinates. A second layer would bring in the larger themes of the event proper, as later narrated by historians and others—people who *did* have the whole picture in their minds (or at least a version of it) and were intent upon *explaining* not only the Boxer phenomenon itself but how it was linked up with prior and subsequent historical developments. The third layer (the one where your own work has been focused) would consist in the symbolic representations supplied in the contemporary news media and in later fictional and nonfictional references to the Boxers and "Boxerism"—representations designed less to elucidate the Boxer past than to score points, often of a political or explicitly propagandistic nature, in the post-Boxer present. My aim, in so juxtaposing these different strata of consciousness, would be to convey something of the elusiveness of the historical enterprise, to illuminate the tension between the history that people make, which is forever fixed, and the history that people write and use, which seems . . . to be infinitely malleable.

4. Mary C. Wright, "Introduction: The Rising Tide of Change," in *China in Revolution: The First Phase, 1900–1913*, ed. Mary C. Wright (New Haven, CT: Yale University Press, 1968), 1.

5. Jeffrey Wasserstrom, "The Boxers as Symbol: The Use and Abuse of the Yi He Tuan," unpublished paper (1984), 10–11.

6. In the United States, the Boxers and their female counterparts, the Red Lanterns, came in for warm praise from radical Chinese Americans in New York and San Francisco. A Red Guard party was formed in San Francisco. In New York, an organization calling itself I Wor Kuen (Cantonese for Yihequan or "Boxers") started publishing a bimonthly (sometimes monthly) bilingual magazine called *Getting Together (Tuanjiebao* in Mandarin) in February 1970. An editorial titled "I Wor Kuen" in the second issue clearly indicated the group's stance:

I Wor Kuen fighters were not frightened away by the foreigners' weapons because they believed that spiritual understanding and unity among people were more important than weapons in deciding the outcome of a war. . . . Tens of thousands of liberated women fought against foreigners alongside of the men in units such as the Red Lantern Brigade. . . . The patriotic rebels of the Taipings and I Wor Kuen lit the spark which started the gigantic fire for the liberation of Chinese [*sic*] and world's peoples. (*Getting Together* 1.2 [April 1970]: 2; English-language section)

7. The "murderous Boxer Uprising" loomed large in part 1 of *Life*'s three-part pictorial survey of the historical background to the emergence of "the young fanatics of the Communist Red Guard." See "Behind Mao's Red Rule: The 100 Violent Years," *Life*, September 23, September 30, and October 7, 1966.

8. See Paul A. Cohen, "Imagining the Red Lanterns," *Berliner China-Hefte* 12 (May 1997): 88–95.

9. Paul Veyne, *Writing History: Essay on Epistemology*, trans. Mina Moore-Rinvolucri (Middletown, CT: Wesleyan University Press, 1984), 40.

10. The film was partly based on a short story, also titled "Rashomon," by the early twentieth-century Japanese writer Akutagawa Ryūnosuke.

11. Paul Ricoeur argues forcefully that even the work of Fernand Braudel and other members of the Annales school, although proclaiming itself to be nonnarrative in character, has embedded in it a concealed narrative structure. See especially Paul Ricoeur, *Time and Narrative*, trans. Kathleen McLaughlin and David Pellauer (Chicago: University of Chicago Press, 1984), vol. 1, chap. 6, on "Historical Intentionality." See also David Carr, *Time, Narrative, and History* (Bloomington: Indiana University Press, 1986), 8–9, 175–77.

12. This problem is encountered in all historical scholarship. It is posed most conspicuously by scholars who are candid about their extraprofessional social and political commitments. See, for example, Gail Hershatter, "The Subaltern Talks Back: Reflections on Subaltern Theory and Chinese History," *positions: east asian cultures critique* 1.1 (Spring 1993): 103–30. Hershatter, a first-rate social historian, raises the problem implicitly but does not actually address it in her article.

13. J. H. Hexter, as quoted in David Lowenthal, *The Past Is a Foreign Country* (Cambridge: Cambridge University Press, 1985), 218.

14. Anonymous, *Tianjin yiyue ji* (An account of one month in Tianjin), in *Yihetuan* (The Boxers), ed. Jian Bozan et al., 4 vols. (Shanghai: Shenzhou guoguang she, 1951), 2:153–54.

15. The distinction between biographical (or autobiographical) and historical consciousness is elaborated in Cohen, *History in Three Keys*, 65–67. It is illustrated in an account that Shen Tong, one of the student leaders in Beijing in the spring of 1989, gave of his participation in the demonstrations. Shen observed that, for him, there were "two Tiananmen Squares," the one he personally experienced, which was full of confusion and excitement and remained an ongoing part of his consciousness, and the one created by the Western media, which quickly faded from view after the June 4 crackdown. Likening his experience to a "voyage" or "journey," Shen noted that although Tiananmen as an event was "over," his own sense of involvement in the movement that resulted in it began before 1989 and continued after it. Talk given at Harvard University, October 24, 1990.

16. The oral history materials, which give us the fullest Boxer evocations of their own experiences, are clearly inadequate for this purpose, because they are not contemporary and because they are substantially structured by the consciousness not of the respondents but of their interrogators. In any case, none of these materials come close to supplying us with the kind of intimate biographical tracking (including pre-Boxer or post-Boxer life experience or both) that is readily available for foreign participants in the Boxer events in Richard A. Steel, *Through Peking's Sewer Gate: Relief of the Boxer Siege, 1900–1901*, ed. George W. Carrington (New York: Vantage, 1985), Eva Jane Price, *China Journal, 1889–1900: An American Missionary Family during the Boxer Rebellion* (New York: Scribner's, 1989), and numerous other published and unpublished accounts.

17. For two examples of this, see Paul A. Cohen, "New Perspectives on the Boxers: The View from Anthropology," in Cohen, *China Unbound*, 84–104 (originally published

in Chinese as "Yi renleixue guandian kan Yihetuan" [trans. Lin Liwei], *Ershiyi shiji* [Twenty-first century] 45 [February 1998]); Paul A. Cohen, "Boxers, Christians, and the Gods: The Boxer Conflict of 1900 as a Religious War," in Cohen, *China Unbound*, 105–30 (originally presented as a talk, subsequently published in Chinese as "Yihetuan, Jidutu he shen: Cong zongjiao zhanzheng jiaodu kan 1900 nian de Yihetuan douzheng" [trans. Li Li, Tao Feiya, and Xian Yuyi], *Lishi yanjiu* [Historical research] 1 [February 2001]).

18. John Noble Wilford, *The Mysterious History of Columbus: An Exploration of the Man, the Myth, the Legacy* (New York: Knopf, 1991), 249–62. The emotions aroused by competing mythologizations of Columbus were very much in evidence in the summer of 1991 in Philadelphia when the City Council voted to change the name of Delaware Avenue (almost four miles long) to Christopher Columbus Boulevard to mark the 500th anniversary of Columbus's landing in North America. Italian-American groups had pushed for the change. But an Apache Indian active in the Stop the Name Change coalition said his group did not wish to honor a man who stood for "the enslavement of people of color." *New York Times*, August 25, 1991, 271. A year later, a group of Native American protesters in Boston elicited the following response from the grand marshal of the planned Columbus Day parade. "We're Italian-Americans, and they've taken all our heroes away from us. . . . Columbus is the last hero we have. . . . He discovered America. Why don't they leave the guy alone?" *New York Times*, October 11, 1992, 18.

19. Don C. Price, "Popular and Elite Heterodoxy toward the End of the Qing," in *Heterodoxy in Late Imperial China*, ed. Kwang-Ching Liu and Richard Shek (Honolulu: University of Hawai'i Press, 2004), 431–62.

20. In the case of the Guomindang, Mary C. Wright discusses the growing shift away from this identification with the Taipings as, under the leadership of Chiang Kai-shek, in the course of the 1920s the party became more and more wedded to stability and order and less to revolutionary change. "From Revolution to Restoration: The Transformation of Kuomintang Ideology," *Far Eastern Quarterly* 14.4 (August 1955): 515–32.

21. Stephen Uhalley Jr., "The Controversy over Li Hsiu-ch'eng: An Ill-Timed Centenary," *Journal of Asian Studies* 25.2 (February 1966): 305–17; James P. Harrison, *The Communists and Chinese Peasant Rebellions: A Study in the Rewriting of Chinese History* (New York: Atheneum, 1971), 128.

22. Lawrence R. Sullivan, "The Controversy over 'Feudal Despotism': Politics and Historiography in China, 1978–82," *Australian Journal of Chinese Affairs* 23 (January 1990): 2–3, 14.

23. Harold Z. Schiffrin, *Sun Yat-sen and the Origins of the Chinese Revolution* (Berkeley: University of California Press, 1970), 23; see also Marie-Claire Bergère, *Sun Yat-sen*, trans. Janet Lloyd (Stanford, CA: Stanford University Press, 1998), 33–34.

24. Harrison, *The Communists and Chinese Peasant Rebellions*, 260.

25. Nicole Constable, "Christianity and Hakka Identity," in *Christianity in China: The Eighteenth Century to the Present*, ed. Daniel H. Bays (Stanford, CA: Stanford University Press, 1996).

26. A much more complicated (and painful) example was the experience of Bob Kerrey as a Navy Seal in the Vietnam War. On February 25, 1969, Kerry's Seal team attacked Thanh Phong, an isolated peasant village in which Vietcong soldiers were reported to be hiding. After the fighting (which took place at night) was over, aside from the Viet-

cong dead, it was discovered that women and children had also been killed. The details of what happened are disputed. For Kerrey's account, see his *When I Was a Young Man: A Memoir* (New York: Harcourt, 2002).

27. Robertson Davies, *World of Wonders* (New York: Penguin: 1981), 58.

28. In her moving ethnography of an elderly Jewish community in Venice, California, Barbara Myerhoff writes that in her subjects' quest for "the integrity of the person over time" the creation of "personal myths" often took precedence over "truth and completeness." *Number Our Days* (New York: Simon and Schuster, 1978), 37, 222. On a more general level, Shelley E. Taylor argues that to a significant degree, the operations of the healthy mind are marked less by a concern for accuracy than by the ability to engage in "creative self-deception." *Positive Illusions: Creative Self-Deception and the Healthy Mind* (New York: Basic Books, 1989). David Carr, while acknowledging that people in the course of "composing and constantly revising" their autobiographies are concerned with coherence, is less willing than Myerhoff or Taylor to yield on the governing importance of truth and truthfulness to people so engaged. *Time, Narrative, and History*, 75–78, 98–99, 171–72.

29. "My paramount object in this struggle," Lincoln wrote Horace Greeley on August 22, 1862, "*is* to save the Union and is *not* either to save or destroy slavery. If I could save the Union without freeing *any* slave, I would do it." In *The People Shall Judge: Readings in the Formation of American Policy*, 2 vols. (Chicago: University of Chicago Press, 1949), 1:768–69.

30. Almost 75 percent of those interned were U.S. citizens. German-Americans, Italian-Americans, and German or Italian nationals living in the United States encountered difficulties only when there were specific grounds for believing them to be enemy agents.

31. Roger Chartier comments that history, while "one among many forms of narration, . . . is nevertheless singular in that it maintains a special relationship to truth. More precisely its narrative constructions aim at reconstructing a past that really was." Chartier's remarks, made in a paper delivered at the International Congress of Historical Sciences in Montreal in 1995, are quoted in Georg G. Iggers, *Historiography in the Twentieth Century: From Scientific Objectivity to the Postmodern Challenge* (Hanover, NH: Wesleyan University Press, published by the University Press of New England, 1997), 12.

32. *New York Times*, June 26, 1989, C13, C17.

33. For a discussion of the many sides of this issue, see Lowenthal, *The Past Is a Foreign Country*, esp. 210–38.

Chapter 7. History in Three Keys

1. Joseph Esherick, *The Origins of the Boxer Uprising* (Berkeley: University of California Press, 1987).

2. Paul A. Cohen, *Report on the Visit of the Young Political Leaders Delegation to the People's Republic of China* (New York: National Committee on United States–China Relations, 1977).

3. Titled "Modern China," it was published in *Humanistic and Social Science Research in China: Recent History and Future Prospects*, ed. Anne F. Thurston and Jason H. Parker (New York: Social Science Research Council, 1980), 38–60.

4. Wang Xi letter to author, January 31, 1991.

5. Wang Xi email to author, December 4, 2003.

6. Letter to Wang Xi, March 1, 2001.

7. My comments in the next few pages are based on the report I wrote for the American Council of Learned Societies, which provided financial assistance for my travel to China to attend the conference.

8. Some thirty-five years after the 1981 conference, the Manchuness of the Qing remains an issue of historiographical debate. See my discussion in chapter 5. Mark Elliott, in particular, rejecting the conventional assimilation or Sinicization model, places a lot of emphasis on the differences between Manchu and Han ethnicities in *The Manchu Way: The Eight Banners and Ethnic Identity in Late Imperial China* (Stanford, CA: Stanford University Press, 2001).

9. Kewen [Paul A. Cohen], "Meiguo yanjiu Qingmo-Minchu Zhongguo lishi de xin dongxiang" (New directions in American historical scholarship on late Qing and early Republican China), *Fudan xuebao* (Fudan journal) 6 (1981): 73–84. The conference papers were subsequently published in the conference volume: Cai Shangsi et al., eds., *Lun Qingmo Minchu Zhongguo shehui* (Essays on late Qing and early Republican Chinese society) (Shanghai: Fudan Daxue Chubanshe, 1983).

10. Zi's initial reaction to my book was expressed in her letter to me, dated July 2, 1997; her review article was published in *Dushu* 1 (1998): 122–30.

11. Australia, for example, with its growing ethnic Chinese population and expanding economic links to China, has had a succession of cases of residents or citizens of Chinese extraction being detained by Beijing. See Chris Buckley, "China Is Said to Bar Professor from Leaving after Visit," *New York Times*, March 27, 2017, A7. The focus of the article is Feng Chongyi, an associate professor at the University of Technology, Sydney, who had often expressed criticism of China's crackdown on political dissent.

12. The substance of this section was originally given as a talk titled "Unspoken Agendas in Historical Reconstruction: Opportunities, Strategies, Risks." I gave the talk in 1999 before the Indiana Association of Historians at Butler University; later I gave it with a different title—"Silences in Historical Reconstruction: A China Historian's Confessions"—at Gordon College in Wenham, MA (2006) and at Shandong University in Ji'nan, China (2011). The latter was translated into Chinese (by Cui Huajie and Qu Ningning) and published as "Lishi shuxie de wusheng zhi chu: yiwei lishi xuezhe de zibai" (Silences in historical writing: a historian's confessions), *Wenshizhe* 3 (2012): 5–12.

13. Paul A. Cohen, *History in Three Keys: The Boxers as Event, Experience, and Myth* (New York: Columbia University Press, 1997), 5, 213.

14. Cohen, *History in Three Keys*, 214, 292.

15. *New York Times*, March 10, 1989, C4.

16. At a videotaping at Shea Stadium in January 1988, TV crew members, during breaks, "peered down at the snow-filled seats and pointed to where they had been when Mookie Wilson's grounder had slithered through Bill Buckner's legs, now a moment in

history, like Pearl Harbor, Bobby Thomson's homer and the death of Elvis." *New York Times*, January 17, 1988, S3.

17. Deuteronomy 11:13–21.

18. Both examples are cited in David Arnold, *Famine: Social Crisis and Historical Change* (Oxford: Basil Blackwell, 1988), 15.

19. R. K. Hitchcock, "The Traditional Response to Drought in Botswana," in *Symposium on Drought in Botswana*, ed. Madalon T. Hinchey (Gabarone: Botswana Society in collaboration with Clark University Press, 1979), 92.

20. Erika Bourguignon, "An Assessment of Some Comparisons and Implications," in *Religion, Altered States of Consciousness, and Social Change*, ed. Erika Bourguignon (Columbus: Ohio State University Press, 1973), 326–27.

21. Arthur H. Smith, *China in Convulsion*, 2 vols. (New York: Fleming H. Revell, 1901), 2:659–60.

22. These examples are all drawn from Richard D. Loewenberg, "Rumors of Mass Poisoning in Times of Crisis," *Journal of Criminal Psychopathology* 5 (July 1943): 131–42.

23. Andrew Gordon, *Labor and Imperial Democracy in Prewar Japan* (Berkeley: University of California Press, 1991), 177.

24. Nwokocha K. U. Nkpa, "Rumors of Mass Poisoning in Biafra," *Public Opinion Quarterly* 41.3 (Fall 1977): 332–46.

25. See Paul Rabinow, "Representations Are Social Facts: Modernity and Post-Modernity in Anthropology," in *Writing Culture: The Poetics and Politics of Ethnography*, ed. James Clifford and George E. Marcus (Berkeley: University of California Press, 1986), 241.

26. Boston radio station WEEI, June 19–20, 1988. The general consensus of the onlookers in Ohio, according to the radio announcer (Charles Osgood), was to believe in rather than doubt the potential efficacy of the rainmaking ceremony.

27. For additional detail, see Paul A. Cohen, "Boxers, Christians, and the Gods: The Boxer Conflict of 1900 as a Religious War," in Cohen, *China Unbound: Evolving Perspectives on the Chinese Past* (London: Routledge Curzon, 2003), 105–30. Originally presented as a talk and subsequently published in Chinese: "Yihetuan, Jidutu he shen: Cong zongjiao zhanzheng jiaodu kan 1900 nian de Yihetuan douzheng" (trans. Li Li, Tao Feiya, and Xian Yuyi), *Lishi yanjiu* (*Historical research*) 1 (February 2001).

28. Jane E. Brody, "Lucking Out: Weird Rituals and Strange Beliefs," *New York Times*, January 27, 1991, S11.

29. Mary Douglas, *Purity and Danger: An Analysis of the Concepts of Pollution and Taboo* (New York: Routledge, 1991), 68, 72.

30. Cohen, *History in Three Keys*, 122. The quoted phrase is from a letter by Protestant missionary Sarah Boardman Goodrich, May 25, 1900, Cohen, *History in Three Keys*, 333, n. 13; see also 319, n. 66.

31. Cohen, *History in Three Keys*, 119–45.

32. The publisher of the 2000 translation (*Lishi san diao: zuo wei shijian, jingli, he shenhua de Yihetuan*) was Jiangsu renmin chubanshe (in Nanjing). A revised and corrected translation (with the same Chinese title) was brought out in 2014 by Shehui kexue wenxian chubanshe (Social Sciences Academic Press) (Beijing).

33. Zhang Jincai (83), Third Brother-Disciple, western suburbs of Tianjin, in "Tianjin diqu Yihetuan yundong diaocha baogao" (Report on the survey of the Boxer movement in the Tianjin area), compiled by Nankai daxue lishixi 1956 ji (Class of 1956 of the History Department of Nankai University) (unpublished), 123. (I used an undated reissue of the original 1960 mimeographed version furnished by my hosts during my visit to Nankai in 1987.)

34. Li Yuanshan (79), Boxer, Tianjin, in "Tianjin diqu Yihetuan yundong diaocha baogao," 134.

35. Charles A. Desnoyers's review, *History* (Fall 1997): 35.

36. Greg Dening, "Enigma Variations on *History in Three Keys*: A Conversational Essay," *History and Theory: Studies in the Philosophy of History* 39.2 (May 2000): 210; see also the comments of Peter Burke, "History of Events and the Revival of Narrative," in *New Perspectives on Historical Writing*, 2nd ed., ed. Peter Burke (University Park: Pennsylvania State University Press, 2001), 295.

37. The shortcomings were actually a matter of the publisher's strictures, not the failings of the translator. The research for the book was carried on in part during the time in 1989 when the Tiananmen prodemocracy demonstrations were taking place in Beijing. In response to the Communist Party's political ruling, all references to the demonstrations, however harmless-seeming, were deleted from the text and notes. Also, all foreign names and book titles were rendered in Chinese characters with no indication of how they were written in their original language, which meant that apart from a certain amount of confusion in the text proper, the lengthy bibliography at the end of the book was rendered useless.

38. Lei Yi, "Shixuejia jiushi fanyijia" (Historians are akin to translators), foreword to Kewen [Paul Cohen], *Lishi san diao: Zuowei shijian, jingli, he shenhua de Yihetuan* (*History in three keys: The Boxers as event, experience, and myth*), trans. Du Jidong (Beijing: Social Sciences Academic Press, 2014), i–v. See also the translator's note ("Yi houji"), which details the shortcomings of the first edition and the improvements made in the 2014 edition, in *Lishi san diao*, 376–79.

39. The quoted phrases are from Sheila Levine's letter to me, November 1, 1995.

40. As will be seen in the following chapter, I published another book, *China Unbound: Evolving Perspectives on the Chinese Past* (Routledge Curzon) in 2003. This was a collection of previously published writings rather than a book on a completely new topic.

Chapter 8. From the Boxers to King Goujian

1. Although scheduled to be published in a volume of conference papers, to the best of my knowledge, this never happened. The third of the three conferences in the series was published under the title *Historical Truth, Historical Criticism, and Ideology*, ed. Helwig Schmidt-Glintzer, Achim Mittag, and Jörn Rüsen (Leiden: Brill, 2005).

2. Lucian W. Pye, *The Spirit of Chinese Politics: A Psychocultural Study of the Authority Crisis in Political Development* (Cambridge, MA: MIT Press, 1968), 71–72.

3. *Gezhong jinianri shilüe* (A concise history of the various commemoration days), compiled and printed by the Political Training Department of the Nanchang Field Headquarters of the Head of the Military Affairs Commission of the National Government (1932?), 103–9.

4. See *Chongbian riyong baike quanshu* (New edition of encyclopedia for everyday use) (Shanghai: Shangwu yinshuguan, 1934), 5792–93.

5. The chart is in the front matter of Liang Xin, *Guochi shiyao* (A concise history of national humiliation), 6th printing (Shanghai: Rixin yudi xueshe, 1933 [orig. ed. 1931]), 1–6. This chart was apparently first issued by the Ministry of the Interior in 1928. See Xu Guozhen, *Jin bainian waijiao shibai shi* (A history of the foreign affairs defeats of the past hundred years) (Shanghai: Shijie shuju, 1929), 203–5.

6. Liang Yiqun, Yang Jie, and Xiao Ye, eds., *Yibaige guochi jinian ri* (One hundred national humiliation commemoration days) (Beijing: Zhongguo qingnian chubanshe, 1995).

7. Twenty-five such days are covered in *Gezhong jinianri shilüe*. On the entire range of national anniversaries and the ways they were observed, see Henrietta Harrison, *The Making of the Republican Citizen: Political Ceremonies and Symbols in China, 1911–1929* (Oxford: Oxford University Press, 2000).

8. See, for example, Liang Xin, *Guochi shiyao* (A concise history of national humiliation); Lü Simian, *Guochi xiaoshi* (A short history of national humiliation), 5th printing (Shanghai: Zhonghua shuju, 1919 [orig. ed. 1917]); Shen Wenjun, *Zengding guochi xiaoshi* (A revised and expanded short history of national humiliation), 11th printing (Shanghai: Zhongguo tushu gongsi heji, 1924 [orig. ed. 1910]); Jiang Gongsheng, *Guochi shi* (A history of national humiliation), reprint (Shanghai: Zhonghua shuju, 1928 [orig. ed. 1926]); Anonymous, *Guochi tongshi* (The painful history of national humiliation) (n.d.); *Guochi tu* (National humiliation illustrated) (Shanghai: Shangwu yinshuguan, n.d. [probably 1931 or 1932]). There were many other works that, although not containing the phrase *guochi* in the title, were focused entirely on the theme of national humiliation. See, for example, Xu Guozhen, *Jin bainian waijiao shibai shi*; Fu Youpu, *Zhongguo tongshi* (The painful history of China) (Shanghai: Xinhua shuju, 1927).

9. See, for example, the reprinted titles in note 8.

10. *Guochi shiyao*, for example, includes a preface by the head of the Guangdong Department of Education, expatiating on the importance of not forgetting the humiliations suffered by China since the Opium War and enthusiastically commending the book to readers.

11. See *Zengding guochi xiaoshi*.

12. Chow Tse-tsung, *The May Fourth Movement: Intellectual Revolution in Modern China* (Cambridge, MA: Harvard University Press, 1960), 22.

13. I am grateful to Jeffrey Wasserstrom for sending me a photocopy of this lesson (no. 23), which is contained in *Shimin qianzi ke*, 20th ed. (Shanghai: Shangwu yinshuguan, January 1929 [orig. ed. March 1927]), 2:52–53.

14. Lesson no. 24, in *Pingmin qianzi ke*, 4 *ce*, 3rd rev. ed. (Shanghai: Zhonghua Jidujiao qingnianhui xiehui, 1924), 4:48–49.

15. He Yu and Hua Li, *Guochi beiwanglu: Zhongguo jindaishishang de pupingdeng tiaoyue* (Memorandum on national humiliation: The unequal treaties in modern Chinese history) (Beijing jiaoyu chubanshe, 1995).

16. Lü Tao, *Guochi de kaiduan* (The beginnings of national humiliation) (Beijing: Zhongguo huaqiao chubanshe, 1992).

17. *Guochi tongshi*.

18. Zhao Yusen, *Guochi xiaoshi xubian* (Supplement to a short history of national humiliation), 5th ed. (Shanghai: Zhongguo tushu gongsi heji, 1924); Zhichishe, ed., *Guochi* (National humiliation) (Taibei: Wenhai chubanshe, 1987?); Guo Dajun and Zhang Beigen, *Wu wang jiuyiba: Liutiaohu shijian qianqianhouhou* (Don't forget September 18: The full story of the Liutiaohu incident) (Beijing: Zhongguo huaqiao chubanshe, 1992).

19. Liang Xin, *Guochi shiyao*, "Zixu" (Author's preface), dated June 30, 1931. Other examples of works that focus on Chinese shortcomings are Fangshi, "Lun xue guochou yi xian li guochi" (To avenge ourselves against our national enemies we must first foster a sense of national shame), *Dongfang zazhi* (Eastern miscellany), 1.4 (June 8, 1904): 65–67; Lü Simian, *Guochi xiaoshi, shang*, 1–3; *Pingmin qianzi ke* (1924 ed.), 4:48–49; Fu Youpu, *Zhongguo tongshi*, 2–3.

20. In one variation or another, the Goujian story has long been a standard part of the repertoire of Chinese children's stories. See, for example, *Woxin changdan* (Sleeping on brushwood and tasting gall) (Shanghai: Zhonghua shuju, 1921); Zhao Longzhi, comp., *Goujian* (Taibei: Huaguo chubanshe, 1953); Yang Muzhi and Huang Ke, comps., *Zhongguo lishi gushi (Chunqiu)* (Stories from Chinese history: Spring and Autumn) (Beijing: Zhongguo qingnian chubanshe, 1986 [orig. ed. 1979]), 115–24. As a rough measure of the wide circulation of the Goujian story, 348,000 copies of the last-named title had been printed as of 1986.

21. *Shimin qianzi ke*, 52.

22. *Guochi tongshi*, outside cover.

23. Many book titles evoked the "do not forget" theme. See Guo Dajun and Zhang Beigen, *Wuwang jiuyiba: Liutiaohu shijian qianqianhouhou* (Don't forget September 18: The full story of the Liutiaohu incident) (Beijing: Zhongguo huaqiao chubanshe, 1992). At the Summer Palace in Beijing, described by Geremie Barmé as having lately once again risen to prominence as "a symbol of aggrieved nationalism and patriotic outrage," a long wall was erected in the 1990s, with a listing of the unequal treaties on its face, introduced by the phrase "Do not forget the national humiliation" (*wuwang guochi*) in oversized characters. Geremie Barmé, "The Garden of Perfect Brightness, A Life in Ruins," *East Asian History* 11 (June 1996): 113. I am grateful to Barmé for sending me a photocopy of a photograph he took of the wall. The slogan "Do not forget the national humiliation" was commonly encountered in the early years of the twentieth century also. (For its pervasive use in 1915 at the time of the Twenty-One Demands, see Chow Tsetsung, *May Fourth Movement*, 22.) The aim of the slogan in the earlier period was to remind the Chinese people not to forget to avenge themselves at an appropriate future date, whereas at the end of the twentieth century the aim of not forgetting was to ensure that the humiliations of the past would never again be visited upon China.

24. Author's introduction, *Yibaige guochi jinian ri*, 11. Reiterations of the same master narrative are found in An Zuozhang's preface to *Guochi: Zhongguo renmin bugai*

wangji (National humiliation: The Chinese people should not forget), ed. Che Jixin (Jinan: Shandong youyi shushe, 1992), 1–2; Zhang Dazhong's preface to *Wuwang bainian
guochi* (Don't forget the hundred years of national humiliation), ed. Shao Rongchang
and Wu Jialin, 2 vols. (Beijing: Zhongguo renmin daxue chubanshe, 1992), 1:i–iii; and
the conclusion to the same work, 2:354–60.

25. A prime example of such efforts was the explosive tract *China Can Say No*. See
Song Qiang et al., *Zhongguo keyi shuo bu: lengzhanhou shidai de zhengzhi yu qinggan jueze*
(China can say no: Politics and choice of sentiments in the post–cold war era) (Beijing:
Zhonghua gongsheng lianhe, 1996). For an insightful analysis of *China Can Say No* and
the victimization-centered nationalism it embodies, see Toming Jun Liu, "Uses and
Abuses of Sentimental Nationalism: Mnemonic Disquiet in *Heshang* and *Shuobu*," pa-
per presented at the annual meeting of the Association for Asian Studies, Boston,
March 1999.

26. Titled "Remembering and Forgetting National Humiliation in Twentieth-
Century China," it appeared in *Twentieth-Century China*, 27.2 (April 2002): 1–39 and
was reprinted in my *China Unbound: Evolving Perspectives on the Chinese Past* (London:
Routledge Curzon, 2003), 148–84. The discussion in the following section of the text
draws mainly on the article's opening pages and conclusion.

27. Prasenjit Duara, "Response to Philip Huang's 'Biculturality in Modern China and
in Chinese Studies,'" *Modern China* 26.1 (January 2000): 32–37 (quotes from 35).

28. Among the first to make the point were Mary C. Wright, in the introduction to
her *China in Revolution: The First Phase, 1900–1913* (New Haven, CT: Yale University
Press, 1968), and John Schrecker, in his *Imperialism and Chinese Nationalism: Germany
in Shandong* (Cambridge, MA: Harvard University Press, 1971). For a somewhat different view, which sees the anti-imperialist nationalism of the late Qing as being centered
in gentry and regional opposition to the central government, see Min Tu-ki, *National
Polity and Local Power: The Transformation of Late Imperial China*, ed. Philip A. Kuhn
and Timothy Brook (Cambridge, MA: Council on East Asian Studies, Harvard University, 1989), esp. 207–11.

29. Mary Rankin is particularly good on this. See her "Nationalistic Contestation
and Mobilization Politics: Practice and Rhetoric of Railway-Rights Recovery at the End
of the Qing," *Modern China* 28.3 (July 2002): 315–61.

30. In his discussion of Ah Q's reaction to being beaten over the head by a man he
had just insulted, Lu wrote: "As far as Ah Q could remember, this was the second humiliation of his life. Fortunately after the thwacking stopped it seemed to him that the
matter was closed, and he even felt somewhat relieved. Moreover, the precious 'ability
to forget' handed down by his ancestors stood him in good stead. He walked slowly away
and by the time he was approaching the wineshop door he felt quite happy again." *The
True Story of Ah Q*, in Lu Hsun [Xun], *Selected Works of Lu Hsun*, 4 vols. (Peking: Foreign Languages Press, 1956), 1:92.

31. Benedict Anderson, *Imagined Communities: Reflections on the Origin and Spread
of Nationalism*, rev. ed. (London: Verso, 1991 [1983]), 159.

32. This tension also existed during the late Qing and the years of the Yuan Shikai
presidency of the new Chinese Republic (1912–16). In regard to the latter, in 1915 the
North-China Herald printed a translation of a telegram that the Yuan government sent

to the provinces for the purpose of containing anti-Japanese activities in the aftermath of China's acceptance of the Twenty-One Demands. "Although we can have no reason to prohibit any declaration of patriotic feelings," the telegram read in part, "yet, for fear of treacherous persons taking advantage of this opportunity, stringent measures should be taken to keep these matters within bounds." *North-China Herald*, May 22, 1915, 546. See also Karl G. Gerth, "Consumption as Resistance: The National Products Movement and Anti-Japanese Boycotts in Modern China," in *The Japanese Empire in East Asia and Its Postwar Legacy*, ed. Harald Fuess (München: Ludicium, 1998), 135.

33. The difficult relationship between popular nationalism and official nationalism is explored in Yongnian Zheng, *Discovering Chinese Nationalism in China: Modernization and International Relations* (Cambridge: Cambridge University Press, 1999), 87–110, 123, 133–34.

34. The government's quandary in this area was illustrated in the immediate aftermath of the collision on April 1, 2001, between a U.S. spy plane and a Chinese fighter jet in the air space between Hainan and the Paracel Islands. Government-monitored Internet chat rooms and bulletin boards, described (with some exaggeration) in the *New York Times* as "an easy barometer of opinion among the country's best-educated young people," were jammed with "furious denunciations of American imperialism" and calls for "retribution," but at the same time, the *Times* noted, "the most inflammatory comments were blocked or deleted." Still more telling, the Chinese leadership reportedly issued strict instructions to universities around the country that there were to be no student demonstrations. Craig S. Smith, "American Embassy Officials Wait to See Plane's Crew," *New York Times*, April 3, 2001, 6; Erik Eckholm, "U.S. Envoy to Meet Chinese Foreign Minister as Negotiations on Plane Crew Continue," *New York Times*, April 6, 2001, A10. A different sort of example was provided in the summer of 1991 when a small group of people met privately in Nanjing to commemorate the Nanjing Massacre of 1937. It was originally to have been a high-visibility conference, with many more delegates, held on the campus of Nanjing University. But the government had recently applied for a favorable loan from Tokyo and an unexpected visit by the Japanese prime minister appears to have persuaded Beijing that this was not the most opportune time for a large-scale, well-publicized conference on Japanese war crimes. Ian Baruma, *The Wages of Guilt: Memories of War in Germany and Japan* (New York: Farrar, Straus, Giroux, 1994), 123.

35. Many writers have touched on this difference in one way or another. Maurice Halbwachs, for example, distinguished between autobiographical and historical memory, the former referring to events that have been personally experienced, the latter to events that have been experienced only indirectly, through books, commemorative rites, and the like. See Lewis A. Coser's introduction to Maurice Halbwachs, *On Collective Memory*, ed. and trans. Lewis A. Coser (Chicago: University of Chicago Press, 1992), 23–24, 29–30.

36. "Since context must, of necessity, constantly change," writes Israel Rosenfield, "there can never be a fixed, or absolute, memory. Memory without the present cannot exist." *The Invention of Memory: A New View of the Brain* (New York: Basic Books, 1988), 80. The point is nicely illustrated by the postwar experience of East and West Germany, where very different presents led to very different patterns of remembering and forget-

ting of the Nazi past. See Claudia Koonz, "Between Memory and Oblivion: Concentration Camps in German Memory," in *Commemorations: The Politics of National Identity*, ed. John R. Gillis (Princeton, NJ: Princeton University Press, 1994), 258–80.

37. Letter of November 1, 2001, from Craig Fowlie, senior editor at Routledge, and Mark Selden, the editor of the new series.

38. Others who were later asked to be part of the series were equally esteemed, including Vaclav Smil, Timothy Brook, and Prasenjit Duara.

39. Benjamin I. Schwartz, "Introduction," in *China and Other Matters* (Cambridge, MA: Harvard University Press, 1996), 1.

40. Email to Jeffrey Wasserstrom, August 21, 1998.

41. Email to Wasserstrom, June 20, 2003, and Wasserstrom email to author, June 23, 2003.

42. On June 25, 2007, I wrote John Ziemer telling him of my decision to go with the University of California Press, to which he responded with his usual graciousness: "Thanks for letting me know. I don't mind losing books to Cal, and I know they will do a good job for you."

Chapter 9. The Problem of Insideness versus Outsideness

1. Originally presented at the conference "1900: The Boxers, China, and the World" held at the School of Oriental and African Studies, London, June 22–24, 2001, the talk was subsequently published under the same title in Robert Bickers and R. G. Tiedemann, eds., *The Boxers, China, and the World* (Lanham, MD: Rowman and Littlefield, 2007), 179–97.

2. Paul A. Cohen, *Discovering History in China: American Historical Writing on the Recent Chinese Past* (New York: Columbia University Press, 2010 reissue), xxii.

3. Arthur Miller, *Timebends: A Life* (New York: Grove Press, 1987), 348.

4. For an account of the process by which stories became elaborated in early China and continued to grow and change thereafter, see Stephen Owen, ed. and trans., *An Anthology of Chinese Literature: Beginnings to 1911* (New York: Norton, 1996), 88. Owen singles out as an example Wu Zixu, who happens to figure very prominently in the Goujian story.

5. In Joan of Arc's case, again, there is no stable text, and so, Mary Gordon tells us, there are as many renderings of her story in fiction, film, drama, and television as there are storytellers. Gordon, *Joan of Arc* (New York: Lipper/Viking, 2000), 148–65.

6. On Lin, see Wen Zhou, "Lun Lin Zexu liufang shi de yongdian yishu" (The art of using allusions in Lin Zexu's exile poetry), *Xinjiang daxue xuebao* (*zhexue shehui kexue ban*) 24.3 (1996): 89. On Zeng, see Xue Qilin, "Zeng Guofan wenhua ren'ge lun" (Zeng Guofan's cultural personality), *Loudi shizhuan xuebao* 1 (1995): 55. On Chiang, see Paul A. Cohen, *Speaking to History: The Story of King Goujian in Twentieth-Century China* (Berkeley: University of California Press, 2009), chap. 2. For references to the Goujian story in poems left by immigrants at Angel Island, see Him Mark Lai et al., *Island: Poetry and*

History of Chinese Immigrants on Angel Island, 1910–1940 (San Francisco: Hoc Doi, 1980), 56, 124–25, 139, 143, 158, 160. On the identification of Chinese immigrants in the Philippines with the Goujian story, see "Kan Huashi lishiju *Yue wang Goujian*" (Viewing the Chinese Television System's [Taiwan] airing of the historical drama *King Goujian of Yue*), http://www.siongpo.com/20070323/forumI.htm (accessed May 5, 2007).

7. The source of the fable is the Daoist text *Liezi*. "Yu gong yi shan," in *Guomin xiaoxue guoyu* (National primary school Chinese), comp. Guoli bianyi guan (National Institute for Compilation and Translation), 13 vols. (Taipei, 1974), 4 (lesson 23): 65–66, and "Zengwenxi shuiku" (The Zengwenxi reservoir), in *Guomin xiaoxue guoyu*, 12 (lesson 6): 17–19; "Yu gong yi shan," in *Guomin zhongxue guowenke jiaokeshu* (National middle school Chinese textbook), comp. Guoli bianyi guan, 6 vols. (Taipei, 1974), 3 (lesson 15): 67–70.

8. An early discussion of this contemporary application of the story is in Mao's concluding speech at the Seventh National Congress of the Communist Party of China, delivered on June 11, 1945. See Mao Zedong, "The Foolish Old Man Who Removed the Mountains," in *Selected Works of Mao Tse-tung* (Beijing: Foreign Languages Press, 1965), 3:321–24. For later references, see "Carry Out the Cultural Revolution Thoroughly and Transform the Educational System Completely," in *Peking Review*, June 24, 1966, 15–17; Liang Heng and Judith Shapiro, *Son of the Revolution* (New York: Vintage Books, 1984), 78, 175.

9. Included in the Chinese cultural world, as used here, were the countries of East Asia (Vietnam, Japan, and Korea) whose scholars were trained in the Chinese classical tradition, much as European elites were schooled in the classical learning of Greece and Rome. See Cohen, *Speaking to History*, 229.

10. "In the present day," a commentator on historical drama observed in the early 1960s, "when the party has called on us to engage in arduous struggle [*jianku fendou*] and to work hard to strengthen the nation [*fafen tuqiang*], the story of King Goujian of Yue's sleeping on brushwood and tasting gall has appeal for large numbers of viewers." Wang Jisi, "Duo xiexie zheyang de lishi gushi xi" (Many thanks to these dramas dealing with historical stories), *Juben* 2–3 (February–March 1961): 121–22.

11. Jerome Bruner, *Making Stories: Law, Literature, Life* (Cambridge, MA: Harvard University Press, 2002), 7, 34–35, 60.

12. For a fuller account of the ancient story, see Cohen, *Speaking to History*, chapter 1.

13. For information on the specific texts used, see Cohen, *Speaking to History*, 242, n. 3.

14. See Cohen, *Speaking to History*, 242–43, n. 4, for more detailed information.

15. David Johnson, "Epic and History in Early China: The Matter of Wu Tzu-hsü," *Journal of Asian Studies* 40.2 (February 1981): 255–71.

16. See Cohen, *Speaking to History*, 243, n. 6.

17. Wen Zhong's ritual suicide, like Qu Yuan's in the third century BCE and Deng Tuo's in the 1960s, "fits the Confucian trope of . . . the tragic rejection of a loyal minister by a foolish ruler." Timothy Cheek, *Propaganda and Culture in Mao's China: Deng Tuo and the Intelligentsia* (Oxford: Clarendon Press, 1997), vi.

18. Cohen, *Speaking to History*, 59.

19. Cohen, *Speaking to History*, 69–71. In ancient China, the removal of one's upper garments was a ritual expression of submission, used to apologize for an offense and re-

quest forgiveness. The bare upper bodies of the Goujian figures in the present case indicate a state of oppression and victimization rather than an admission of fault. Like Jesus, Goujian, during his stay as a prisoner in Wu, was made to suffer the mockery of the subjects of King Fuchai when they saw him driving the king's carriage.

20. Yang Tianshi, "Lugouqiao shibian qian Jiang Jieshi de dui-Ri moulüe: Yi Jiang shi riji wei zhongxin suo zuo de kaocha" (Chiang Kai-shek's Japan strategy prior to the Marco Polo Bridge incident: An examination mainly based on Mr. Chiang's diaries), *Jindaishi yanjiu* 2 (2001): 10. The quotations in this paragraph are found in Cohen, *Speaking to History*, 72–74.

21. The comic book, compiled and illustrated by Lan Hong, was titled *Woxin changdan*. For details and illustrations, see Cohen, *Speaking to History*, 124–26.

22. Wang Jisi, "Duo xiexie zheyang de lishi gushi xi," 121–22. See also Cohen, *Speaking to History*, 270, n. 8.

23. Mao Dun, *Guanyu lishi he lishiju: Cong "woxin changdan" de xuduo butong juben shuoqi* (On history and historical drama: With special reference to the numerous different librettos on the *woxin changdan* theme) (Beijing: Zuojia chubanshe, 1962). Mao's book appeared originally as an article in *Wenxue pinglun* 5 (1961): 37–65 and 6 (1961): 1–57.

24. On Cao Yu and his play, see Cohen, *Speaking to History*, 155–76.

25. Xiao Jun's *Wu Yue chunqiu shihua* (A story from the annals of Wu and Yue) and Bai Hua's *Wu wang jin ge Yue wang jian* (The golden spear of the king of Wu and the sword of the king of Yue) are dealt with in Cohen, *Speaking to History*, chap. 5.

26. Much of the detail in the ensuing paragraphs is drawn from Cohen, *Speaking to History*, chap. 6.

27. Cohen, *Speaking to History*, 203–5 (including an image of the graffiti on the wall at Hu Xiaolong's home).

28. *China Academic Journals* (Beijing: Tsinghua Tongfang Optical Disc Co.) is distributed in the United States by East View Publications in Minneapolis.

29. Cohen, *Speaking to History*, 222, 283, nn. 50–51.

30. Zhongli, a fictional master sword maker of Yue, was the title character in the early 1960s opera *Zhongli jian* (The swords of Zhongli). In the opera, he passes on his craft to his granddaughter, whose skillfully fashioned swords—she made 8,000 of them—were said to have been an important factor in enabling Goujian to vanquish Wu. See Zhao Cong, *Zhongguo dalu de xiqu gaige: 1942–1967* (Opera reform on the Chinese mainland: 1942–1967) (Hong Kong: Zhongwen daxue, 1969); Liu Naichong, "Kan pingju *Zhongli jian* hou manbi" (Notes jotted down after viewing the northern opera *The Swords of Zhongli*), *Zhongguo xiju* 14 (1961): 22–25.

31. Cohen, *Speaking to History*, 219–27.

32. The Masada and Kosovo examples are dealt with in Cohen, *Speaking to History*, 228–29, 236–39; see also (on Masada) Lewis A. Coser, "Introduction: Maurice Halbwachs 1877–1945," in Maurice Halbwachs, *On Collective Memory* (Chicago: University of Chicago Press, 1992), 32–34; and (on Kosovo) Avishai Margalit, *The Ethics of Memory* (Cambridge, MA: Harvard University Press, 2002), 96–98. The Obama talk is excerpted in David Remnick, "The Joshua Generation: Race and the Campaign of Barack Obama," *New Yorker*, November 17, 2008, 69–70.

Chapter 10. The Power of Story

1. Simon Schama, "His Story, Our Story," *Financial Times*, June 9, 2012. My thanks to Chris Munn for calling Schama's article to my attention.

2. Jerome Bruner, *Making Stories: Law, Literature, Life* (Cambridge, MA: Harvard University Press, 2002), 27.

3. There are a number of important exceptions to this assertion, which I touch on later in this chapter in my discussion of popular memory.

4. Bruner, *Making Stories*, 27.

5. The ensuing account of the Battle of Kosovo and Serbian history is drawn from Paul A. Cohen, *History and Popular Memory: The Power of Story in Moments of Crisis* (New York: Columbia University Press, 2014), 1–32.

6. He gives as examples the Battle of White Mountain (Bílá Hora) near Prague in 1620, which is still actively commemorated by the Czechs despite their having been decisively defeated in it by the forces of the Habsburg Empire, and the massacre of Lakota Indians by the United States 7th Cavalry Regiment at Wounded Knee (South Dakota) in 1890—an event that continues to be memorialized by the descendants of the Native Americans killed.

7. Vamik Volkan, "Chosen Trauma, the Political Ideology of Entitlement and Violence," paper presented at conference in Berlin, Germany, June 10, 2004; also his "Large-Group Identity and Chosen Trauma," *Psychoanalysis Downunder* 6 (December 2005).

8. The ensuing account of the Joan of Arc story during World War II is drawn from Cohen, *History and Popular Memory*, 109–48.

9. "Those genetic lines that did not find their infants cute no longer exist, because their young were not properly cared for." David Eagleman, *Incognito: The Secret Lives of the Brain* (New York: Pantheon Books, 2011), 99.

10. One of the most informative and persuasive accounts of storytelling's role in the earliest evolution of *Homo sapiens sapiens* is Michelle Scalise Sugiyama, "Narrative Theory and Function: Why Evolution Matters," *Philosophy and Literature* 25.2 (2001): 233–50. She writes, "The universality of narrative suggests that those individuals who were able (or better able) to tell and process stories enjoyed a reproductive advantage over those who were less skilled or incapable of doing so, thereby passing on this ability to subsequent generations" (235). Also of interest are some of the essays in Jonathan Gottshall and David Sloan Wilson, eds., *The Literary Animal: Evolution and the Nature of Narrative* (Evanston, IL: Northwestern University Press, 2005).

11. Scalise Sugiyama, "Narrative Theory and Function," 234. David Bordwell and Kristin Thompson describe narrative as "a chain of events in cause-effect relationship occurring in time and space" (*Film Art: An Introduction*, 4th ed. [New York: McGraw-Hill, 1993], 65).

12. The Jewish leader at Masada was Elazar ben Yair. There is an excellent historical novel on Masada by Alice Hoffman, *The Dovekeepers: A Novel* (New York: Scribner, 2011).

13. Avishai Margalit, *The Ethics of Memory* (Cambridge, MA: Harvard University Press, 2002), 95. See also Jan Assmann, "Collective Memory and Cultural Identity," trans. John Czaplicka, *New German Critique* 65 (Spring–Summer 1995): 125–33.

14. Ernest Renan, *What Is a Nation? Qu'est-ce qu'une nation?*, trans. Wanda Romer Taylor (Toronto: Tapir Press, 1996), 47. Kwame Anthony Appiah discusses Renan's ideas in his review of Margalit's book, *New York Review of Books*, March 13, 2003, 35–37. See also Joep Leerssen, *National Thought in Europe: A Cultural History* (Amsterdam: Amsterdam University Press, 2006), 227–31.

15. Bruner, *Making Stories*, 25.

16. Jonathan Gottschall, *The Storytelling Animal: How Stories Make Us Human* (Boston: Houghton Mifflin Harcourt, 2012), 177; see also 28, 197.

17. Mark Elvin, *Changing Stories in the Chinese World* (Stanford, CA: Stanford University Press, 1997), 5.

18. Benedict Anderson, *Imagined Communities: Reflections on the Origin and Spread of Nationalism*, rev. ed. (London: Verso, 1991), 5–7.

19. Margalit, *Ethics of Memory*, 99.

20. See *History and Popular Memory*, 208–12.

21. Chartier's remarks, made in a paper delivered at the International Congress of Historical Sciences in Montreal in 1995, are quoted in Georg G. Iggers, *Historiography in the Twentieth Century: From Scientific Objectivity to the Postmodern Challenge* (Hanover, NH: Wesleyan University Press, University Press of New England, 1997), 12.

22. Iggers, *Historiography in the Twentieth Century*, 119; see also 12–13, 145. My own understanding of the relationship among historical reconstruction, reality, and truth is found in *History in Three Keys: The Boxers as Event, Experience, and Myth* (New York: Columbia University Press, 1997), esp. 3–13.

23. David Lowenthal, *Possessed by the Past: The Heritage Crusade and the Spoils of History* (New York: Free Press, 1996), 162–63.

24. The comments on the distinction between history and memory in this paragraph and the following one by J. H. Plumb, Pierre Nora, David Lowenthal, and Bernard Bailyn are drawn from an important review of Jill Lepore's *The Whites of Their Eyes: The Tea Party's Revolution and the Battle over American History*, in Gordon S. Wood, "No Thanks for the Memories," *New York Review of Books*, January 13, 2011, 41–42. For a clear and useful account of the history/memory issue, see also Pierre Nora, "Between Memory and History: *Les Lieux de Mémoire*," *Representations* 26 (Spring 1989): 7–24.

25. Jonathan Safran Foer, "Why a Haggadah?," *New York Times*, April 1, 2012.

26. For an excellent probing into the fiction–nonfiction issue, see Beverley Southgate, *History Meets Fiction* (Harlow, UK: Pearson/Longman, 2009).

27. While following Maurice Halbwachs up to a point, Schwartz goes beyond Halbwachs's extreme presentism, arguing that alongside the transformations the image of Lincoln has undergone, there are also basic American traits and values that have persisted unchanged through time. See the discussion of Schwartz's views in Lewis A. Coser, "Introduction: Maurice Halbwachs 1877–1945," in Maurice Halbwachs, *On Collective Memory*, trans. and ed. Lewis A. Coser (Chicago: University of Chicago Press, 1992), 30.

28. Ken Burns, "A Conflict's Acoustic Shadows," *New York Times*, April 12, 2011, A21. See also the account of changing perceptions of the Civil War in Harvard University president Drew Gilpin Faust's lecture "Telling War Stories: Reflections of a Civil

War Historian," delivered at the Cambridge Public Library in Cambridge, Massachusetts, January 10, 2012, reported in Katie Koch, "The Civil War's Allures and Horrors," *Harvard Gazette*, January 12, 2012; and Andrew Delbanco's review of David W. Blight's *American Oracle: The Civil War in the Civil Rights Era* (Cambridge, MA: Harvard University Press, 2011) in "'The Central Event of Our Past': Still Murky," *New York Review of Books*, February 9, 2012, 19–21.

29. As quoted in Wood, "No Thanks for the Memories," 42.

30. J. H. Plumb, *The Death of the Past* (1969; reprint, New York: Palgrave Macmillan, 2004), 106–7. Plumb makes a similar comment in regard to Edward Gibbon, who in the second half of the eighteenth century, in Plumb's view, "raised the writing of history to a new level": Gibbon "sought a detached and truthful past, free from preconception or the idea of inherent purpose. Yet his detachment was infused with a warm and generous attitude to mankind in spite of its immeasurable follies and iniquities" (129–30).

Chapter 11. Then and Now

1. Author email to Vogel, April 18, 2000. I was certainly right about Ezra, who after retiring published (among other writings) his magisterial *Deng Xiaoping and the Transformation of China* (Cambridge, MA: Harvard University Press, 2011).

2. I have in mind a reflective piece that Jeff Wasserstrom asked me to write assessing the contributions of journalist/author Peter Hessler to the deepening of U.S. understanding of the complexities of contemporary Chinese life. See Paul A. Cohen, "Peter Hessler: Teacher, Archaeologist, Anthropologist, Travel Writer, Master Storyteller," *Journal of Asian Studies* 72.2 (May 2013): 251–72.

3. Paul A. Cohen and John E. Schrecker, eds., *Reform in Nineteenth-Century China* (Cambridge, MA: East Asian Research Center, Harvard University, 1976), x.

4. See Philip Kuhn, "The Taiping Rebellion," in *The Cambridge History of China*, vol. 10, *Late Ch'ing, 1800–1911*, Part 1, ed. John K. Fairbank (Cambridge: Cambridge University Press, 1978), 264; William Rowe, *China's Last Empire: The Great Qing* (Cambridge, MA: Harvard University Press, 2009), 198–200.

5. Paul A. Cohen, "Nineteenth-Century China: The Evolution of American Historical Approaches," in *A Companion to Chinese History*, ed. Michael Szonyi (Hoboken, NJ: Wiley, 2017), 154–67.

6. Rowe, *China's Last Empire*, 149–85.

7. See Lin Tongqi, "Yizhe daixu 'Zhongguo zhongxinguan': tedian, sichao, yu neizai zhangli" (Translator's preface to the "China-centered approach": Distinguishing features, ideas, and internal tensions), in Kewen [Cohen], *Zai Zhongguo faxian lishi: Zhongguo zhongxinguan zai Meiguo de xingqi* (Discovering history in China: The rise of the China-centered approach in America), trans. Lin Tongqi (Beijing: Zhonghua shuju, 1989), 1–34.

8. Paul A. Cohen, *Speaking to History: The Story of King Goujian in Twentieth-Century China* (Berkeley: University of California Press, 2009), 232–33.

9. Cohen, *Speaking to History*, 233; Marina Warner, *Joan of Arc: The Image of Female Heroism* (New York: Knopf, 1981), 131–32.

10. Cohen, *Speaking to History*, 233–34. "On the Media" was produced by WNYC in New York City. Its website (http://www.wnycstudios.org/shows/otm) contains the transcript of the Charles Lewis interview, titled "The Digging Life."

11. Paul A. Cohen, "Wang T'ao's Perspective on a Changing World," in *Approaches to Modern Chinese History*, ed. Albert Feuerwerker, Rhoads Murphey, and Mary C. Wright (Berkeley: University of California Press, 1967), 134.

12. Paul A. Cohen, *Between Tradition and Modernity: Wang T'ao and Reform in Late Ch'ing China* (Cambridge, MA: Harvard University Press, 1974), 69, 181, see also 138–39, 152–53, 235.

13. For a detailed examination, see Paul A. Cohen, "Boxers, Christians, and the Gods: The Boxer Conflict of 1900 as a Religious War," which forms chapter 4 of *China Unbound: Evolving Perspectives on the Chinese Past* (London: Routledge Curzon, 2003).

14. Cohen, *China Unbound*, 106; 126, n. 5.

15. Cohen, *China Unbound*, 108; 126, n. 8.

16. A portion of one of the most widely disseminated examples of a Boxer notice follows:

They proselytize their sect,
And believe in only one God,
The spirits and their own ancestors
Are not even given a nod.
Their men are all immoral;
Their women truly vile.
For the Devils [foreigners] it's mother-son sex
That serves as the breeding style.

. . .

No rain comes from Heaven.
The earth is parched and dry.
And all because the churches
Have bottled up the sky.
The god[s] are very angry.
The spirits seek revenge.
En masse they come from Heaven
To teach the Way to men.

The translation is by Joseph W. Esherick, in his *The Origins of the Boxer Uprising* (Berkeley: University of California Press, 1987), 299; reprinted in Cohen, *China Unbound*, 108–9.

17. Cohen, *China Unbound*, 109.

18. Cohen, *China Unbound*, 112–18.

19. David Carr, *Time, Narrative, and History* (Bloomington: Indiana University Press, 1986), 9, 16, see also 65, 73, 168–69, 177. For White's views, see his "The Question of Narrative in Contemporary Historical Theory," *History and Theory* 23.1 (February 1984):

1–33. For a more detailed comparison of White and Carr, see Jeremy D. Popkin, *History, Historians, and Autobiography* (Chicago: University of Chicago Press, 2005), chap. 2. On Carr, Popkin writes: "The importance of Carr's approach is its forceful reminder that all the forms of literary narrative do grow out of what we might call a more basic, preliterary experience of storytelling, whether we take this more basic experience to be rooted in reality itself or to be a fundamental aspect of human culture" (55).

20. In the final part of his book, Carr explicitly acknowledges some of the characteristics of historical narration that seem to set it apart from participant narration. The differences, however, are of a practical rather than a formal sort, and form, rather than practice, is what counts for the author. Thus, in practical terms, the historian has hindsight, while the subjects about whom he or she writes do not. But in formal terms people in the present also have a kind of hindsight—Carr calls it "quasi-hindsight"—inasmuch as they are able to anticipate future outcomes and act as if the future they anticipate will be realized. See Carr, *Time, Narrative, and History*, 168–77, also 60–62.

21. Paul A. Cohen, *History in Three Keys: The Boxers as Event, Experience, and Myth* (New York: Columbia University Press, 1997), 4.

22. Daniel L. Schacter, *Searching for Memory: The Brain, the Mind, and the Past* (New York: Basic Books, 1996), 308.

23. Cohen, *History in Three Keys*, 4–5; see also Julian Barnes, *Flaubert's Parrot* (New York: Vintage, 1990), 168.

24. A major criticism that John Fairbank made of my doctoral dissertation years ago, the reader may recall, was that I failed to convey a sense of the build-up of tension in the course of the 1860s culminating in "that excellent and horrifying Tientsin Massacre which wraps up all the angles of analysis in one crescendo. If you can pull this off as an editorial *tour de force*, you will have almost a best-seller because the story is one that builds to a remarkable climax." Fairbank, letter to author, November 15, 1960.

25. Cohen, *Speaking to History*, 229.

26. Cohen, *Speaking to History*, 229.

Index

national humiliation (*guochi*): and
Chinese intellectuals, 169, 170, 172,
174; in communist vs. Republican
periods, 167–69; Days of, 162–69, 179,
194; and experience, 174; and Goujian
story, 166–67, 169, 177–80, 185, 192–95,
230; and Guomindang, 162, 163, 165,
171, 172, 173; and imperialism, 163, 165,
166, 167, 169, 171, 174; as internal
Chinese problem, 169–70, 175; and
Japan, 163, 165, 167, 172, 173, 195, 209,
243; literature of, 165–69, 194–95; in
PRC, 167–68, 169, 171; remembering
vs. forgetting, 169–75; in Republican
period, 164–65, 166, 169–70, 171, 174,
175; and the state, 171–74; and story,
243, 244
National Humiliation Illustrated
(*Guochi tu*), 195
nationalism: popular vs. official, 172–73;
Serbian, 213–14, 216; and stories, 210
nationalism, Chinese, 112, 139, 177, 201,
281n28; and national humiliation,
163, 165, 166, 170, 171; and the state,
171–73
Nee, Victor, 66–67
Needham, Joseph, 82, 265n7
Nevsky, Alexander, 210, 212, 222
New England China Seminar, 36
Nguyen Trai, 244
Nian rebellion, 72
Nigeria, 143, 145
Nixon, Richard, 17, 28
Njegoš, Petar Petrović, 214–16
Nora, Pierre, 224
North Vietnam, 59
Northwestern University, 27

Obama, Barack, 207
Obilić, Miloš, 214
Olivier, Laurence, 209, 210, 222
Opium War (1839–42), 62, 97, 235; as
critical turning point, 71–72, 135–36,
234; and Goujian story, 186, 194; and
national humiliation, 165, 166, 169

oral history, 186, 214, 220; of Boxers, 120,
129, 137–38, 153–54, 273n16
Origins of the Boxer Uprising, The
(Esherick), 158
Ottoman Empire, 213–14, 216

Painful History of National Humiliation
(*Guochi tongshi*), 167, 168
Palau, 144
Palestine/Israel, 207, 210, 214, 245
Pantheon Books, 89
Papers on China (journal), 13, 15, 16, 183
Peck, James, 66–67
Peng Dehuai, 200, 201
Pétain, Philippe, 216–17, 219
Pi-hsieh shih-lu (*Bixie shilu*; *Death Blow
to Corrupt Doctrines*), 28, 259n16
Plumb, J. H., 224, 226, 288n30
Polachek, James, 97
Pomeranz, Kenneth, 97–98, 99, 267n8
Popkin, Jeremy D., 8, 257n1, 262n3,
290n19
Possessed by the Past (Lowenthal), 224
Pye, Lucian, 162–63

Qing dynasty, 43, 54, 70, 135, 136, 194;
documents of, 15, 16; historiography of,
97, 101–2, 234–35; national humiliation
in, 169, 170, 171–72, 175. *See also*
Boxer uprising; Manchus; Taiping
Rebellion
Qu Yuan, 284n17

Rabinow, Paul, 145, 146
railways, 47
Rankin, Mary B., 84, 97, 258n9
Rao Shurong, 7
Rashomon (film), 114
*Rebellion and Its Enemies in Late Imperial
China: Militarization and Social
Structure, 1796–1864* (Kuhn), 67
Red Guards, 112, 152, 272nn6–7. *See also*
Cultural Revolution
Red Lanterns, 112, 122, 125–26, 208,
272n6. *See also* Boxer uprising